Miles Franklin in America

Her Unknown (Brilliant) Career

Miles Franklin in America
Her Unknown (Brilliant) Career

VERNA COLEMAN

A SIRIUS BOOK

To the memory of my mother

Angus & Robertson Publishers
London • Sydney • Melbourne • Singapore • Manila

First published in the UK by Angus & Robertson (UK) Ltd, 1981
First published in Australia by Angus & Robertson Publishers, Australia, 1981

© Verna Coleman 1981

National Library of Australia
Cataloguing-in-publication data.

Coleman, Verna
    Her unknown (brilliant) career.
    Includes index.
    ISBN 0 207 14536 9.
    1. Franklin, Miles, 1879-1954. 2. Novelists,
        Australian-Biography. I. Title.
A823'.2

Typeset in 10 pt Garamond by Graphicraft Typesetters, Hong Kong
Printed in Hong Kong

Acknowledgements

My thanks are due firstly and pre-eminently to the Mitchell Library, Sydney, for the use of its resources, for permission to quote from the Franklin Papers, from the pocket diaries of Miles Franklin, 1909-16, and from other manuscripts, and for permission to reproduce pictures from the Miles Franklin Collection, and to its unfailingly courteous and efficient staff. I should like to thank also, in Australia, the National Library of Australia, Canberra, for permission to quote from the Kate Baker Papers and other documents; the State Library of New South Wales; the Perpetual Trustee Company, Sydney; and Angus & Robertson for permission to quote from the works of Miles Franklin. Among individuals, I owe a great debt to Leslie Bridle who shared her time and knowledge with me.

In America my special thanks are due to the Department of Rare Books and Manuscripts and its staff in the University of Florida Library, Gainsville, and to Sam Gowan for permission to quote from the Margaret Dreier Robins Papers, University of Florida Libraries, and to Lisa von Borowsky, executor of the Robins estate.

I should like to thank the Library of Congress, Washington, DC, particularly the manuscript division, for its help and advice, the Chicago Historical Society for permission to quote from the Agnes Nestor Papers, the New York Public Library, and the Library of the University of South Carolina.

I am grateful to Mr Lee Major and Mr R.V. Twilling of the *Chicago Tribune* for their help and for permission to use quotes and photographs from that paper. Lastly I should like to thank Mr William Bross Lloyd Jnr of Winnetka for his courtesy.

Contents

Foreword

In a remote area of the snow-topped Southern Alps of New South Wales, a traveller of the 1880s got off his horse at Talbingo Station in the Monaro district and entered the comfortable homestead. He was greeted with great courtesy and aplomb by a tiny person who, in the absence of the lady of the house, entertained him with all proper attentions. When finally his adult hostess appeared, the puzzled visitor turned to her and enquired, "Is she really a child or a dwarf?"

Never one to hide behind her grandmother's skirts on any occasion, or behind anyone else, skirted or not, this "brave, clever little girl", as a beloved aunt termed her, confronted and dealt with the strange gentleman with the same eager courage and competence which she showed in dealing with the experiences of later life as Miles Franklin.

Feminism today is chic, one of the staples of the glossies and even of some of the popular type of women's magazines, along with their "personalities", royalty and diets. In the narrow, cut-off communities of the Australian countryside in the 1880s a little girl who thought a woman might be a head of state equally as well as a man was laughed at. Such a view was thought weird, unnatural and pretentious, at best a diverting piece of nonsense. The simple beliefs of this girl, that a woman could have brains and talents, that she could use these attributes to make a brilliant career and do fine things in the world were regarded as foolish and rebellious, even by strong women like her severe mother and her forceful, matriarchal grandmother. Only her gentle, generous-natured father gave her some support.

To be a girl with these notions in that society was startling enough; to be a writer as well was something at which to gawk. In the battle for freedom and self-expression, as woman and artist, it took great courage, a strong will and a limitless belief in herself to persevere as Stella Miles Franklin did. But talent and intelligence, backed by an unshakable determination to succeed, brought her recognition firstly and briefly as Miles Franklin, novelist, then as Stella Franklin, feminist and labour leader, then as that curious and mysterious old party, Brent of Bin Bin — though the identity of this storyteller was kept secret for many years — and, rounding the circle, as Miles Franklin, writer and patron of Australian literature.

Miles Franklin said to a girl whom she had met in London in 1922: "You were the last person to call me Stella." Except to her family, the girl Stella Franklin was swallowed as the years passed by the more familiar Miles. This book aims to tell the story of young Miles in Australia and of her second career, as Stella Franklin, in the United States. It also traces the development of the young novelist through the American years to London, where Brent of Bin Bin emerged.

The American experience, when she was the often anguished, but always brave and vibrant Stella, was a vital part of the life of Miles Franklin. There her nature was torn between the writer and the activist, causing much pain. Eventually she made her choice and, in London, though still intensely committed to feminism, withdrew gradually from any active involvement and returned to her craft, and to success in the guise of Brent of Bin Bin.

It was when she returned to live permanently in Australia that she became the Miles Franklin of legend, the "infatuated Australian", the apostle of Australian literature and an institution amongst the Australian writers of her day. But that is another story.

1 The Monaro and the family

In the winter of 1879 a young woman, seven months pregnant, rode south-west from her home in the rugged Brindabella Ranges, on the western edge of the limestone plain, over which today the city of Canberra sprawls. There was then no sign of Burley Griffin's airy city, only a windy bare plain, former haunt of escaped convicts and bushrangers, with the spire of St John's Church of England and a few scattered farmhouses the sole signs of human occupation.

On a sturdy mountain pony, Susannah Franklin travelled 110 kilometres along high and difficult bridle tracks, often through snow-drifts, to Talbingo Station, some twenty-four kilometres south of Tumut (but only as the crow flies). She rode with difficulty, for not only was the terrain treacherous, but in the fashion of the day she was seated side-saddle and laced into an elegant riding habit. She jolted along with effort and discomfort as she travelled to her mother's home to await the birth of her first child. It was a bruising, dangerous, fatiguing journey, broken only for a desperately needed rest period at Argalong with the Herlihy family, where Mrs Herlihy was so touched that she put her own baby into the bed at the traveller's feet to warm them.

The tough pioneer stock from which Susannah sprang carried her through. She had been born in these mountains in 1850 at icy Cooma, where her Prussian father Oltman Lampe had been overseer at Wambrook Station. In her teens she had been forced to carry a large part in the running of the family property at Talbingo when her father, after a fall from a horse, was stricken with paralysis and blinded. With her unconquerable mother and her younger brothers and sisters she had laboured as hard as any adult male. She had toiled as farmhand, gardener, laundress and housemaid until Talbingo Station with its gardens, orchards and dairies was a byword in the district for comfort and hospitality. On 26 November, 1878, Susannah Lampe married John Franklin and moved to Brindabella, even more lonely a place than Talbingo. Now, after the ordeal of her journey, she found pleasure in the order and decency of her old home and support in the birth of her child.

The baby was born on 14 October, 1879, and was baptised on 6 December by the Reverend George Spencer as Stella Maria Sarah Miles Franklin. The names largely represented the intertwining pioneer families which had put down roots in the still shallow soil of this remote region.

Stella and Maria were mysterious choices, almost a Catholic aberration in this staunchly Protestant family, although Grandmother Mary Franklin was also known as Maria. Perhaps the romantic father who loved stars, sunsets and poetry chose Stella. But Sarah was for grandmother Lampe, Susannah's supremely practical mother, who had been born Sarah Bridle at Macquarie Fields, New South Wales, in 1831. Sarah's father, William Bridle, the baby's great-grandfather, born in Somersetshire in 1798, had arrived in the colony on the transport *Larkins* in 1817. There was a family tradition that he was of French descent. In the colony he received a small land grant near Liverpool and in 1823, married a locally-born girl.

The early settlement around Sydney had been built up mostly with small free land grants for crops and pasturage, but after the barrier of the enclosing Blue Mountains was breached in 1813, a big push westwards began in an endeavour to open up new sheep grazing areas to supply wool for the English and Indian markets. Many stock owners occupied, without any title, land not yet surveyed, earning the nickname "squatters". In 1829 geographical limits to settlement were proclaimed, but enterprising spirits often overran the legal rim, grazing at will as squatters. The position was legalised in 1836 and these adventurers were given some security by the issue of licences for grazing.

Whereas formerly the care of outback runs had been left to isolated shepherds, squatters now began to move their families to these regions and to build homes there. One such family was the Bridles, who moved into the high Monaro district in the early 1840s.

Sarah Bridle, the tiny Stella's maternal grandmother, married Oltman Lampe at Gundagai on 12 February, 1850. Lampe, a migrant from Bremen, had arrived in the colony in 1841 and after working for a time at Wambrook Station, near Tumut, finally bought his own property in 1865 from his father-in-law William Bridle — Talbingo Station. The story of the early settlement of this wild and mountainous district is one of cruelty and courage, of rough living and rough justice. The last of the Aboriginal tribes were being pushed further out, and stock stealing and bushranging were rife. As late as 1865 Ben Hall held up the township of Collector in the northern Monaro and a local constable was shot dead. Eight days after the Lampes moved into their home at Talbingo, a former inn on Jounama Creek, they were held up by bushrangers. Undeterred they added to, rebuilt and improved the old building, until the tragic accident which left Oltman Lampe blind and bedridden for the rest of his life.

Miles, the last of the baby's list of Christian names, was for her earliest Australian ancestor, William Bridle's wife, Martha Miles, born at Prospect in

top: William and Martha Bridle, Stella Franklin's great-grandparents, Fitzroy Cottage, Tumut.
bottom: Joseph Franklin, Stella's paternal grandfather.

New South Wales in 1807, the daughter of a Firstfleeter.

Finally, there was the family name of Franklin, defined in the dictionary as a freeholder, one not liable to feudal service. Stella's paternal grandfather, Joseph Franklin, from County Clare in Ireland, arrived in Sydney in April 1839. Son of a teacher, he had married Mary Hogan and their first child was born on the voyage out. Joseph worked for a time for the Marshall and Williams families near Yass, then began cattle trading.

He settled his family at Condor Creek, past the Cotter River (where Canberra citizens now find recreation), in high country near Mount Franklin which is part of the southern chain dominated by Kosciusko. He spent much time away from home, moving mobs of stock about the country, and returned from one of these trips to find his house burned to the ground and his family gone. He took such things in his stride, and having located his family sheltering with the McDonalds of Uriarra Station, about twelve kilometres away, he built another house, before setting off once more, exploring westwards to the beautiful Brindabella Ranges where he began running stock.

A man born to adventure, or misadventure, on another trading trip he was thrown from his horse on to a bull-ants' nest, where, unable to move because of injuries from the fall, he lay in agony for twenty-four hours until rescued by one Mr Grosvenor of Gunning. The Grosvenors tended him for nine months until his strength was restored, but for the rest of his life he limped badly.

Even this escapade did not prevent adventure-loving Joseph from joining in the rush to the Victorian goldfields in the 1850s. Fortune befriended him just a little this time and after eighteen months of endeavour he returned with £200. It was enough to secure some land at Oak Vale, near Yass. In addition he was able to buy the squatting rights of the settlers Hall and Webb at Brindabella, for although he had made use of the run there he had no title to it. He also leased the adjoining runs of Bramina and Bin Bin. There in the lovely valley, with the bright Goodradigbee River running its length, he raised stock with his sons Thomas and John. They dealt in cattle but also horses, in particular the "walers", the sure-footed, rugged horses of the ranges, much sought after by the Indian army buyers as cavalry mounts. George, the eldest son, looked after the property at Oak Vale, where Joseph lived out his not-so-quiet days, which were brightened by visits to the clan at Brindabella.

Thomas, the second son, built a homestead at Brindabella for his family, and about two and a half kilometres up river the youngest son, John Maurice, Stella's father, established a house on the Bin Bin run for his bride.

So around the cradle of the new baby gathered the spirits of endurance and enterprise, fortitude and courage, and of the steely will to survive and succeed in a new and difficult land. The gentler elegancies of an older tradition were elbowed out by these tough, though often kind-hearted, survivors.

Outside the homestead, however, were other magical influences which would leave their delicate mark on the fragile infant mind. There were the snow-fringed mountains, with their space and grandeur, the unspoiled forests of great gums, the trailing ferns and limpid streams, and there was the cutting brilliance of the air and sky, by night and by day.

When Susannah had recovered sufficiently to make the trek back home, the little caravan of mother, baby and attendant uncle set off from Talbingo Station. Three-month-old Stella nestled into a purple sateen pillow stuffed with feathers, and travelled securely on the horse of her mother's young brother, William Augustus Lampe, while Susannah cantered ahead in the hot summer sunlight, across the plains this time, avoiding the mountains, until they began the climb to the new house at Brindabella.

It was built in the typical pattern of one-storey bush homesteads of the day, out of hand-cut slabs of mountain-ash and stringy bark, with a neat pitched roof of mountain-ash shingles and a wide chimney piece at one side. Traditionally the kitchen was set at a distance from the living quarters in case of fire, and the water supply flowed a few hundred metres away. The baby's new home was rough in structure but superior to the two-roomed humpy in which many a young pioneering couple began their married life in the bush.

The isolation of these ranges was such that dry supplies of flour, sugar, rice, tea and other necessities could be brought in only once or twice a year by bullock team. The small homes had to be as self-supporting as possible, with vegetables, milk, eggs, bacon, meat and fruit produced on the property. The kitchen smoke-room held hams, sides of bacon and drying bullocks' tongues, while light came from tallow candles supplemented by kerosene lamps. The dead standing timber provided the logs for heating and cooking. Back-breaking labour raised and attempted to civilise these little homes, yet "The pioneer houses like the nests of birds rarely lasted beyond one or two generations".[1]

This particular pioneer shelter was, however, a wonder to other nesters for it contained those admired symbols of far-away middle-class civilisation and respectability—a sewing machine and, wonder of wonders, a piano, dragged up the ridges on drays, without a scratch, by gentle, agonised bullocks, and guarded at night like jewels along the track by the rough-tongued bullocky beneath the glittering stars.

These unusual items were precious to Susannah. She had sweated and laboured with her mother at Talbingo to establish a comfortable home. Here she had to start again. Bit by bit, even though baby followed baby fairly quickly, she created around her roughly-hewn new house vegetable and flower gardens. She planted orchards. She sewed, cleaned, cooked and as far as she was able brought the decencies of life and some of its beauties to her lonely dwelling. From her teens there had never been a moment free from responsibility and effort. Ceaselessly energetic, she strove to instil in her children the same severe standards of cleanliness and correct behaviour, unknown to many pioneering families, by which she herself had been raised. Despite the pressure of unending fatigue, she created for her little daughter a legacy of energy, endurance and bravery.

Susannah's only help in a household where facilities were minimal was a little nursemaid, just a child herself, yet the mother provided snowy pinafores and clean linen as well as nourishing meals and warmth. She also entertained on Saturday nights various neighbours and visitors with all the grace possible in the primitive circumstances. Precocious, wide-awake baby Stella, in a long gown, loved to sit beside her mother at the piano while Susannah attacked the "Maiden's Prayer" and similar ballads, and the candles flickered in the goldly-gleaming brass holders. Outside, encircling the little home, stretched the dark, empty land and the boundless starlit sky.

As the years passed, elegant and talented Susannah found little romance or humour in life. She did her duty for her growing brood without tears, strongly disciplined and ferociously energetic. All the same, the armour of self-control did not entirely suppress marked artistic impulses. She painted in watercolour, read Shakespeare and Milton and sewed garments of practical beauty for her children—linen pinafores and fine cotton underwear trimmed with *broderie anglaise*, kilted frocks and pink dresses for best, and Stella's own small riding habit, floor length of black-braided serge. In another age and place this fine craftswoman might have achieved the recognition of the world. Here her reward was the knowledge of duty well done, as she mixed *Mrs Beeton* with the Bible, *Modern Etiquette* with music practice.

But above all she found release for her love of beauty in a garden, weaving around the simple house a pattern of shade and colour. Daffodils, sweet williams, honeysuckles, roses, overhung by a lilac and a golden laburnum, mixed the tints and perfumes of a gentler landscape with the grey-green tang of the bushland. She introduced her little daughter to the delights of the seed catalogue, laying the basis for a life-long passion.

Yet a sadness hung over the spirit of Susannah, as it did over so many of those pioneers who struggled with the harshness and coarseness of primitive bush life. Order and beauty, even basic cleanliness, meant an unending expenditure of self. She was not happy in this life though she never spared herself in her duties. Capable, practical, sensible, at this period she may well have won the approval of even that crisp critic of incompetent motherhood, Jane Austen. Her daughter remembered her as "the wonder of her region", "beautiful and accomplished",[2] yet she recalled also Susannah's sense of dismay in her struggles.

The father, John Maurice Franklin, born at Yass in 1847, was a more

Stella's mother, Susannah Franklin, in 1895.

obviously romantic figure. He was a superb horseman in a time when all rode well, and he was an expert bushman with a deep love and knowledge of the wide, wild countryside. Tall and handsome in the Celtic style with blue eyes, black hair, and a classic profile, he was also blessed, or cursed, with a generous, easy-going Irish charm. His relationship with Stella as a tiny child had much of the playmate about it. He carried her sunbonneted figure on his shoulders on Sunday walks while he chatted about the ways of flowers and plants. He pick-a-backed her as she clung round his neck on morning swims in the river, and he took her with him at times on his work, on exciting excursions to the far extremes of the property.

He imparted to her his sense of marvel at the glory of the heavens, the moon, the stars, the sunsets. It has been said of him that he was a hundred years ahead of his time in his intellectual tolerance and broadness of outlook, and that he had a sweetness of disposition unusual in any society where opinions are held rigidly and bitterly. He encouraged Stella in her unorthodox little ambitions, agreeing that girls could be dragons, whereas commonsense Mother had said no, she could not be a dragon: "Dragon is *he*". A kindly, dreamy man, fond of the poetry of Byron and Henry Kendall, John Franklin never punished his child, and the only instance of corporal punishment was at the mother's hand.

At Brindabella Stella's father led the usual outdoor life of the squatter, riding, shooting, droving, felling timber, fencing, burning off—all the strenuous athletic pursuits of the bushman were the stuff of each day. He raised blood horses and cattle and was known as a reckless, daring rider. "The Man from Snowy River is a common feat with him,"[3] wrote Stella proudly. A superman indeed for a small girl to idolise.

Both John and Susannah Franklin were gifted and striking people but there were strains within the marriage caused by temperament and circumstance. Both parents were hedged about by the stiff behavioural barriers of Victorian bush morality. Susannah's self-disciplined Lampe coolness was matched by the reserved Irish puritanism of the father. Fear of touch kept parents and children apart. "My mother was revolted to see old people kissing little children," wrote Franklin. "We kissed chastely if separating for the day or longer and on returning, and, while very small, on going to bed. We did not cling around our parents and hug them."[4] John's elder brother George when leaving home would merely shake hands with his children, even the toddler, but there were no embraces. Love was there but restrained as dangerous and explosive in its physical manifestation.

Though she was unromantic in attitude and controlled in expressing physical affection Susannah merged her austere principles of conduct into a broader morality of courage, independence and endurance. Lines of conduct were drawn clearly, giving a basic security and some freedom within limits. A child might wander and explore the station within sensible boundaries. Stella

Stella's father, John Franklin.

could roam through this paradise at will, through communities of pansies, lilies, roses and honeysuckles, through colonies of vegetables and settlements of pigs, cows chickens, kittens, dogs and peacocks. But monarch of the territory was the horse. Everyone rode, from childhood. It was a necessity, the lifeline between the isolated mountain domain and the outside world. Dressed in a dark blue hand-me-down habit, the intrepid little Stella was taken for her first canter without a bearing rein at the age of four.

The station drew its greatest excitements from the horses. When the buyers for the Indian army visited the neighbouring squatters and station hands, boundary riders and horse fanciers gathered from all over the Murrumbidgee and Monaro districts to yarn and reminisce, and judge the horses, their riders and the "breakers". The country of "Clancy of the Overflow" and "The Man from Snowy River" teemed with splendid horsemen and it was a time for daring and display. Stella Franklin became a superb and fearless rider. On horseback she found freedom from Victorian rigidities, excitement and challenge. She loved all animals but horses most intensely, and as a child they were her preferred companions.

So she grew in this strange combination of freedom and constraint, a friend to every man on the station in a natural, frank way. Yet the early discipline of strict bush codes and their physical reserve were to imprison her all her life. Friendly and flirtatious, affectionate and candid, she never lacked admirers but kept them at a certain distance. Nevertheless the bright, brave little rider inevitably won the admiration and respect of the hardy bushmen, and her self-confidence and individuality blossomed in the small secluded world of up-country station life. There were as yet no buffeting winds from a broader domain.

2 Talbingo and Brindabella

In spite of the pleasures of her home station, Stella Franklin as a tiny child often longed for the place of her birth, Talbingo. This predilection was bound up with her relationship to her sister Linda. At almost two Stella was robbed of her mother's lap and concentrated attention by a supplanting little creature, Linda Lampe Franklin, born on 12 September, 1881, and the baby jealousy which flared then mixed with her love for her sister for many years. At this time Stella was sent to Talbingo where she sought the security of her grandmother's love, and determined to live forever in the old house where she had been born and had known no rival. On Grandmother Lampe's formidable silken lap, playing with her impressive golden watch-chain, the sleepless toddler (for Stella was of a hyperactive nature) kept late hours with the adults, having her say in the grown-up conversation and earning a reputation as an entertaining little being.

There in her earliest years she reigned alone over her six young aunts and uncles to whom she was "a little tin god", as she recalled in her memoirs, *Childhood at Brindabella*. Her small ego could expand blissfully on visits there, whereas at home Mother was preoccupied with babies. Brother Mervyn was born on 3 October, 1883 and sister Una on 15 March, 1885. At Talbingo Stella could avoid her rivals and was petted and pampered in the warmth and sprawl of a Victorian family. Grandma had eight married sisters and brothers, all occasional guests, making seventeen quasi-grandparent figures in all. Stella's self-image was nourished also by the admiration and encouragement of visitors whom she met aplenty, for it was an unusual week when no stranger arrived with the mailman to spend a night or two before journeying on. An essential stimulus to writing, that sense of the importance of the communication of experience, was given early by the amused admiration of her sayings and doings offered by her elders. Linda wrote some years later, "Granny was telling us the other day the funny things you used to say as a child, and we all shrieked with laughter."[1]

Grandma Lampe enjoyed the company of her quaint grandchild and to

top: Talbingo Station.
bottom: Grandmother Lampe.

Stella she was a cherished idol. Short in stature, she towered in competence and authority, the archetype of the Victorian matriarch, God fearing, energetic, hard-working and hospitable, with a name for fairness in all her dealings whether with station hand or small child. But there was no profanity, no drunkenness and no loose conduct allowed in her strict domain. Religious fervour was expressed in morning and evening Bible readings, and every Sunday there was a service in the drawing room. The rector took this once a month. At other times Grandma assumed his role while the young aunts played selections from *Hymns Ancient and Modern* on the piano.

In spite of the rigidity of the morality, temporal comforts were not neglected. While there was always grace before and after meals, there were also the refinements of proper table manners, and a well laid and bountiful table. Even the pieties of the Sabbath were succeeded by the delights of Sunday dinner, cooked on Saturday and kept hot in brick ovens so cooking did not sully the holy day.

However conservative and uncompromising Grandma Lampe was in matters of religion, in practical affairs she was shrewd and flexible and in day to day discussions of earthly matters outspoken and forthright— and she approved of such qualities in others. The constriction of her severe Victorian morality was loosened by a plain-dealing and straight-talking element in her personality. Everyone throughout the clan, from herself to lisping baby, was free to express his or her opinions and ideas. The motto ''Children should be seen and not heard'' was not to be found embroidered on her wall hangings. However uninformed a small person might be, he or she could have a say, and a sharply observant child with an amusing twist of tongue was encouraged in self-expression, and the habit of truthfulness.

Stella conversed with many of the visitors both at Talbingo and at home, from the local Member of Parliament and the Crown Land Commissioners to the remittance men, swaggies and Indian hawkers wandering the land. She heard the cantankerous controversialists of her family and friends argue the questions of the day. Religion was still one of the bitterest subjects with the Catholic Irish being at the bottom of the social barrel in the eyes of the descendants of Northern Irish Protestants and Prussian Lutherans, though the isolation meant that many a bigoted family had to come to terms with a mixed marriage.

Whatever the heat of the religious debate among some settlers, it could not match the burning obsession of all with the basic issue of land and its leasing. The Commissioner for Crown Lands who had the power to reassess the value of runs held, so raising or lowering the fees to be paid, was a person to be courted.

As the 1880s proceeded, the arguments even in remote homesteads such as Talbingo began to change, for a new instrument was stirring the community. In Sydney, three months after Stella Franklin's birth, a weekly magazine, *The*

Stella Maria Sarah Miles Franklin, aged four.

Bulletin, appeared for the first time, in January 1880. In its first years this controversial journal, founded by John Haynes and twenty-four-year-old J.F. Archibald, was bedevilled by libel suits and money problems to such an extent that in the cause of a ''free press'' (and publicity) Haynes and Archibald ended up in Darlinghurst Jail for a period in 1882. Bolstered by the commonsense and financial help of William Traill, a new, pink-covered version appeared in May 1883 featuring a brilliant cartoonist, American Livingston Hopkins, ''Hop'', and the magazine began to pull through its difficulties. When J.F. Archibald became controlling editor in 1886, *The Bulletin* was set fair on its long course as the foremost weekly in Australia.

Determinedly contentious, cheeky and abrasive, it attacked the heavy questions of the hour from one side or another, free trade, protectionism, republicanism, socialism, nationalism, federation and immigration. It also pummelled the lighter topics of the monarchy, the Queen, royalty and vice-regality, the clergy, the judiciary, temperance, and the ''new woman''. It prided itself on its bush readership, describing itself on 15 December, 1888 as the ''Bushman's Bible''. The title stuck. ''Slangy, pungent, irreverent, cynical, often sentimental, sardonically humorous, witty'',[2] it was written largely by the hardy men who lived in and knew the bush. Its tone seems to have appealed strongly to young Stella Franklin and to have influenced her attitudes.

But across its bright and impudent pages fell a shadow. ''Australia for the Australians'' and ''Australia for the White Man'' were its slogans. Its fervent nationalism was tainted with racism. The ''yellow peril'' as seen by *The Bulletin*, particularly by its cartoonists, was not a pretty sight. As early as 1860 there had been serious disturbances at Lambing Flat when Chinese miners were chased off the goldfields. A big interstate conference held in Sydney in 1888 backed the trade union view that coloured immigration should be restricted, and the so-called White Australia policy was taken up by *The Bulletin* and supported by the community in general. Seeds of this development seem to have lodged in a corner of little Stella's brain, to sprout decades later in some cranky ideas on population and eugenics.

Federation was another issue discussed. The air of the fresh ranges became thick with the issue in the 1890s. ''What do you think of Federation and War?'' Linda was to write from Talbingo in the 1890s. ''I am sick of hearing of nothing else.''[3]

There were other rumblings reaching up-country areas in the 1880s and 90s. The ideas of social reformer Edward Bellamy advanced in *Looking Backward* (1888), and of single tax theorist Henry George would have been part of the background of debate at this time, with the even heavier thought of Karl Marx appearing in William Lane's journals *The Boomerang* (founded 1887) and *The Worker* (founded 1890), perhaps finding an exasperated reader or two among Stella's phalanx of relatives.

Increasing unemployment strengthened trade unionism, and even a small girl pondered in her secluded ranges the problem of the men and boys tramping the country in search of work and food.

The "new woman" with her breeches and bicycles gave much joy to *The Bulletin*, and the more serious ideas of John Stuart Mill on the position of women were drifting inland, puffed along by the efforts of Australian exponents of the cause—Louisa Lawson, Rose Scott, Lady Windeyer and her daughter Margaret. The question of higher education for women had been taken up in Sydney, and, after Chancellor William Manning's enlightened memorandum of 6 April, 1881 to the Sydney University Senate, women were admitted to university privileges. Maybanke Anderson (wife of the first Challis Professor of Philosophy at Sydney, Francis Anderson), suffragette leader Dora Montefiore and Louise McDonald, first principal of the Women's College (founded 1892) in the university, were all working for the extension of women's rights in education and in the professions, but though the first woman graduate in law, Ada Evans, took her degree in 1902 state laws prevented her from practising as a barrister until 1921.

Through the tonic air of the mountains blew these seeds of ideas and some found lodgment in the heart and head of Stella Franklin as she grew. There was a flowering some time later of mildly radical views on politics and religion, a stalwart growth of republican feeling and a little weed of racism, all tangled together with an overwhelming luxuriance of nationalism, though her patriotism was not of the florid sort. Living for her first nine years in the beauty of the unspoiled high Monaro had soaked the child's heart with a passion for that place, that land, which had little to do with flag-waving or pompously-expressed sentiments or any of the ideas of nationalism held by conventionalists of the left and the right.

There was another idea that took strong root, that somehow, in some way, women were not as free as men. This was no mere intellectual notion but part of her experience, for seeing her beautiful, talented mother and other bush wives worn and soured in their marriages by the pressure of frequent childbearing, in circumstances of crushing drudgery, was a much more effective introduction to feminist ideas than any theoretical article.

Against the backgrounds of Talbingo and Brindabella, Stella's first nine years passed idyllically with an ecstatic visit to the zoo in Sydney the only venture afield. At home on wintry mornings in her early years her mother would read to her by the fire, *Tales from Mother Goose* in particular, though impractical fairies and frightening witches were banned. Stella, a besotted animal lover, found endless delight in a *Picture Alphabet of Birds, Dr Wood's Natural History*, in *Aesop's Fables* and in the saga of that roistering, wandering, a-wooing frog, Rowley. She learned her pot-hooks and hangers, her alphabet and some figures at her mother's knee and then it was time for formal education to begin at the little school at her Uncle

Thomas' home, Brindabella Station. Daily she walked the kilometre and a half across the paddocks, "a very small girl, mostly sunbonnet, moving at a pace scarcely perceptible."[4] In this isolated valley, far from any literary centre, the child had the good fortune to come under the care of a fine teacher, Charles Blyth.

Disguised as Mr Auchinvole in the book *Childhood at Brindabella* and as Old Harris in *My Career Goes Bung*, Charles Blyth was a learned but impractical Scottish gentleman of good education who had landed up somehow, some said pursued by the demon drink, in this cut-off corner, tutoring small children. The position was rumoured to have been found for him by a distant relative, a leading politician who in time became Premier. (Mr Blyth was certainly a fiery supporter of Premier George Reid. "I am specially glad," he wrote in 1895, "that Premier Reid gained such a signal victory over that jealous old humbug Sir H. Parkes, whose virulent detractions and abuse of a better, abler and honester politician than he ever was, were disgusting."[5] Gentle, well-bred and literary, the elderly man was heartened by the intelligence and ability of Stella, though like the best of teachers he was concerned for all his pupils. Little Linda had supplanted her elder sister again, this time at Talbingo, but the pain of the loss of her grandma was soothed by the interest of the new world of the classroom, which occupied a room at one end of the long sprawling house, and opened on to a verandah where at certain times Mr Blyth also presided over Her Majesty's Post Office. Stella shared the only table, set near the fireplace, much-needed for the snowy winters, with her four cousins, children of Thomas and Annie Franklin. There were three boys, Thomas Ernest, Joseph Michael and George Donald, and Stella's admired and protective older cousin Annie May, later Mrs H.E. Bridle.

She loved her lessons, and showed ability early in composition and literary appreciation. "You were the smartest and best little pupil I had or can hope to have in Brindabella[6] . . . the only one of all my pupils here and elsewhere that I would or could write to expecting to be understood,"[7] was her teacher's assessment. "You had not only the ability to succeed but the desire to do so and the energy to persevere."[8] He summed up a large part of Stella's nature in that one sentence.

Taking her cue from her mother, Stella despised juvenile stories but responded enthusiastically at school to more difficult literature, revelling particularly in the poignancy, the heroism, the bitter bravery in loss and defeat of the Scots ballads. She also fell head over heels in love with the dictionary. Words were fascinating objects, the more unusual, the more exciting. "Do you remember convicting me of having omitted the last h in ornithorhynchus on the authority of Chambers?" Blyth asked.[9] Publishers and editors in following years often lost patience over her esoteric and unorthodox vocabulary. Happily, Aunt Annie was a reader too, with a taste

The jacket of *Childhood at Brindabella*, first published in 1963.

for such *avant-garde* writers as Zola and Walt Whitman. Even so, her pre-adolescent niece found it necessary to purloin *Esther Waters* and read it under the spare room bed. Other adults observed the child's skill with words. "What a remarkably clever little girl!" declared that august person-age, the Commissioner for Crown Lands. "I think you are going to be an author."[10]

The childish world was not all words and sums. Just before her sixth birthday, loss by death touched her for the first time. Baby sister Una died on 11 September, 1885, aged six months. Mourning was simple in the bush. The men of the station fashioned a tiny coffin, lined with white satin, and the women scattered a profusion of spring flowers, snowdrops, violets and daffodils around the little form. Then Una was buried on part of the property, on a plot surrounded with palings of mountain ash, and Susannah Franklin planted an elm tree in memory of her child. It was one of the few times in her life that Stella saw her mother's face wet with tears, though there was no wailing or breakdown from stern, courageous Susannah.

The baby's death brought a moment of sadness to her sister, but an incident involving a doll, not a living creature, aroused a far more passionate resentment against the Fates. Stella had few toys, and when Grandma gave her a doll, won in one of those wicked games of chance, a raffle (almost respectable because it was for the church bazaar), Stella cherished it and lovingly shared her bed with it. This wonder was dressed as a bride of the 1880s, in pink sateen with a train, and had long wavy hair and a delicate china head and feet and hands on a sawdust body. Inevitably in the manner of china dolls, it fell to the ground one day and a tiny hand parted from a sawdust arm. Assured by adults in a general way that the Almighty could do anything, Stella trusted God with this disaster, putting the beloved in her cot, putting the hand at the end of the arm and praying for a miracle. Next morning's disillusionment was never forgotten, for in later life she still talked about the incident. So great was the passion of disappointment that it even affected her religious faith.

On a somewhat higher theological level, Stella announced some years later at Talbingo that she was not going to church one Sunday as she no longer believed in a good God because of his cruelty to his dear son on the cross. Grandma's immediate answer to that crisis of conscience was a resort to the broomstick, knocking the heretic into the mud in her best dress, then locking her in the pantry. Stella was confirmed at All Saints Church of England, Collector, in 1894, and though she retained a kind of broad religious belief, it depended to a large extent on the idiosyncrasies of her own passionate nature and its demands, rather than on a set of creeds.

Such childish sorrows and problems mingled with the delights of the countryside and the discoveries of the classroom. At home she learned to cook and sew, even winning a darning competition in a local show on one

Bullock team, branding calves, and breaking a horse at Brindabella.

occasion, and all her life she prided herself on being deft and neat in housekeeping without fussing about it.

Enfolded in a happy family, she wrote in the winter of 1887 when she was seven to her aunts at Talbingo. She was proud of nine-month-old Norman's prowess in crawling. Father had not come home yet and the weather had been rough: "... the snow lay very deep for a whole day—we had such fun snow-balling but it was so cold ... Linda is getting on very well with her lessons which she learns at night, she has had her hair cut again and she looks much better when she has it cut.''[11] In the spring she told them of the young calves, fresh butter and eggs and the lushness of the grass: "... the grass is so long everywhere that you would think that it was a fattening paddock more than a flower garden.''[12] In the summer she rejoiced in her garden, in the fox-gloves, sweet william, roses and poppies, the red, the white and the purple.

It was a happy, busy life. For a time the pleasant pattern had been marred by the barbed teasing of her cousin George, to such an extent that, sobbing, she had shirked school. "All boys are teases. You'll have to endure them or keep away from them,'' was the dry and practical advice of her mother, and reinforced by this calm, if prejudiced view, she coped with the trouble and it subsided.

The free and glowing years of childhood passed peacefully in a beautiful setting, in the security of a wide family. But in the late summer of 1889 there seemed a breath of unhappiness in the air. Mervyn and her mother both had the blight on the lip. Father was away with cousin Joseph Vallance of the Bramina run, voting for some Member; Linda was reigning again at Talbingo; and Mr Blyth was in bad health and going away to see a doctor. The child seemed to sense that changes were approaching. Perhaps she had heard discussions between her parents. In her tenth year the idyllic golden days ended. The family left Brindabella.

Stella Miles Franklin wrote many years later: "I was leaving the place where I had been a child in exceptional circumstances. There I had never suffered discomfort, ill health, deprivation. There I had known no sordidness, sorrow, humiliation or discontent.''[13] However misted by the haze of time that view may be, it still seems clear that for Stella Franklin leaving her childhood paradise was an expulsion from Eden. Already, at this early age, that longing for the happy past, which lasted life long, began to grip her heart. Some six years later, when the troubles of adolescence clawed her, Charles Blyth wrote, "Your looking back regretfully to earlier days shows you had a happy time there, and I agree with you in thinking that there is a sadness in reflections as to the days that have gone and will never recur again in this life.''[14]

3 Stillwater and Linda

On 30 April, 1889, John and Susannah Franklin and their family left their secluded station in the ranges and moved down and north-eastwards to the flatter and more settled country around the railway town of Goulburn, centre of a prosperous agricultural and pastoral district. The new territory was about 110 kilometres from Brindabella and 220 by rail from Sydney.

The first sight of her new home filled Stella with a sense of desolation. The scenery was drabber, the trees scraggier, no clear streams flowed, no fresh ferns cascaded. The house itself was a poorly built wooden structure of ten rooms with only the most rudimentary facilities. Worse still, the descent from the mountains to the tablelands was combined with a slide down the social scale, from the comfort, hard-won by Susannah, and the standing of a minor up-country squatter, to the circumscribed hard labour of a farmer and his family on a small selection and the lowly status of a "cockatoo", scratching for a living. In this district even the horses were inferior and the liberation of the saddle, one of the great joys of Stella's life, was denied her for a time. "Only men rode." Later she wrote of this experience: "I was going to a life changed in situation and routine, a life more restricted in territory, finances and social association."[1]

What reasons prompted such a move? They were probably associated with the need for proper education for the growing family, particularly the precocious "first born" and Linda, who was now ready for school. Mr Blyth was not in good health and could not be relied on forever. As well, John Franklin, now past forty, was restless and wished to attempt something new. He thought he would do better for himself and his family in a more populated district where, with his fine knowledge of stock, he could try his hand at auctioneering.

So, on an autumn afternoon, 7 May, 1889, father, mother and the two little boys arrived by sulky at the drab home near Thornford, which Susannah, ever a fighter, named Stillwater after some clogged waterholes. Stella rode down from her mountains on a lady's hack, Zephyr, accompanied by the maid, Mary Boyd. Then came Grandma Lampe, bringing Linda back after two years at Talbingo, and escorting a midwife to help with the birth of the baby to be born on 3 July, who was named Hume Talmadge after his grandfather Franklin's explorer friend, Hamilton Hume. Distressed by the abrupt changes, Stella pleaded to visit the familiar old station at Talbingo again, and to her delight Grandma Lampe granted her wish. By train and sulky she flew back in the crisp winter cold for one more taste of her childhood joys.

By now she was almost ten and when her proud rendition of a piano piece was disregarded by her relatives for the excitement of the first crawling of a new grandchild she was stunned, and must have realised that for her that endearing stage of childhood, when just to be new and young is to be a marvel, was over. A smashing blow on her way home, the death of a loved but maimed chicken which was to haunt her for many years, was another symbol of the end of a golden age. The freedom, the indulgence, the admiration, the protection were left behind. She had now to make a place in a wider circle, a harder world.

> For this rude change I was as lacking in protective worldliness as a bird reared in a boudoir might have been when released to normal living. For one thing I had no knowledge of evil either as sin or vice, nor any understanding that ill-will and unfriendliness could exist.[2]

After Christmas 1889, she returned reluctantly to Stillwater, to the discipline of a real school, to an increasing perplexity about life and to a growing rebellion against the restrictions at that time placed on maturing girls. Even in her last days at Talbingo Grandma had reprimanded her for being "froward" or mutinous when Stella questioned these codes. Her mother discouraged her views as impractical. In recalling this time Stella remarked: "The artificial bonds called feminine were presented to my understanding. I must become genteel as befitting a young lady. A good deal was attributed to God's will, and did not turn my heart any more warmly to that gentleman." Women were to be womanly which meant devoted to household chores, to marriage and to babies. But if a girl was not attracted to these pursuits, what then? Most girls of the day did seek happiness in marriage and a family, but Stella was not willing to comply.

> It was the humbug in 'womanliness', the distorting and atrophying of minds on a sex line, the grinding superstition that all women must be activated on a more or less moronic level, the absence of fair play between men and women when the masculine and feminine issue arose that was at the root of the trouble, though I did not know so much in my first decade.[3]

At ten, bewildered, rebellious, she was leaving the clear reaches of childhood behind. The world was becoming deeper, dark and clouded, adult behaviour puzzling and confusing. Beloved parents were showing feet of clay, turning from trusted gods into ordinary mortals, with ordinary faults, turning even into tyrants. The whole world was heaving threateningly. For Stella Miles Franklin that move into adolescence which we all make coincided with the abrupt loss of the home of her happy past. All her life she was to be nostalgic for a place and time, the high Monaro country of her childhood years.

In spite of wrenching changes, the persevering, industrious little girl settled well into life at tiny Thornford Public School, well-equipped with her quick mind and eager attitudes for the new tasks. Again she was most fortunate in finding an appreciative and devoted teacher, Mary Gillespie, who remained a friend when schooldays were over. Susannah was proud of the impression that her small daughter made on the inspectors in 1890, and Stella was soon winning her fair share of prizes.

Her quirky, questioning mind still meditated on the theological problem. Thornford School was asked by a clergyman on one occasion to pray for a sick child. During the following week the child died. When the rector reappeared to tell the children the sad news, the eleven-year-old doubter in his flock said: ''I knew it would do no good. It was none of our business. It was God's business.''

The rebel, the feminist and the writer in the little girl were all burgeoning. Her scrapbooks of these years, while crammed with cutouts of posies of flowers, butterflies, birds, aristocratic elegant ladies and beautiful, round-cheeked toddlers, all washed with the gentle sentimental pastel glaze of Victorian taste, also include astringent counters culled from the journals of the day, such as: ''What this country needs is a religion which will make a man feel that it is just as cold for his wife to get up and light the fire as for himself.'' Pressed ferns and seaweed are neighbours to some unconventional rules for behaviour in high society.''Salute the hostess by saying 'Cully, how's his nibs!' It has an offhand informal pleasantry about it that makes everyone feel easy . . . Shout 'Woof' as you sit down.'' Some comic verses on the anomalies of English grammar and pronunciation show her interest in language, and, touchingly, a short girl in an age of tall, willowy beauty, she included a cheer-up verse on the ''little woman'' and how she gets her man.[4]

There is also a paragraph on the importance of loving words and deeds in the home. Unfortunately the move to Stillwater had not been a success. The background of life there was darkening. Susannah Franklin had laboured to create a pleasant home at Brindabella. But now after years of effort, with six children of whom the eldest was twelve when baby Laurel was born on 20 July, 1892, her energies were depleted, and to her Stillwater became a place of heartbreak and disappointment. A long disastrous drought struck the dairying and pastoral industries (deepening the depression which had followed the bank crashes of 1893) and John Franklin, no businessman, failed in his auctioneering venture.

Stella's carefree early childhood had vanished with her father's decision to

Scenes of Tumut and surrounding district, 1900s.

leave Brindabella. The freedom-loving little girl of the ranges had become a drudge on a cow cockie farm. There was milking before school and feeding the calves, then a long walk in summer heat or winter frost, a day's lessons, the walk home, milking again, washing the dishes, homework and piano practice. It was the life of many Australian bush children of the day, but where most accepted their fate stoically, if grumblingly, Stella raged against the oppression of this harsh and dreary state. At thirteen she sought escape from the sordidness surrounding her in scribbling romances of silken English high life, full of lords and ladies and grand mansions with butlers.

She also found release and joy in music. Her examination results were creditable, ninety-five percent in the Junior Exam on 9 June, 1894, and seventy-one percent in the Intermediate on 6 June, 1896. She played piano and sang in an unusual contralto. Music books surviving from that day include such songs as ''Just Before the Battle'', ''In Her Little Bed We Laid Her'', ''Weep Not For Me'', ''Cherry Ripe'', ''The Bluebells of Scotland'' and many more of the sentimental airs which flowed through the little parlours or grander drawing rooms of Victorian Australia. (That fine film, *My Brilliant Career*, seems to me to have struck a false note when it had puritanical Sybylla-Stella sing a ribald ditty in order to shock. Stella-Sybylla had no need of such devices to raise eyebrows. Her shockingness lay in her whole unusual way of thinking and feeling.)

Meanwhile, Charles Blyth encouraged her reading, *Vanity Fair* and Dickens, and praised her writing. Her first published piece, a report on the Thornford Public School picnic, was printed in the *Goulburn Evening Penny Post* in 1896 when she was sixteen. That same year she showed one of her high-life efforts, probably ''For Sale to the Highest Bidder'', to T.J. Hebblewhite of the *Goulburn Post*. Wisely, he strongly advised her to leave the unfamiliar world of lords and ladies and to deal with the material at hand. She also sent a manuscript to Angus & Robertson, and Blyth thought the reader's report encouraging.

At home things were not happy. Between the parents there must have been recriminations. To have left the comfort and status of Brindabella for the poverty of Stillwater must have been distressing and hardening to Susannah in particular, and Stella's image of her father as god-man seems to have crumbled. Sybylla Melvyn's words, ''He was my hero, confidant, encyclopedia, mate, and even my religion till I was ten. Since then I have been religionless''[5] might have come from Stella's lips. The disillusionment with her father may have led to her tartness concerning the abilities of men in general. To Blyth she wrote, in 1894, of the speech void of sense or wit prevalent at election times among the males of the community.

At sixteen, with her schooling over, it was time for the daughter of a poor farmer to look for work. The helpful local MP, E. O'Sullivan, recommended her to the Education Department on 26 June, 1896 as a pupil teacher and she

Linda Lampe Franklin, Stella's sister.

was invited to attend a competitive examination for applicant pupil teachers at the Goulburn Superior School on 7 July, 1896.[6] However, in February 1897 she was teaching her Franklin cousins privately at Yass. She found it very hard going, and in comforting her Blyth urged her to keep a diary of thoughts, feelings and remarks, and to look upon her disappointments and worries as useful material for literary purposes in the manner of Charlotte Bronte. Tactlessly, he also remarked that Charlotte was small, plain and short-sighted. The adolescent concern with looks is a venerable chestnut. In Stella Franklin's case the matter was an anguished issue, distressingly complicated by her relationship with her sister Linda.

Stella thought herself plain and her sister beautiful. The girls were less than two years apart in age, close in their affection, but utterly different in looks and temperament. Adolescent Stella longed for Linda's traditional style of beauty, for her classic profile, oval face, golden hair, slender figure and gentle, delicate manner. Short and dumpy in contrast with Linda's willowy elegance, she was convinced that the younger girl was her mother's favourite.

In looks Stella's conviction of plainness was quite unbased. She was short, certainly, only 157 centimetres (5 feet 2 inches), but her figure was trim and well proportioned. Her complexion, always well protected from the sun in spite of her outdoors life, was fine and fair, her teeth white and even. Her blue-grey eyes slanted slightly beneath well-marked brows and a determined little chin supported a mobile mouth. Though the character and intelligence evident in the face were not in the more insipid style of beauty then popular, she also had one noticeable conventional claim to contemporary loveliness. At seventeen her mid-brown hair, glinting with copper lights, flowed over 100 centimetres (forty-three inches) down her back. She thought it her best feature, while her worst she considered to be her "Bridle nose", short, buttonish, even cute, but without the classic line of Linda's "Wilkinson nose".

Charles Blyth had tried to reassure Stella about her looks—"I never thought you were or would be plain"[7]—but perhaps the best appraisal of Stella's style comes from one of her novels in a discussion of a heroine named Ignez:

> "What's she look like?"
> "Some think she's wonderful, and others call her quite plain. She has a different kind of face, but you like to watch it. She says the terriblest things straight out to men as well as to women, but I don't think she would go astray with men—she's not fast that way."[8]

If the sisters differed in looks, in character they were also far apart. Linda lacked the force and fire of the elder girl and her docile, sweet-tempered gentleness and happy nature were more understood by, and more comforting to, the much-tried mother who found Stella wilful and difficult. Soft-hearted Linda idolised her sister. When Stella was ill in the latter half of 1897 Linda

Stella Franklin at eighteen.

wrote from Talbingo that her eyes were sore from crying — ''When I get home I will cheer you up and make you laugh . . . I do miss you. I don't know what I would do without you.'' In 1899 she wrote: ''I have not recovered from the loss of you either or ever will.''[9]

Stella's reciprocating love was strong, but interwoven with the jealousy she had experienced at being supplanted first in her mothers's arms and then at Talbingo. There was the awareness too that Linda was all she could not be, gentle and accepting, mixed with the suspicion that her mother did not love her as she did Linda. After trying her hand at some short Australian sketches, such as ''Within a Footstep of the Goal'', she began to pour all the adolescent rage and pain she felt into a burlesque autobiography of a girl very like herself, Sybylla Melvyn, living on an impoverished dairy farm in a district called Possum Gully, the daughter of a strong, austere mother and an incompetent father who has come down in the world and finds comfort in drink. She entitled her book *My Brilliant (?) Career*.

4 *"My Brilliant Career" and Henry Lawson*

Stella Miles Franklin began *My Brilliant Career* on 20 September, 1898, when she was 18, and finished it on 25 March, 1899.[1] Into this book she put all her feelings of oddness, of plainness, of unlovedness. She put in also her passionate ambition; her terror at the transience of life; her revolt against a God who seemed uncaring about the suffering of his creation, human and animal; her anger at the condition of women in the harsh, restrictive bush society; her puzzlement in sexual matters; and her general adolescent unhappiness and confusion. It was a novel of egotism, self-centred and powerful; all the agonies of a brilliant being crushed pell-mell together in a breathless rush of words. The force of the work lies in the strength of feeling expressed honestly and unselfconsciously, without guile.

Sybylla Melvyn, sixteen years old, drudging daughter of a poor farmer, finds that her ambitious wishes for a career in the arts, and her impatient demands on life, clash with her late 19th century society's narrow notions of what is proper for a girl. In deep distress, she wins no support even from much-loved members of her family. Her adored Grannie, her beautiful and sad Aunt Helen, and her over-worked, respected mother urge her to conform. Her once-worshipped father, now a broken-down farmer-cockatoo, well known for his sprees around the commonest pubs in town, cannot help her; nor can wealthy squatter Harry Beecham who wishes to marry her, and is dependable and kind, but who does not understand her. Sybylla's younger sister Gertie, "so pretty, so girlish, so understandable, so full of innocent coquetry", only points up the difference between Sybylla and what is expected of her. The clash between her tormented rebellion and her love for her family is set against a realistic background of the varied Australian countryside, the dreariness of the drought-stricken dairy farm contrasting with the beauty and fullness of the stations in the ranges. But the sombreness is relieved by bursts of unquenchable high spirits and love of life, for Sybylla's vitality is her essence.

In 1899 Stella Franklin sent this MS to Angus & Robertson, to *The*

Bulletin and to her mentor T.J. Hebblewhite. Angus & Robertson returned it with an encouraging comment. Hebblewhite thought it a big advance on her earlier work but worried that she was fretting her heart out in the bush. Montgomery of *The Bulletin* returned it for Archibald (who did not have time to read it), and gave some useful advice. She revised the work quickly, probably acting on this counsel, between September and November, 1899, and in a last throw approached Henry Lawson, then at a peak of success in his writing. The draft of this letter reads:

> This is written to ask if you will help me. I will explain. For some years I have been scribbling and have written a book. My trouble is that I have lived such a secluded life in the bush that I am unacquainted with any literary people of note and am too hard up to incur the expense of travelling to Sydney to personally interview a publisher on the matter. As for posting a story to them with a hope of it being read unless one has swell influence one might as well try to sell an elderly cow for a race horse — thus I have conceived the idea of beseeching your aid.
> Perhaps it is a foolish notion as probably you will have neither time nor inclination to extend a hand to me but if you would be good natured enough to read my yarn you would be helping me out of a deep hole. I merely ask you to run through it and state whether you think it twaddle, interesting or trash and allow me to use your opinion. Do not be annoyed at my presumption, believe me it has taken me some time to pluck up sufficient courage to ask this of you and my only excuse is that I am in a fix and though I have not had an opportunity of reading your prose have gained such help from your poetry that I feel as though I have known you for many years. This is not my first attempt at writing. When a youngster I gained a prize in an Australian story competition [the Amykos Competition, 1896] also for several essays and local penmen have pronounced my yarn as containing ability, originality.
> Awaiting reply
> Sir
> Faithfully yrs,
> Miles Franklin.[2]

She did not mention her age or sex.

Something about the letter he received appealed to Lawson. In December 1899 he wrote back to Mr M. Franklin, asking for the manuscript. Upon reading it his praise was high. He asked if the writer were man or woman, and said he thought the book was a big thing.

At the same time a minor success came from another direction. The MP O'Sullivan had recommended her to several of the big city hospitals for a position as trainee nurse in October 1897. But the waiting list was long as nursing represented about the only escape from the dullness of country life for genteel girls. It appears that Stella began nursing training about this time, for Lawson in a letter of January 1900 thought she would be put upon considerably by the head and other nurses, until she knew the ropes. Her nursing experiences lasted only a few weeks for in February there was a saddening shock. Her eldest brother Mervyn died of typhoid fever at 16. Stella returned home but the short episode was a landmark. (''Once was in Sydney

Henry Lawson.

for three weeks. Met H. Lawson. Big, large, immense, GREAT event for me . . . ''³) She wrote up her nursing experiences in a serial ''Ministering Angel'', published in *New Idea* years later. Lawson wrote to her care of Mrs Gill, 235 Victoria Street, Darlinghurst, inviting her to visit him and his wife, Bertha, and in his kindly way came to escort her to their home at Chaplin Cottage in Charles Street, North Sydney, reached by ferry across the harbour.

He tried to place ''the little bush maid's'' book with Angus & Robertson but, when George Robertson hummed and ha'd, offered to take it with him to England to seek a publisher there. Although Bertha had been gravely ill after childbirth and their financial affairs were shaky, the Lawsons left Sydney in April 1900 to try their luck in chancy London, where they did not even have an address as yet. Their generosity in the midst of their own difficulties to a young unknown was remarkable.

Back at Stillwater by April, Stella kept herself busy with a series of sketches and stories, but her main concern was with her manuscript, now in Lawson's hands. She was steadfastly against any toning down in her draft letters. ''Please you and you alone keep an eye on it, don't trust it to those people who don't understand.'' She continued,''I will not despond while you have me in hand.''⁴

Lawson placed the work with the famous pioneer agent J.B. Pinker. Pinker was something new in the literary world, a go-between, mothering and protecting writers in their dealings with publishers. Joseph Conrad, Henry James, Somerset Maugham, Arnold Bennett, H.G. Wells and many other authors sought his help and advice. To have him as an agent was thought to be an enormous help. He had helped Lawson and now began negotiations with Blackwood of Edinburgh about the Franklin book. On 1 September, 1900, Stella signed an agreement with him, though she was still against any toning down and did not want ''Miss'' on the title page as she wished to pose as ''a bald-headed seer of the opposite sex''.⁵ Blackwood accepted it in January 1901, and by April it was printed. Lawson sent a parcel of reviews and urged her to look after her pronouns and write a lot like M'Swat. The M'Swat family, ignorant, dirty but not unkindly bush folk, had peopled some lively chapters in *My Brilliant Career.*

At Stillwater in September Stella confronted with mixed emotions six brand new copies of her surprising offspring. For her began a period of joy mixed with anguish; joy at her final triumph and anguish at the thought of the explosion the book might cause in her family circle. ''Those poor lost girls who have a baby without being married must feel like I did. There would be the baby but all the wild deep joy of it would be disgrace and trouble.''⁶ The words are those of fictional Sybylla Melvyn in a similar situation but there can be little doubt that they echoed Stella's emotions in her success. In her headlong rush to express her own passions she had given no thought to the feelings of others, some of them very close and dear to her. The consequences of that insouciance had now to be faced.

Inevitably, since supposedly fictional Sybylla's life so closely paralleled Stella's, the unsophisticated country people of her blood or acquaintance saw themselves caricatured in the book. There was very little understanding of the artist's use of exaggeration, transposition and simple imagination. The George Franklins of Oak Vale, who had given her a job teaching their children, thought themselves parodied and outrageously insulted in the M'Swat portrayal as ignorant and slatternly and could not forgive her. It was a family breach which could not be mended.

Her humourless mother was furious at the picture given of their lives and at the trouble caused in the family. Unworried by what people might say, adoring Linda was delighted and even Grandma accepted it, not without a chuckle.

> Thank you for that lovely, lovely present. I am so proud to be the sister of an authoress . . . Grannie nearly killed herself laughing at parts of it . . . Grannie hides it when anyone comes in but tells them about it not what's in it . . . She looks at the business side. Let 'em buy it she says . . . You are pretty hot on me in places, not to say anything of poor Father![7]

Linda saw herself in gentle Gertie, pretty, soft-hearted but a butterfly of life.

Aunt Helena Lampe, possibly model for Aunt Helen in the book, was concerned too, not for herself but for Father. She wondered what he would think, and felt sorry for him as he must have been hurt to be used as material for a somewhat disreputable character. Amiable dreamer John Franklin may have been upset at the portrayal of Sybylla's father as an incompetent drunk, but if so he laughed it off. Certainly he was no great success in business, having the reputation even with loving Linda of being feckless and a poor manager. Linda wrote to Stella some months later in June 1902:

> I think it would be a mad idea F having a butcher's shop as even good business people generally fail at that. He being *no* business man and inexperienced into the bargain. It would be a mess. And being in town would never do him. Poor you would have all your time taken up pulling him out of pubs. No matter where we go it will always be the same while F manages. I wish M could take it all in her own hands.[8]

Adolescence is given to censoriousness, and to ruthless, relentless judgments. Whatever his failings, John Franklin must have been a man of generous and loving nature not to react to some degree in the manner of his brother George. To be even thought by friends and neighbours to have been exposed in a cruel manner by his daughter must have put him in an unpleasant position. Yet there was no break. Some acquaintances were disposed to think he had helped her write the book. In a later work Stella Franklin made amends. In *My Career Goes Bung* the tolerant, encouraging, understanding side of the man ''a hundred years ahead of his time'' is made plain.

As word of that Franklin girl's latest exploit spread, the whole district was abuzz. From an unusual child she had grown to a remarkable girl and now into an extraordinary young woman. As a little girl her quaintness had been appealing, especially in her family circle. As a schoolgirl she had been the joy of her teachers, if somewhat resented by less gifted pupils. As a teenage girl she had alarmed family and neighbours by being outspoken on such matters as suffrage for women and other odd ideas that did not enter the heads of most girls. She was well known as a superb and daring horsewoman though she had caused some scandalised comment by riding astride. ''She was by far the best horsewoman in the Goulburn district, famous as a local show-rider before she became more famous after all that fuss about her book . . . She used to race the train into Goulburn . . . and loved a joke.''[9]

Daring, high-spirited, lacking in girlish meekness, she had as well unusual ideas on marriage and religion, though she never had a reputation for ''fastness''. Station-reared in a male world, she was as free and friendly in her manner with men as with women, but fastidious in her own sexual behaviour to the point of primness. Her entertaining liveliness attracted a number of male admirers and the district speculated on the identity of Harry Beecham. Linda wrote to her sister about the names mentioned, Splendid Alex McDonald from Uriarra Station, a certain J.B. reported as spoony over her in 1898, or Philip B. — '' . . . everybody thinks he is Harry,'' wrote Linda, ''it does make me wild.''[10] The gossip was not about Stella's sexual behaviour but about her outrageous ideas in general. Some girls of that harsh environment, resenting their life of dull poverty, might slip away to seek a brighter future and jollier time in the more dubious trades of the city, perhaps becoming in the odd phrase of the day ''no better than they should be''. But Stella Franklin's revolt was not of that kind. A friend of later years, Beatrice Davis, described her aptly as ''a rebellious puritan''. Stella Franklin's virtue was not in question. Her defiance was intellectual. Iconoclastic, satiric and abrasive, she was yet chaste, loving and generous. Hers was a personality to bewilder the simple rural community.

She was different from the conforming girls around her in the quality of her mind, the range of her talents (for she could sing as well as write and had hopes of developing her voice to concert level), and in the strength of her ambitions. Passionate in her love of music, she yearned to do something big in life, perhaps like the Australian heroine of the hour, Madame Melba, then the rage in the opera houses of Europe and the United States. Most daughters of poor farmers would have been glad of the opportunity of training as a nurse, content to serve in a modest way and escape the tedium of bush life, but Stella had rejected this career very quickly. ''I could have made a nurse and a good one . . . But it is a profession demanding the whole of

Franklin at the time *My Brilliant Career* was published.

one's time, thought and energy and — well — life is fleeting and there were about 678 things more or less, that I wished to do or become.''[11]

No ''flower child'' or ''drop-out'' ambition influenced her behaviour, and good manners, the niceties of life were important to her, as was her standing as ''a lady''. What she hated and spoke up against was the coarseness and ugliness of the life in which the people around her were entangled.''It would be terrible to live all one's life here and get old and growly like the women with horrible things the matter with their insides from having too many children or to take to drink like the men,''[12] said another of her alter-ego heroines, Ignez. Primarily she sought for herself the heroic possibilities of life. Deeply troubled as she was by the anger and offence she had caused within her family, still she could not but rejoice in the acclaim of the world.

Overseas reviews were stunningly enthusiastic. The London *Sun* described her book as being '' . . . as good as Dickens in its touches of humour''. *The Spectator*, while acknowledging its defects, talked of its passion and power, and *The Manchester Guardian* wrote of its strength and vitality. *Blackwood Magazine* compared its forcefulness with Emily Bronte, and there were reviews in other leading papers — in *The Yorkshire Post*, *The Daily News*, *The Glasgow Herald*, *The Literary World* and *Pall Mall Gazette*.

In Australia, the Melbourne *Age* made comparisons with the Russian writer Marie Bashkirtsheff (1860-1884), whose posthumously-published autobiography had aroused extraordinary interest, and *The Barrier Truth* compared the author with Olive Schreiner, who had written *Story of an African Farm* in her teens.

The accolade in Sydney was bestowed by A.G. Stephens of *The Bulletin*'s ''Red Page'', who headed his review of 28 September, 1901, ''A Bookful of Sunlight''. He dubbed the work ''the first Australian novel . . . as tonic as bush air, as aromatic as bush trees and as clear and honest as bush sunlight''. Such praise must have been as balm to her. In impish delight Stella wrote to the editor of *The Bulletin*, J.F. Archibald, Esq. The draft of 5 September, 1901, reads:

My dear Sir,
Per same post I send you a copy of a self-written yarn entitled ''*My Brilliant Career*''. If you would kindly do me the honour of accepting same you will afford me much gratification. Don't for a moment imagine me so unsophisticated and green as to think the ignorance and inexperience of a bush 18 yrs (most unadulterated bush too) could produce anything interesting to a litterateur of yr experience. But spare me a moment and I will explain. In '99 I sent you an MS; you, or Alex Montgomery for you — wrote to me and said you had not time to read the MS but from occasional glances you considered it fairly well written and gave me some good information — advice. It was the first honest letter I received from anyone in the ink and paper business and I shall always remember it. The scribblings submitted to you was this yarn. I re-wrote it and appealed to our poet Lawson for help. You must know him as your name is in the front of his book so you will know he did not hum or haw but came to my

rescue oh! so kindly and sympathetically as only Henry Lawson could or would. This book is the result.[13]

Though *My Brilliant Career* had been written as a protest, as the desperate cry of a talented girl against her imprisonment in a flat society, it was not a tract. The message and the melancholy were mixed with an attractive exuberance. The book was also a celebration of the pleasures of youth and flirtation and romance. The rebellion was well laced with humour and high spirits.

As Sybylla said in one of her bursts of happiness: ''What a delightful place the world was! — so accommodating, I felt complete mistress of it. It was like an orange — I merely had to squeeze it and it gave forth sweets plenteously.''[14]

After the unhappiness and frustrations of her adolescent years, after her resolute struggle to succeed, in spite of the turmoil which she had roused within her family, at twenty-one Stella Miles Franklin held the juicy golden orange of the world in her hands.

5 Sydney and A.G. Stephens

She had arrived. This small girl, looking younger than her years in white muslin frock and cotton stockings, with her long dark hair still flowing down her back in schoolgirl fashion, bounced into Sydney like her fictional heroine Sybylla Melvyn as an acclaimed author, yet a "girl not out", and was scooped up by some of that brash, pleasure-loving city's most notable citizens.

At the turn of the nineteenth century Sydney was still what Norman Lindsay, then a fledgling illustrator with *The Bulletin*, has described as a sailor town. Distinguished literary visitors such as Joseph Conrad and R.L. Stevenson had delighted in the zest of the waterside life of this hurly-burly port and in the beauty of its vast, unbridged harbour. Though the wool-clippers no longer anchored at Circular Quay, their place having been taken by regal liners and scudding commuter ferries, a great deal of the city's life still focused there. Looking down the lines of the main streets from the heart of the town, the glance expanded into the freedom of blue, green or grey waters and the bustle of the harbour. The Quay was a meeting place, a melting pot of sailors of all nations and races, the link with imperial "home", a gateway to the world. The usurping airport at suburban Mascot which destroyed this vitality was far off in the future, and the dull heaviness of Circular Quay Railway Station had not yet stretched itself across the edge of the square, obliterating the vista of water and shipping. Nearby in lower George Street a Chinatown flourished, and though an attempt was being made to clean up the Rocks area (today a trendy tourist centre) after the bubonic plague of 1900, it was still a dangerous haunt of violent "pushes", the roving and restless gangs of the young.

Around the corner from the bustling Quay, at 214 George Street, *The Bulletin* had its offices. A.G. Stephens wrote to Stella, and invited her to lunch on 12 April, 1902. He had already written to congratulate her on her book and they had exchanged photographs and letters. He told her that her face reminded him of Olive Schreiner, but not her book, and presented her with a copy of Will Ogilvie's poems, *Fair Girls and Grey Horses*.

Further up-town from the Quay lay a different city. Victorian sandstone buildings stood square and grave, and graceful iron railings rimmed the formal green of Hyde Park. The *beau monde*, the beautiful people, hoping to be noticed or to see someone worth noticing, ''did the block'' in their finest array, strolling down King Street, along George, up Hunter and along Pitt, chatting, window shopping, hailing friends and striking up acquaintances. The city was small enough to be intimate but large enough to be interesting, a business-like Victorian city, though the age of the grand old Queen was ending and Sydney was no longer a colonial town but one of the two leading cities of a new country.

The year of *My Brilliant Career* was the year of the proclamation of the Commonwealth of Australia. The six separate colonies, suspiciously jealous, with rival economies and their own postal and defence systems, even with customs checks at their borders, had finally united, after much argument and discussion, into a federation. With all the pomp and ceremony that the newborn country could muster Federation Day was duly celebrated. On a hot and sticky summer morning a procession led by twenty-two unions, with fire brigades in their splendour of scarlet and brass, decorated floats and troops in full dress, preceded the Governor-General's carriage through the crowded streets of Sydney to the broad green expanses of Centennial Park. There, from an ornamented rotunda a new nation was proclaimed on 1 January, 1901 and the Earl of Hopetoun was sworn in as first governor-general. The citizens of Sydney were full of pride in their new nationhood and hope for the new century. The vitality and beauty of the sea-port and the dignified briskness of the commercial centre combined to make what its inhabitants thought to be a very special city.

To Stella Miles Franklin it was certainly special, a first conquest in a hoped-for dazzling career. But though the critical acclaim was glorious and the personal interest delightful, she was still the daughter of a hard-pressed small farmer. There were no royalties as yet from her book and trips to the city were expensive, while living there permanently was out of the question for the moment. The help of patrons and friends was necessary in the furtherance of her ambitions.

At Lynton, a two-storey cottage in the discreetly elegant suburb of Woollahra, she found an especially helpful patron who became a dear friend. The intellectual and artistic élite of this special city gathered at Lynton to float all the lively new ideas, to meet all the new and interesting people against a background of Victorian dignity and solid worth. In feminist Rose Scott's pretty drawing room flourished the nearest thing to a French *salon* that Sydney has seen. Politicians, poets, feminists, artists, judges and journalists, simple working girls and famous overseas visitors gathered there to show off their wit and brilliance, to listen, to argue. Stella's conquest of the city was signalled when kindly, impeccable Rose Scott, the *grande dame* of this coterie, wrote enthusiastically to the latest sensation in March 1902: "Your book is *wonderful*. If you come to Sydney will you come to see me?"[1] Stella came to Lynton later in the year and found there then and on her later sallies into the metropolis a friend and a home.

Other important citizens promoting her reputation were Alex Montgomery, a powerful member of *The Bulletin*'s staff who sent his congratulations, Professor Mungo MacCallum of the University of Sydney who was heard to say that there was genius in her work, and Ethel Turner, queen of writers for juveniles, author of *Seven Little Australians* and many other bestsellers, who thought it the best thing for local colour she had ever read.

Such sweet and potent praise might have turned a girl's head, except for the fact that there were two Stella Franklins. An old friend remarked perceptively: " . . . knowing your bright and cheerful nature I was surprised by the melancholy nature of your book."[2] Outwardly merry, teasing and confident, inwardly, as her book had shown, she was sad, perplexed and lonely. The double aspect of her nature tended to bewilder and mislead many men. Though she responded warmly to people there was also a reserve. Any personal passion was cooled by her dislike of intimate physical contact, while her vivid pleasure in life was clouded by awareness of the shadow of time, decay and death. When Harry Beecham said of Sybylla, "You're the queerest girl in the world. One minute you snub a person, the next you are the jolliest girl going and then you get as grave and earnest as a fellow's mother would be",[3] he could well have been speaking of Stella Franklin.

The "great hard rock of the world" had not crushed Franklin's spirit but had left already marks of pain. Even in the midst of one of Rose Scott's *soirées* she slipped away with a young male guest, and after talking of her life, her work and her ambitions, she showed him a photograph of her sister Linda. " . . . a lovely face, classic in perfection of features and fair. It was, I think obvious that there was some resentment that this beautiful girl had been spared the harder, dirtier farm work because of her beauty."[4] Franklin's feeling of being unloved, discriminated against by her mother, had not been wiped away by the praise of newfound admirers.

There were plenty of these. In the just-born nation of Australia in 1901 the youth and energy and intensity of Franklin's heroine drew a response from her own generation. Young women from all over the country wrote to Sybylla Melvyn of Possum Gully, to tell her that she had expressed for them their emotions and ambitions. "How I long to do something glorious and here I am twenty-three and nothing done," came a plaintive cry from Melbourne. At the great girls' high school in Sydney, Fort Street, according to a letter " . . . one of the teachers got your book. She read pieces from it while we were at lunch and it affected us all". An exile wrote from London, "It carried me back to my own land with a reality and truth that says everything for your way of telling it,'' and in that great sophisticated city also it drew attention—'' . . . it is being talked about by everyone in London as the cleverest novel of the season,'' reported Martha Garnett, sister-in-law of powerful literary figure Edward Garnett.[5]

Another young admirer, artist Norman Lindsay, had the pleasure of an unexpected encounter with the "infant phenomenon" when he came across her as he walked up *The Bulletin* stairs. The outward, physical Stella Franklin dazzled him. "She was very short but pleasingly plump, and she wore a large flowered hat, a summery ankle-length frock, and a superb mass of black hair in a cascade that reached her pert rump, to match a pert nose, with fine eyes and arched eyebrows and an alluring pair of lips.'' But watchdog A.G. Stephens restrained the young blood's pursuit of this vision with the stern command, "You come here,'' further insulting the twenty-two-year-old married man by adding, "I'm not going to have you interfering with that girl . . . I wouldn't trust you with her or any young girl.''[6]

Stephens, then thirty-six, was a champion to be prized by a new writer. With his weapon of the "Red Page" he was the terror of the literary world, and the maker of reputations among Australian authors at this time of the emergence of a determinedly nationalistic literature. A later writer, mauled by AGS, as he was known, testified to his power: "He could make or break. And it is no exaggeration to say that literary aspirants actually trembled in his presence.''[7] A Queenslander by birth, he worked first as a printer and compositor in that state, moved into journalism, travelled abroad to Chicago and Europe, and then in 1884 joined *The Bulletin* on the invitation of J.F. Archibald. He was well read in several languages and ruthlessly devoted to the development of a serious Australian literature. His ferocity and pompous personal style reportedly cloaked a basic timidity, especially with women, though Lindsay testified to AGS's somewhat martinettish behaviour to his wife and children in the rural suburbia of his Gordon home.

With Stella Franklin the "three-initialled terror of *The Bulletin*" put away his arrogance and austerity. This bush girl's freshness and verve softened his severity. He addressed her waggishly as Dear Miss Stella, Miles and Franklin, and welcomed her visits. Since there were still no royalties Franklin continued to live with her parents at Stillwater, Bangalore via Goulburn, for most of 1902. The friendship with Stephens was conducted largely by letter, enlivened by the occasional call at his office. He was affectionate and somewhat arch in his correspondence, refusing to call her Miles, as too boyish, and though at times he was touchy and peevish he was a sturdy friend. To have his goodwill and admiration, as she sought to strengthen her position in the Sydney literary circle, was tremendously encouraging.

She could not rest on her laurels, for as early as November 1901 people were asking about a sequel. Though Linda begged her to put her writing aside and come up for the Tumut Show in February 1902 she did not do so, but

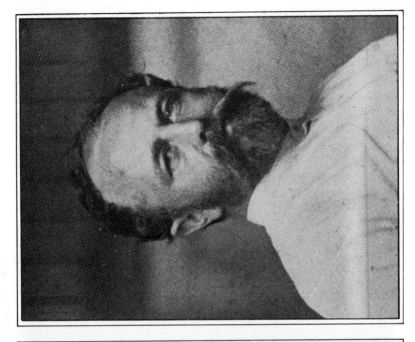

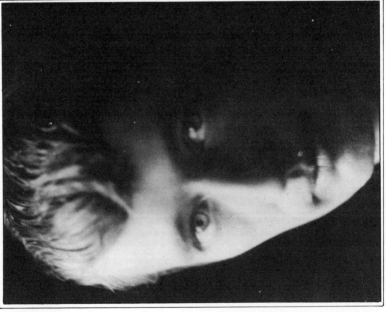

left: Norman Lindsay. *right*: A.G. Stephens.

knuckled down to her new manuscript in the hope of another success. Fred Maudsley of the Melbourne-based *Booklover* enquired in March 1902 how her new manuscript compared in length with *My Brilliant Career*, and her Aunt Lena commented waspishly that having made a reputation she would have to live up to it. Much was expected of her. Arthur Macquarie of Florence who had worked on her first book, presumably for Pinker, and had called her ''a little firebrand of genius'', offered to correct her next work free, before passing it on to Pinker. ''We'll call it a debt of friendship.''[8] As an agent Pinker was of enormous help to many writers, but for Franklin he was too far away. She needed guidance and advice on the spot, and in provincial Sydney AGS was the only mentor to whom she could turn.

Speaking of his standing in the writing world of that city, Franklin later said:

> The importance of A.G. Stephens lay in his courage and acumen in setting up standards in the void. He did not lose his sense of literary proportion by over-indulgence towards local attempts, nor limit his taste and judgments to them. He had an acute interest in European literature and was so ahead of the local mentality in regard to it that by male adults he was considered 'wrong-headed', even immoral, certainly no mentor for young girls. One of them had to make her own way to him to find a puritanically conventional uncle, a tutor, a friend, generous and stable from the first day she sought him till a last meeting shortly before his death.[9]

She was grateful all her life for his kindness but did not become involved with him at a deeper emotional level during the main years of their friendship, 1901-05. Her encounter in the year of her triumph, 1902, when she was still the vogue, with a more genuinely fierce and dangerous literary lion was much more exciting and risky, though it left a certain long-lasting bruising.

6 "The Banjo"

"Banjo" Paterson, poet, clubman, war correspondent, lawyer, author of the best-known Australian poem of the day, "The Man from Snowy River" (and of the now world-famous words of the ballad "Waltzing Matilda"), wrote to Stella Franklin in her guise of Miles from his patrician club, the Australian, on 25 March 1902. He had heard that she wanted his advice about a publishing agreement. He had not yet read her book but had heard it spoken of highly, and he enquired when she would be down in the city.

Born at Molong, New South Wales, in 1864 into a well-to-do grazing family, Andrew Barton Paterson attended Sydney Grammar School while living with his grandmother, Mrs Barton (who wrote verse) at Rockend, on the Parramatta River in Gladesville. He combined the skills of the countryman, being a fine rider and a good shot, with the gloss of city sophistication. After studying law at Sydney University he began practising as a solicitor while writing verse as a sideline. His first well-known poem "Clancy of the Overflow" appeared in *The Bulletin* in December 1889 under the pseudonym of "The Banjo". In 1895 his collection *The Man from Snowy River* was a runaway success. In 1899 he travelled to South Africa to report the Boer War for *The Sydney Morning Herald*, then on to China to cover the Boxer Rebellion, though the uprising was over by the time he arrived. Back in Sydney he gave up his law practice in 1900 to devote himself to poetry, to journalism and to lecturing on his experiences.

For Stella Franklin this romantic, glamorous figure had a special allure, since he celebrated the Monaro country in his verses. He was the singer of the valorous bushmen among whom she had grown up, such as her father. Physically Paterson was commanding, tall and muscular, with black hair and dark eyes, and with the casual detached manner and dislike of excessive emotion in life or art which Lindsay thought marked him as an "aristocrat". The interest of such a paragon was a tribute to Franklin's promise. He invited her to lunch with him at an ABC tea shop in Pitt Street, near King Street, in April 1901, saying she would easily know him, a sad-looking person with a hard face.

She gave him some stories and sketches for an opinion. These were "Match Breaking", "One Bushman's Wooing", "How Dead Man's Gap was Named", "The Tin-potting of Tim Jones", "Gossip by the Way", "Of Love", "Of Humanism", "An Old House Post" and "Jilted". He was brusquely straightforward in his criticisms, saying that some was average stuff and some was sheer drivel, just what every schoolgirl wrote. But he found a country sketch or two quite admirable.

Paterson took the trouble to submit the "Dead Man's Gap" sketch to Rowlandson's magazine, as pioneer publisher A.C. Rowlandson was always on the alert for material for his paperback books, and to have talks with publisher George Robertson. Nevertheless, the stinging criticism of this highly successful writer, together with the stalemate in her career and financial pressures depressed her considerably. She turned for advice to another celebrated author. Ethel Turner in her bracing reply urged her not to be downhearted for her autobiography would be very dull if there was no struggle to record, "nothing reminiscent of Grub Street". Feeling rather flat after an illness, Stella returned to "grinding away", writing to Tossie O'Sullivan, daughter of the helpful MP, that there were "no circuses or harbour picnics or lunches at Shadlers or enjoying ourselves round town now".[1]

Then on 31 May, 1902 Paterson, who had been writing 2,000 words a day of "very unambitious" work in his Bond Street apartment, made an exciting suggestion. He had to leave for the New Hebrides immediately but he asked if on his return she would collaborate with him on a literary venture. He had written a racing and sporting yarn but felt it was a bit flat. George Robertson thought she might take it, and perhaps add a little more plot and thrill. If that went well they might liven up another of his works. They would have to toss up for whose name went first on the book "but place aux dames, eh?" quipped Paterson.

It was a most tempting offer from a mature, established writer to an almost beginner. Franklin found it difficult to decide and canvassed opinions. Fred Maudsley of the Melbourne *Booklover* was emphatically against it. Blasting Paterson's idea as cool and selfish cheek, he warned her of the dangers of collaboration in general, and said Paterson's literary opinions were not worth a brass farthing. Linda did not know what to think of Paterson—"one thing he must think a lot of your brains"[2]—and wondered who would get all the honour and glory. Franklin seems to have been vexed that the autocratic Banjo had sent her his manuscript without waiting to see whether she would agree to his collaboration proposal. When he returned from the New Hebrides and found she had not accepted the suggestion, he asked for the return of his material. That letter of 25 July, 1902 is marked in her writing "FINALE".

But it was not the end, as it was all too exciting and interesting to let go

"Banjo" Paterson.

completely. She wrote suggesting a joint play. Paterson was puzzled by the lack of reserve in her letters compared with her guarded conversation, but the play idea appealed and he was so anxious to begin work that he offered to pay her expenses for a week in Sydney, as though they were two tradesmen starting a business. Still she did not come and in August he sent her two plays and suggested she might accompany him on a six-week lecture tour of Fiji, chaperoned by his sister Jessie. This was perhaps too unusual a plan for a strictly-raised bush girl, as he left Sydney without her towards the end of August, after sending her a cheque on 18 August for five pounds so that she might come down and work with him. Strong-willed Banjo was determined on a joint venture.

It was a heady situation for Stella Franklin and she took those whom she trusted into her confidence. There is some evidence that this attractive, glamorous man of the world had proposed marriage to Stella Franklin. Certainly her sister Linda and Linda's fiancé Charles Graham thought so, as did Bertha Lawson. In September the Lawsons, now back in Sydney and living at Manly, were concerned for her. In their letters to her Henry advised her strongly against changing publishers and warned her to keep away from other writers. He felt responsible for her welfare and happiness and worried about this naive girl in the big city. Bertha asked if the person Stella was involved with and had rejected was Banjo. She thought any romantic connection with him would be a mistake and harm her work. Linda Franklin and Charles Graham (who was an admirer of both sisters to the extent that their Uncle Theo referred to them both as the two Mrs Grahams), were consulted and Linda in her joyous way was delighted. "When are you going to be Mrs Banjo? My word the next generation ought to be something. Mum an Authoress and Dad a Poet."[3] Charles Graham scolded Stella for her impulsiveness, for rushing into the dark without a thought and appearing eager for the Fiji trip. He asked if she would like to see Linda take such a trip with a man, and said she had been right to refuse Banjo, for if it was really love he would ask again. Perhaps partly because of the lack of enthusiasm shown for the association by those she loved and trusted, the relationship faded away.

In November Paterson had a visit from Lawson, "reeking of beer", and a month later he thanked Franklin for the cheque, with interest, which she had returned and wished her luck on a plan to go interstate. The episode was over. Linda summed up, "So poor old Banjo went off."[4] A true gambler, he could cut any losses without too much pain. Early the following year he happily took up the position of editor of *The Evening News* and later married and settled down contentedly.

Stella had been flattered and excited by the interest of this dashing man, but once the relationship was over her sharp, satiric pen went to work and she wrote a farewell letter to Banjo Paterson at the Australian Club, a parody of the letter in which he had sought collaboration. The draft reads:

> I am leaving for a ride on a 'steeple chase crack' immediately. Don't write back until return post because I won't be back until then to get it. Now, there is another matter.
>
> I have written a book of 'pomes' which I am sending you. They are full of good stuff but want more rhyme and metre. They are O.K. as 'pomes' but a little more grammar and rhythm would make them A1. My Scheme is this. You take and convert them into sonnets and odes and incantations and I shall be glad of the collaboration.
>
> We would have to toss up for whose name goes first on the book but place aux preux chevalier, eh; We will have to agree on terms when we see how it looks.
>
> If this goes let's make a dictionary.
>
> I hope to find some Byronic odes when I come back.
> SO THIS IS THE END of your little bush girl,
> Miles.[5]

But did she send the letter? That might have been too forward.

It was the end of the idyll of the bushmaid and the handsome chevalier, but Stella Franklin was still brimming over with energy. While dallying with the poet and charming the critic she had been working on two novels, *The End of My Career* and *On the Outside Track*. The first of these was not published until forty years later, when it appeared, in an amended form, as *My Career Goes Bung*.[6] The second, *On the Outside Track*, was apparently an early version of *Cockatoos*, a novel first published in 1954. *Cockatoos* carried a preface dated 1927-8 stating: "The young author wrote this story contemporaneously with the happenings involved" and that the manuscript "lay undisturbed by anything but silverfish for twenty-five years." This would date it as written in 1902-3, and like *On the Outside Track*, *Cockatoos* dealt with the era of the Boer War. The later work was different in some ways no doubt, but it is reasonable to assume that the two have a fair amount in common.

The End of My Career, of which only an incomplete version remains, was a sequel to *My Brilliant Career*. Country girl Sybylla Melvyn, after the success of her first book, comes to Sydney and is taken up by the social and literary set. She has various encounters, with writer Mr Zither Qualey, with poet and South African war correspondent Mr Violin Dadson, and with editor Aijee Refuseem. She is scratchy about the women journalists who seek interviews, saying: "Fancy a writer who could contribute to the *real literature* of Australia under the headings, 'Hints to tired mothers', 'How to drape a baby's cot', 'Splendid recipe for taking grease spots out of cashmere etc' being so gracious." Sybylla is secretly engaged to Harold Beauchamp of Five Bob Downs, though she is repelled by the complacent malice of bush attitudes which see a woman's first child as "something to break the spirit and tether (her) to domestic slavery", rather than as "an ecstatic and glorifying experience". But Sydney disappoints her, for, though she is "charmed with the material difference of life when compared with Possum Gully'', she finds that city people are ''cut from the same calibre of mental cloth'' and she returns to the country and to the prospect of marriage with Harry Beauchamp. In the 1946 version of the story, renamed *My Career Goes Bung*, Harry, now pompous Henry Beecham, is repudiated, and Sybylla, determined to escape overseas, faces life alone.

When Stella showed the first draft of *The End of My Career* to George Robertson, he threw cold water on her enthusiasm: ''It isn't feasible . . . you've made me jolly glad I didn't meet you.''[7] He had picked out most of the Sydney personalities satirised, including feminist Rose Scott, and declared, ''not even 200% would induce me to publish.'' The writer's ruthless naivety in the open use of friends and acquaintances as material was part of that egotism that had blinded her to the likely reaction of her family and neighbours to *My Brilliant Career*.

The artlessly flirtatious but fundamentally innocent and puritanical young woman had cast a cold eye over the city's best and fairest and had found them not much to her liking, coming to the conclusion that: ''Few of the people I had met in Sydney had any more in them basically than those around Possum Gully.''[8]

In the 1946 version of the story, A.G. Stephens appears under his own name as a kindly adviser, but the author is resentful about a character labelled the ''Great Name in Australian Literature'', Goring Hardy, who may have a touch of Paterson about him, being an ex-war correspondent, ''a sizzling imperialist'', country born and university educated, magnetic and exciting. Sybylla says of this man, ''In thinking of him in the years that have gone I know it was his unalloyed maleness that hurt me. He would appraise women in the light of the pleasure or service they could give him. He had no scrap of that understanding for which I was hungry.''[9]

Whatever may be the truth as to the fault or blame in the Franklin-Paterson relationship, it was bound to collapse, involving as it did the clash of two strong-willed and strongly-opposed personalities. They shared a love of the Snowy country, and a passion for horses and horsemanship, but little else. Their literary styles and interests were different, their natures in conflict. Independent feminism was a vital part of Stella Franklin. She resented fiercely the accepted male dominance of the period, and rebelled against any show of male arrogance. In her sexual attitudes she was puritanical, though not prudish. Paterson, fifteen years older, with a much wider experience of the world, described by Lindsay as an aristocrat, implying an unquestioning self-confidence, was terse, factual and practical, a man of action, not given to self-pity or self-examination. Of optimistic temperament himself, the problems which had been real for inexperienced Stella Franklin, the attempts to understand the meaning of life, love and religion, he dismissed as drivel, wounding without intent.

Their political attitudes were opposed. Stella was a pacifist and had taken an anti-Boer War stance, whereas Paterson enjoyed the risk of the battlefield. "Wherever there was a war, or a revolution, or any other state of human conflict he was first in the ring as a newspaper correspondent,"[10] said Lindsay. Courageous and fearless himself (he had been a steeple-chase jockey) and coming from a comfortable background, he had little understanding of the less brave and the less fortunate, though he had a special regard for unhappy Henry Lawson and defended him to Franklin. She, though also physically brave and daring, had brought with her from the dreary dairy farm a feeling for the drudging lot of the disadvantaged and a simple democratic faith verging on republicanism.

The man she sought was not the Paterson type, whatever his brilliance and distinction. Her ideal man appeared late and briefly in *My Career Goes Bung*, in the father-figure of Renfrew Haddington, "tall and broad and brown . . . a soul and mind in which one could take refuge", also a famous Australian writer and war correspondent who unfortunately already had a fine wife and a grown-up family. "Manliness seemed to emanate from the man, with patience and strength as well as kindliness."[11] Renfrew Haddington may owe something to another writer who later won her warm affection, Joseph Furphy.

But romance or flirtation with Paterson notwithstanding, Stella Franklin had not let the grass grow under her feet. She packed off the two novels she had been engaged on to Pinker in quick succession. On 31 August she drafted a letter to him. "I have completed an Australian novel regarding which immediately want yr advice as should Messrs Blackwood or any other home publisher not wish to take it up I want to settle the disposal of Australian rights." On 27 September she was equally crisp:

> Am herewith despatching 'On the Outside Track' as I have decided should prefer all my business in the one place. Wish it printed as I have arranged with one portion entitled 'Bush' the other 'City' with the dedicating and prefatory verse. If possible no 'toning' as I have taken great pains to express the war fever as it actually was—the pro-Boer feelings etc.
>   P.S. In *On the Outside Track* I have carried on characters used in *My Brilliant Career* but on no account is the book to be called a sequel.[12]

The original manuscript of this novel has been lost, but *Cockatoos*, the final version, published fifty years later, retains the smack of the period. The heroine, Ignez Milford, who lives with relatives on an impoverished farm at Oswald's Ridges in the Goulburn district, at the turn of the century, is another rebellious, talented, tantalising bush girl in the mould of Stella Franklin and Sybylla Melvyn. "Oswald's Ridges was indebted to Ignez Milford for adding spice to the daily round. Her lively and unconventional ideas caused commotion among tamer fowl." Ignez objects to women being classed with children and lunatics in suffrage matters, despises the mindless small talk of the women of the community, fears the traps of marriage, is determined to pursue a musical career, and in the midst of the country's jingoistic fever is distressed by the Boer War. "It's dreadful to go to shoot people in their own country."

Ignez writes a successsful book, visits Sydney, is taken up by the smart set, has her ambitions for a career in music crushed because her throat has been damaged by bad training, is dismayed and disillusioned by city life, particularly by the sordidness of its sexual attitudes, and returns to the country. But she feels imprisoned by the life there and evades marriage to a bush stalwart, Arthur Masters, by fleeing abroad, to lonely independence in the United States. The book's theme is therefore much the same as that of Franklin's two previous novels, that of the vital outsider in a flat society. But *Cockatoos* attempts to cover a broader spread of Australian life than *My Brilliant Career*. All attention is not focused on Ignez. The embittered drudge, Blanche, and her pretty, dainty sister, Sylvia, who flirts, falls in love and marries, provide contrasting types to the strong-willed Ignez. The novel is interesting for the light cast on the society of the time, but does not possess the emotional concentration of *My Brilliant Career*.

Even so, it appears that the original 1902 manuscript was thought strong stuff by publishers. According to the *Cockatoos* preface, it was shown to one of London's leading publishers, but he was disgusted by its frankness and said the author should not be encouraged to write. Certainly, though the agent (Pinker) acknowledged receipt of *The End of My Career* and *On the Outside Track* on 27 November, 1902, he had no success in placing them. Perhaps he was irked by Stella Franklin's high-handed tone, for in the draft of her letter of 29 May, 1902 she wrote that contemporaries had informed her that "the book, *My Brilliant Career*, was badly engineered from a business point of view . . . I should have thought that you would have seen that it was put upon the market properly."[13] But, well seasoned as he was in the scoldings and ingratitudes of authors, the agent's silence probably resulted from the fact that the works were not suitable. Stella, no doubt, felt that she had reason to be snappish, since her first royalty cheque, of 31 July, 1902, when finally received, amounted to £16-5-6.[14]

Her disappointments, literary and financial, were soothed somewhat by the affection and attention of a new friend, for, while she was still entangled in the Paterson imbroglio, another admirer, had welcomed her enthusiastically as an ally to that centre of feminist causes, "Lynton". All her life Stella Franklin charmed both men and women, and when she went in August 1902 to spend a month or so with Rose Scott at her home, she enchanted that warm-hearted idealist. Scott, who greeted the girl's arrival with a telegram, "Welcome, welcome", began to exert a strong influence on the inexperienced young writer. The older woman's passionate views on the wrongs done to their sex reinforced the feminist in Stella Franklin, and drew her towards the causes which Scott espoused so vehemently. This process made even more obvious that splitting of concentration which bedevilled Franklin's work both as a creative writer and as a feminist activist. Too much of the soap box was to find its way into her creative work and too much of the artist's complexity and doubt into her career as an activist.

7   Rose Scott, Vida Goldstein and Mary Anne

My Brilliant Career had shown a passionate preoccupation with the position of women. The views attributed to its young heroine were bound to raise conventional eyebrows because of their divergence from the accepted patterns of behaviour for women in that era. "Marriage to me," opined Sybylla, "appeared the most horribly tied-down and unfair-to-women existence going. It would be from fair to middling if there was love; but I laughed at the idea of love, and determined never, never, never to marry."[1]

The ambitious heroine, shaken by the tide of creative urges, yearned for greatness and action. But her observations of life at Possum Gully led her to a disheartening conclusion.

> It came home to me as a great blow that it was only men who could take the world by its ears and conquer their fate, while women, metaphorically speaking, were forced to sit with tied hands and patiently suffer as the waves of fate tossed them hither and thither, battering and bruising without mercy.[2]

The common lot of women in general, and of the women of the bush in particular, seemed to Franklin to be a kind of slavery, and it was a slavery with a sexual basis that was distasteful to her fastidious nature. "A man can live a life of bestiality and then be considered a fit husband for the youngest and purest girl!"[3] The two novels written in 1902 continued to deal with the problems of the talented, unconventional girl who shrinks from the sexual norms of her society and from the restrictions placed on women. The growing friendship with Rose Scott reinforced Stella in her belief that women were sexually exploited and that men were often brutish.

Rose Scott had spent the first ten years of her life in the bush. Born in Singleton, New South Wales, in 1847 and therefore more than thirty years senior to her protégée, she had grown up in the unsettled period of bushrangers, ticket-of-leave men and women and Aboriginal tribal destruction.

Her grandfather had been an outstanding British doctor, and a one-time president of the Medical Board of Bombay. Her father, Helenus Scott, a man

Rose Scott.

of capital and social standing, arrived in New South Wales in 1821. He had farmed, bred horses and grown some of the first wines in the Hunter River district.

Rose Scott was a precocious, well-read, thoughtful child to whom the family home at Glendon was stimulating since visitors there included artists, writers, philosophers and bookpeople. This liberating background with its emphasis on the worth of ideas produced a serious girl whose first heroine was Florence Nightingale, symbol of independence, bravery and competence to those young Victorian women who sought a new way of life. Reading J.S. Mill's *The Subjection of Women* at the age of twenty-one turned Scott into an intense and life-long feminist.

In 1857, after a financial failure, the Scott family moved to the nearby port of Newcastle where Helenus Scott was a magistrate for twenty years. When her father died in 1879 thirty-two-year-old Rose came to Sydney with her mother and settled in the pleasant house, set in a garden of fuchsias, roses and camellias, at 294 Jersey Road, Woollahra. Her inheritance enabled her to establish a comfortable and beautiful home and allowed her to devote herself to good causes.

Foremost among these were franchise and higher education for women, and the protection of children. She advocated children's courts, prisoners' aid and early shop-closing hours. She championed the young, the unprotected, the poor and women. In a time when such a beautiful, wealthy, well-bred girl as she was would be expected to marry well, she remained resolutely single, being in the fortunate position of having means enough to live elegantly and social position enough to have some influence in the world of affairs.

In 1889 she had worked with another early Australian feminist, Louisa Lawson, Henry Lawson's mother, in the Dawn Club which produced a magazine, *The Dawn*, edited, printed and published by women. In the 1890s she had conducted a high-powered campaign over the conditions and hours of shopgirls, lobbying shopowners and politicians and inviting them to her home to meet the girls and to discuss the situation. It was said that leading politicians B.R. Wise and W.A. Holman had drafted the Early Closing Act of 1899 at Rose Scott's rosewood table.

Upon the formation of the Woman's Suffrage League in 1891, with Lady Windeyer as president, Rose Scott became secretary. She felt that if women obtained the vote they could use it as a weapon to bring change in the areas of most concern to them, especially the protection of children. The battle for franchise in New South Wales was won in 1902. As early as 1894 South Australian women had secured the right to vote. The new Commonwealth of Australia of 1901 guaranteed the franchise to all who already possessed it, so to obtain uniformity on a federal level extended the vote to all. New South Wales then granted the vote to women at a state level, but not the right to sit in state parliament. This latter was a cause Rose Scott could still pursue, and there were many other battles to be fought.

Her energy was impressive. She was secretary of the Literary Society, member of the Women's Guild and active in the cause of higher education for women. She was tireless in good works ranging from obtaining seats for the elderly in parks to founding and presiding over the Prisoners' Aid Society. The situation of women prisoners and of ''fallen women'' aroused her particular pity, and the men involved in their crimes and ''fall'' provoked her special scorn. By reason of her unsparing service Rose Scott had become a symbol of goodness in the community. Beautiful as well as intellectual, a fine public speaker, an undaunted fighter though no fanatic, she was one of Sydney's foremost citizens.

This high-powered reformer swept Stella Franklin into her set. One of her friends, Florette Murray-Prior, offered help with the girl's musical studies at her Palings studio. Palings music shop was at that time also a centre of musical practice. Eminent geologist Professor Edgeworth David and his wife Caroline befriended her. There were dinners and *soirées* in grand homes, where Stella Franklin was a centre of attraction but the paradoxical young girl who had longed for the excitements of the city gradually became critical and disillusioned. Her immense pride, moreover, would not allow her to accept Rose Scott's hospitality indefinitely, so the end of September 1902 found her back home at Stillwater, where Scott admonished her in a letter, urging her dear little girl to cheer up.

That year had opened optimistically for her, with acclaim and acceptance into a new milieu, but as it drew towards its close Stella Franklin was dejected. There was no word from Pinker about the prospects of British publication for her two manuscripts; Robertson, in Sydney, had bluntly rejected *The End of My Career*; the Paterson affair had fizzled out. And she was still dependent for support on her parents, which meant exile at Stillwater.

She was so depressed that she thought of giving up her literary hopes and going as a companion to England. All she had received in royalties was one meagre cheque. The rebel who had striven for freedom and independence was still in financial bondage. To escape from the constraints of life at home she must earn a living. She had tried teaching and nursing, and found them both chafing. The pressure of the expectations of admirers added to her unhappiness. She wrote many years later:

> A *succès d'estime* often becomes a burden to the writer, even if he has a private income to support it, because, unless he can follow it with a fresh success, he has to dine-out too often on the same bone. It places the writer without adequate means in a situation better eased by anonymity or avoided altogether.[4]

She hit upon a seeming solution to all her problems. Coming from a "family of illustrious housewives", she had been well trained in the domestic arts by her capable mother. Good household help was sought after and there lay her escape route. She could live in the city, earn her own living, disappear for a time and avoid the plaguing questions about her next work.

At the beginning of 1903, with a reference from the ever helpful O'Sullivans (this time Mrs E.), the brilliant young author quit the literary scene and vanished into Sydney suburbia, disguised in white frilly cap and apron as "Sarah Frankling", general maid. To a trusted few she confided that her aim was to obtain copy for a book on the adventures of Mary Anne, parlourmaid.

Her mother, at first averse to the idea, had finally agreed, but Grandmother was shocked. "I have not told anyone out of the house that you left home," she wrote. Her grandchild's flightiness worried her too. "No, I would not advise you to marry a man you don't like. If you don't like them why do you lead them to believe you do?"[5]

This fresh escapade of Stella's may have played a part in her parents' move from the Goulburn district in March 1903 to a small property near the rural town of Penrith, only fifty-five kilometres from Sydney, close enough for their difficult child to fly home to if in difficulties. Grandma was withering about the new house—only five rooms and a kitchen—and hoped Stella's father would be able to keep bread to eat.

The new maid—in a world of black dresses and white aprons, of wood-fired coppers for washing, with stoves to be black-leaded and silver to be polished, with carpets to beat and mistresses to please—had her own troubles, and was not finding the life an easy one. Hours were long, with only one day a week free, and wages were low, around ten shillings a week. Of this time, Stella wrote: "I was exhausted at the start . . . The first six months were dreadful . . . Miss Scott had a task in soothing me . . . while I grew so thin that Mrs O'Sullivan fed me Bovril."[6] But she had strength enough to keep up her correspondence with A.G. Stephens and others. Grandma thought her base, writing to two or three men at once. At night she also wrote up her day's experiences.

At first Rose Scott was unaware of the new career and had difficulty in locating her protégée.[2] She wrote to Penrith in April 1903 asking when her little girl was coming to stay again. Susannah Franklin let Rose into the Mary Anne secret and the famous and formidable Miss Scott tracked her little friend down to a household at 34 Brae Street, Waverley, where she joined in the masquerade, calling herself Rachel Scoot. She was eager for a visit and in her letters was sure that the missus would let Stella come all day and as often as she liked to visit Miss Scott. She became very heated about conditions in domestic service and their effect on the girl's health and started looking for a new place for her. In June "Mary Anne" moved with a good reference as honest, obliging, clean, quick and competent to a new position at 53 Campbell

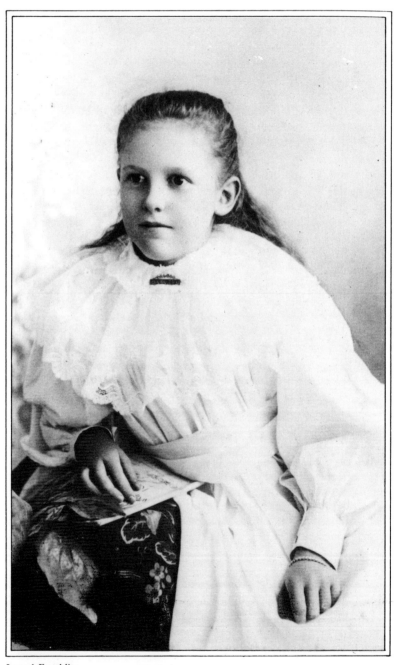

Laurel Franklin.

Street, North Sydney.[7] Though the work was hard "Sarah Frankling" took a gleeful interest in the dinner conversation as she served at table, for it sometimes centred around Miles Franklin's book.

For all her rebelliousness and hunger for independence, the family bond remained strong. Utterly untouched by jealousy, Linda wrote that as far as her fiancé Charles Graham was concerned it was all Stella from morning to night and that he wore a guard on his watch-chain made of Stella's hair. Gentle Linda's love for her sister was so deep that no envy stirred it, but she was anxious about the health of her younger sister Laurel. "The dear little sister. It will be the last straw if anything happens ... I know how you will feel it though you won't show it."[8] Because of the child's illness Stella went home in September, to Chesterfield at Castlereagh Road, Penrith. Laurel, aged eleven, a child of beauty and intelligence, "our pride," said Stella, died on 4 October, 1903 and was buried at St Stephen's Church of England in Penrith.

Stella returned to her role of Mary Anne, this time at Keston, Carabella Street, Kirribilli.[9] Ironically, in November a new journal, *His Excellency*, a society chronicle, invited her to contribute. But the seemingly luscious orange of Sydney had been squeezed and found dry. "Banjo" had married, the sorrowful Lawsons mourned a child still-born in September, Laurel had died in October and while Stella scrubbed and polished her mother worried about Linda's health: "[I] never let her wash or iron she vomits so much."[10] Good friends had not liked her new manuscript. In November Mrs Edgeworth David, who reported that Rose Scott had sent her the manuscript without a word, advised her not to risk her reputation by publishing it, remarking that she saw Miss Scott's influence in a good deal that she said about woman's position and man's vileness. This work, which appears to end in the suicide of the despairing heroine, may have been *On the Outside Track*, the early version of *Cockatoos*, for in that novel the heroine Ignez "abandoned the thought of suicide in favour of exile across the seas". Or it may have been *Some Everyday Folk and Dawn*, which deals with women's issues and includes a suicide in a subplot.

In December 1903 Stella Franklin was lacerated further by a condescending interview in Zara Aronsen's magazine *The Home Queen*, for while its general import was fairly flattering it contained some deeply wounding thrusts: "The Literary Bush Girl ... displayed but few outward points that the woman of fashion would welcome ... somewhat hard outward appearance ... The idea that Miss Franklin is uneducated is erroneous." Mild enough criticisms, but coming on top of a previous comment to which she had taken exception, it rankled so that she never forgave Zara Aronsen.

Clearly it was time for some reviving stimulus, such as a change of city. In the New Year of 1904 "Mary Anne" sailed steerage class to Melbourne

Stella as ''Mary Anne''.

where she spent a lively time as a nursemaid in a wealthy Toorak family and a period with a kind and refined family in less affluent East Richmond. The Melbourne excursion lasted only three months but produced two friendships of the deepest significance, with Vida Goldstein, a feminist activist, and with Joseph Furphy, a novelist. The city of Melbourne she remembered later as an enchanted land.

The Goldstein family, in the person of Elsie Belle Champion, sister of Vida and Aileen Goldstein, had contacted Franklin soon after the publication of *My Brilliant Career*. Elsie Belle Champion, proprietor of the Melbourne-based Booklovers' Library, was married to the English socialist and journalist H.H. Champion, one of the leaders of the big English dock strike of 1889. H.H. Champion had settled in Melbourne in 1893, first running a weekly called *The Champion*, and then *The Booklover*.

Vida Goldstein was already very well known as a suffragist and activist. Ten years older than Stella Franklin, she was born in Portland, Victoria, of an Irish-Jewish father and a mother of Scots descent, and after leaving Presbyterian Ladies College, Melbourne, had run a preparatory school for girls and boys with her sisters, in Alma Road, St Kilda. After five years of teaching her fiery crusading spirit drew her into working full-time for the cause of women's franchise. From 1899 to 1905 she owned and edited a serious woman's monthly, *The Woman's Sphere*. In February 1902 she had appeared as a witness on the question of the franchise before the US Congress hearings on the subject, for by this time Australian women had the vote and Vida Goldstein was well informed on the matter. The famous suffrage worker, Carrie Catt, was another witness and she and Goldstein became friends.

The Goldstein sisters warmly welcomed Stella Franklin to Melbourne as a supporter of women's causes. In *The Sphere* of 15 April, 1904, Vida published a story on Mary Anne, parlourmaid, kitchenmaid, cook, nurse, general . . . who had "a voice of peculiar power which would have won her a place on the concert platform or stage".

These feminist activists and associates of Rose Scott were also devotedly religious, being vigorous advocates of the then fashionable creed of Christian Science. They hoped their new friend might become a "practitioner" though there was little likelihood of a conversion as far as sceptical Stella was concerned. Vida Goldstein argued that Science made one look at the troubles of this life from an entirely new viewpoint. This was true for her. After years of disappointment in public life, for she stood for Parliament three times unsuccessfully, and after the financial losses incurred in her crusading magazines, *The Sphere* and *The Woman Voter*, she decided to retire from pacifist and suffragist activities and to give all her time to Christian Science. She became reader, then president of the First Church of Christ (Scientist), Melbourne.

In early 1904 the likable, fervent Goldstein girls, with whom Stella stayed for part of her time in Melbourne, helped consolidate her in her feminist position, and with their sincerity and kindness won her friendship, a friendship which was to be life-long.

8   Joseph Furphy, romance and failure

Another meeting in this Melbourne period was of importance to Franklin, the novelist. Joseph Furphy, author of the bush classic *Such Is Life* (the title was taken from bushranger Ned Kelly's final words before the gallows trap opened), wrote congratulating Miles Franklin on her book on 17 February, 1904, and pointed out parallels with his own recently published novel. He arranged a meeting on Easter Friday, 1904, in the Melbourne Art Gallery. There, in front of Longstaff's "Sirens" sat the sixty-year-old, lean, laconic, "squinny-eyed" Furphy surrounded by five girls (including his devotee Kate Baker and a number of her friends who wished to meet Miles Franklin), while Stella's merry laugh resounded through the gallery.

He always called her Miles and he described her as slight, slender-waisted with the action of a greyhound. He was impressed with her spontaneity. "In two minutes she had poured out a torrent of commonsense, pathos, humour, wit, clothed in mingled poetry and slang and delivered in a deep, sweet contralto."[1] Kate Baker on that occasion christened her Merrily Miles but Furphy believed that the buoyancy was a mask assumed for protection against life's blows.

The brief encounter left a deep mark on Stella Franklin. She never met with Furphy again but he encouraged her as an artist in his letters, warning her against her passionate self-pity. Furphy had been born of Irish immigrant parents in Victoria in 1843 and had been a selector, golddigger, bullocky and foundry worker while he struggled to maintain a family and to write. His own code was rueful stoicism in his somewhat unhappy relationship with his wife and in his difficulties in achieving publication of his work. Though he had previously written pieces for *The Bulletin*, *Such Is Life* was his first book.

Franklin returned to Sydney on the SS *Peregrine* on 13 April, 1904, as guest of the shipping company, having emerged from the kitchen in Melbourne in Easter week in time to have a *succès d'estime* for a few days. "The most exclusive people want to meet me tho I have nothing but Mary Anne clothes."[2]

Furphy continued to advise, urging more construction in her work and more faith in the universe and the value of life in her philosophy. For her troubled, restless nature he was a refuge. "[I] will always miss him," she declared to Kate Baker years after, ". . . that kindliness and loveliness of disposition that was balm."[3] Renfrew Haddington of *My Career Goes Bung* was endowed with many of the virtues of Joseph Furphy. ". . . there was something restful and enfolding about him so that I ceased to be driven to act any role whatsoever," sighed Sybylla. His qualities of manliness, patience, strength and kindliness caused her to say after one meeting: "I like him better than any human being I ever met."

Joseph Furphy had a similar emotional impact on Stella Franklin. Sybylla said of Renfrew Haddington that from his existence "the world lit up with new possibilities . . . I was refilled with the false hope of youth that happiness could come to me some day with shining face as a prince or knight".[4] In a similar manner, Joseph Furphy gave Franklin a model of an ideal man, a hero, a friend. "Furphy understood women as human beings to a depth unusual with men,"[5] she wrote of him.

On the return to Sydney Rose Scott welcomed but also scolded her, saying she felt sad that Franklin had not come to see her on the way to Melbourne. Other acquaintances, including elderly Sir Francis Suttor, president of the Legislative Council, and a friend of Rose Scott, and Caroline Edgeworth David, who had both been in on the "secret", were intrigued by the Mary Anne episode and the press revived its interest in her briefly. On 26 March, 1904, *The Australasian* printed the first work by Miles Franklin since *My Brilliant Career*, a story, written in 1901, "The Old House Post". A feature on the heroine of the white cap and apron appeared with a picture on the "Red Page" on 31 March, and *New Idea* ran an interview on 6 May. But that was the sum of the success of the Mary Anne undertaking, for the series of sketches did not take with any publisher. Franklin had decided to place no more work with Pinker, so the only word from him was a royalty statement dated 7 April, 1904, showing royalties of £8-3-10 for 1902, and £2-19-6 for 1903.[6]

Depressed, she returned to live with her family at Penrith. Linda wrote from Talbingo that she had been besieged at the Tumut Show by people asking when the next book would be out, and was sure there would be millions of copies sold. Even the Goldsteins enquired in November as to when they might have a peep.

Linda was worried about her sister. "Why don't you tell me something when you write? You only ask me questions about nothing." She was also uneasy about her marriage, set for a few months' time. "I am often of a good mind to throw the whole business over. [Her cousin, May Bridle, nearly died in childbirth.] It is a terrible thing when the first one happens that way."[7]

Rose Scott and A.G. Stephens continued to be Franklin's faithful friends. Stephens invited her in July 1904 to take tea at his new office in Australian Chambers, in tiny, slightly Bohemian Rowe Street, where Stephens held his celebrated "men only" symposiums on Friday nights with poets such as Victor Daley and Rod Quinn, and artists like Julian Ashton and Norman Lindsay as guests. Stella Franklin was invited only by day. Perhaps irked by this she was elusive and it was not until August that she called, chaperoned by Rose Scott.

Comrade-in-arms in the feminist cause, Vida Goldstein, was staying with Rose Scott in October, to give a series of lectures in Sydney on the best use of the vote by women. She was distressed to find that Franklin was feeling so depressed by a problem she shared — the need of a reliable income. Influenced by her friend, Franklin thought of going to America, though Furphy disliked the idea and Linda feared her sister might leave before her wedding ceremony, set for November.

Furphy's faith in her never faltered. He urged her not to write to anyone but to concentrate on her work. "You cannot help doing great work yet, your work ... bears the stamp of genius."[8] He warned her in his letters against both "Lower Bohemia" and "Colonel Birdsfreedom Z. Peanut with $1,000,000". Furphy left for distant Western Australia in December 1904, but continued to write to Franklin from his new home in Fremantle. His courage in his own troubles (*Such Is Life* sold two copies in the last half of 1904) and his belief in her promise stiffened her resolution and she wrote to him: "I have time to fail to all appearances and then succeed again before I'm thirty,"[9] to which he replied that her best work would be done after she was forty.

During these months of dejection she continued working on a novel (which eventually became *Some Everyday Folk and Dawn*) dealing with women's issues, particularly the double sexual standard and the exercise of the franchise. Vida Goldstein's visit to Sydney had been a complete failure because of faction fighting among women's groups, but it provided a character for this novel, Ada Grosvenor, women's activist.

There had been a state election to use as material for the political side and Rose Scott's views on the baseness of men as an influence on the subplot. This latter theme was an obsessive subject with both women. Scott thought that men did not regard women as human beings but as objects for use and pleasure, and that women were a deeply degraded sex. The question of the sexual abuse of women disturbed Franklin greatly and, in comforting her, Scott wrote that she too had wept and been unable to sleep.[10]

Linda married Charles Graham at Penrith on 23 November, 1904 and wrote in December that she was quite happy but very homesick. She added cryptically that she hoped Stella would never go through the awful agony of the first week. Loving, clinging Linda possibly referred simply to

Joseph Furphy in 1903.

homesickness but her sister could have interpreted the remark as having a sexual meaning.

Rose Scott's condemnation of the male sex did not prevent her being friends with many men, and at a ''Poets' Eve'' in November, where Rod Quinn, Victor Daley and politician Bernie Wise were also present, she introduced her young friend to a ''great-souled man with a big brain'', poet Sydney Jephcott. Here was another conquest and counsellor.

1904 rolled into 1905. Friendly Sir Francis Suttor who was distressed at the Mary Anne failure, thought in February that he might help Stella Franklin get her foot on the ladder of a stage career by introducing her to theatre managers. He proposed that she come to Sydney for a week to discuss the matter, but by March this correspondence seems to have ended without results. A.G. Stephens suggested in March that T.W. Heney, the editor of *The Sydney Morning Herald*, might like to get hold of a young, attractive, stylish, good-looking person to do a series of Mary Anne style articles, but though she contacted Heney she had no success there. She sent half of her new manuscript to J.B. Symons at Robertson's in Melbourne on 13 March, 1905 and another manuscript, probably part of the same book, to Stephens.[11]

Some Everyday Folk and Dawn is set in a little town, obviously Penrith. The most lively character is Grandmother Clay who runs a boarding house. Plain, no-nonsense, irascible, funny, austere but with a tender heart, she bears quite a resemblance to Stella's vision of Grandma Lampe. There is a villain, Mr Pornsch, ''a heavy swell'', who has seduced a boarder, Miss Flipp, who is all bangles, rings and golden pompadour. After the abandoned Miss Flipp drowns herself, Mr Pornsch, ''fifty-five if a day and a repulsive debauchee at that'', has his eye on Grandma's granddaughter, Dawn, ''a star she verily was'', who yearns for a stage career while flirting with available young men. Meanwhile the women of the town, helped by visiting activist Ada Grosvenor, are preparing to cast their first vote in a state election.

The narrator of the story, a sad and world-weary lady, is so cynical about the worth of the candidates, all males, that, though she claims her ballot paper, she puts it unmarked in the ballot-box. Except for Grandma Clay there is little to the novel. The brilliance had faded. There was still talent, the ability to entertain by rattling along, creating some amusing characters and incidents, but the explosive literary power which marked the first book was dissipated. The anger had been replaced by irritation and distaste, and the power by preachiness.

Stephens, whose praise had once been so exhilarating, returned the manuscript on 19 May, 1905 with a frosty note saying it did not do justice to the hopes he had formed for her, but he was still glad to see her whenever she came to Sydney, as she cheered him up. Like her two previous efforts, this novel was not acceptable to publishers at the time. However, *New Idea* took her series of nursing sketches, ''Ministering Angel'', and ran it from June to

December 1905, while good-natured Paterson wrote in August saying he could do with some sketches on life in country towns for the *Evening News*.

But the key-note of her feelings at this time was failure, failure in her writing and in love. She confided in Sydney Jephcott that she had experienced her life's master passion at twenty-two and lost. At that age she was flirting with Paterson, but she had a tendency to be vague about age, so perhaps she meant Furphy whom she met at twenty-four. Jephcott thought it too early to judge as at twenty-two we are little more than children. He was right of course, and in the spring of 1905 Stella Franklin became romantically involved once more, this time with a man more her age, her cousin Edwin Bridle, grandson of Grandma Lampe's brother, Thomas.[12]

Edwin Bridle was five years older and a countryman from Wilga Vale near Peak Hill, where Stella's uncle, Gus Lampe, lived. Stella was on holiday there and the wattles were in golden bloom. There were gallops for the two young people and emu hunts. Caught in a hailstorm, they sheltered and dried off in a little red humpy by the creek. They gathered ferns together and talked of love.

In November Edwin visited Sydney and they took trips to Manly and went to the theatres. But he felt the letter which he received from her a few days after his return home in mid November too unreasonable to understand, and he reminded her of the promises she had made. Unfortunately her letters to him have disappeared, but he believed that she returned his affection, and was willing to marry him. He was deeply, genuinely and generously in love, willing to wait until she was ready and concerned not to interfere with her work. She was not nearly so emotionally involved and talked about his meeting someone else, but for him it seemed then that there was only one love in his life and it would last to the end. They parted on Penrith railway station on an early summer morning with not a soul on the platform except the porter calling the stations. Still Edwin continued to write faithfully and passionately.

Stella, though fond of him, was wary of matrimony, and the fire of ambition still burned bright. But like her heroine Ignez:

> what she wrote was not what editors or publishers expected. She diligently tried to please these mentors and her work lost life and originality. There were platitudinous opinions from the cognoscenti, the gist of which was that she would be ruined by remaining in Australia among illiterate station hands.[13]

The great early success had become a burden. There were stinging questions from friend and foe alike about when her next book might be expected. In *Some Everyday Folk and Dawn* there is a sentence applicable to her mood: "In the career of a prodigy there invariably comes a time when it is compelled to relinquish being very clever for a child and has to enter the business of life in competition with adults." That time had come.

She was now twenty-six, still young enough, in spite of her seeming failure since *My Brilliant Career*, to make another career in another country. She could not imagine living the life her mother had lived. "The life of the married woman in the working class where she is wife, mother, cook, laundress, needlewoman, charwoman and often many other things combined is the most heart breaking, cruel and tortured slavery."[14] Her heroine Ignez, a twin-soul in a similar position, ruminated: "Suppose by some horrible mischance she should find herself married to a man of Oswald's Ridges and clamped down to this forever. It frightened her as a bad dream and as a bad dream it fled." Ignez also thought: "I want to get away somewhere so that I'll be able to use my talents without being thought mad or unsexed."[15] For Stella Franklin the decision was the same as that of Ignez, and as Old Harris' advice to Sybylla, "to make no entanglements to cripple the power of long distance flight".[16] As her heroine left behind patient, thoughtful Arthur Masters, so Stella forsook devoted Edwin.

For some time she had been considering leaving Australia and had thought of New Zealand, Canada and England. But now, under the influence of Vida Goldstein, America had displaced those countries as a goal. Joseph Furphy, who had opposed the idea of America strongly, began to believe that she should go abroad or she would feel imprisoned. Vida could smooth her path by giving her introductions to some of the leading activist women in San Francisco and New York. It was a momentous decision, but as she later wrote: "A writer cannot live for long on one book: it gives but temporary relief . . . Also, the appreciation of a published book and the fellowship it brings flowers only for a season."[17] Nothing had gone right for her since the first acclaim but she was still young and full of force. Convinced that in the great, robust republic a girl of her talent and energy would find a place, she planned her departure.

Like so many of the heroines of her novels, like Sybylla, like Ignez, like Freda, Molly and Laleen, she would seek success and liberation abroad.

> Sculptors, writers, singers, actors, painters, educationists, politicians all depart inevitably. I have been going with them in imagination ever since I saw the Heads standing up there with the spray playing around their base and the Pacific beyond like a high blue plateau.[18]

So, as Laleen dreamed:

> She would walk up the gangway and in slow and stately measure glide down the Harbour, past Mrs Macquarie's chair, past Government House and Pinch Gut and Clark Island and Taronga Park out through the great Heads at last . . . Thus to step into real life, to claim fame and love and all that she had dreamed.[19]

On 7 April, 1906, full of such fancies, Stella Miles Franklin boarded the two-funnelled, 6,000 tonnes SS *Ventura* to attempt to take her place in that other world. From Auckland she sent a postcard to Linda on 12 April, 1906 then continued across the heaving ''blue plateau'', bound first for Honolulu, then for legendary San Francisco and the mysterious, challenging continent beyond.

9 San Francisco and Chicago

Eleven days after Stella left Sydney in the SS *Ventura*, at 5.12 am on 18 April, 1906, the earth quaked beneath San Francisco, that simmering mixture of the vice of the Barbary Coast, the gilded elegance of Nob Hill and the romantic squalor of Chinatown.

The great tremour split and shook the city from foundations to skyline. Theatres, churches, schools, homes, emporiums and public buildings collapsed. Then came the fires and in four days much of the largely timber-built city was burnt out. With burst water mains, ruptured gas pipes and the death of Fire Chief Sullivan following the first blast, the conflagration had the advantage, until martial law was declared and the army moved in using dynamite.

On board ship, still twelve days out from her destination, Stella Franklin was sharing a cabin with a jolly, religious Seventh Day Adventist country girl whom she had tagged affectionately ''my big brown girl, Jonesie'' (later Mrs H.P. McKenzie). Though Stella had been half sick all the way across the two girls had joined in the game of shipboard romance with an insurance agent, Oscar Unmack , Allan Levick and a journalist named Ryan (probably Daniel Ryan who later became a Queensland Labor MP) who thought he had proposed to Stella . . . or perhaps to Jonesie, as Stella Franklin later recalled in a letter to Edith McKenzie in 1937.

Stella had sent postcards home and written virtuously to anxious Edwin. On her dairy farm she had longed for adventure and excitement. There could scarcely be a more dramatic landfall than the arrival on May 1 in the grand foggy harbour of a beautiful city shattered by earthquake and fire. R.L. Stevenson had written of the romance of San Francisco, of its vibrancy, its misty bay and orange-coloured dawns, with the ships of all the exotic ports of the Pacific gathered together in the grey-green light. This literary glamour must have been eclipsed by the eeriness of the actuality.

Though much of the waterfront had been saved there was great disorder. Dauntless Carrie Whelan, a friend of Carrie Catt, managed to charter a tug and went out to take Stella Franklin and Jonesie off the ship.[1] The girls stayed with the Whelan sisters in Oakland for some weeks and were always grateful for their kindness and help. Edwin wrote to Oakland that though the broad Pacific rolled between them he was still as much in love as ever. He felt that their love would overcome all obstacles and that they would be reunited. But his sturdy constancy could scarcely compete with the excitements of a Phoenix-city rising and with the exhilaration of new experiences.

Nearly 500 people had lost their lives in the disaster, thousands had been injured, 120 square kilometres had been burnt out and 300,000 were homeless. The people of San Francisco rallied to the work of clearing away rubbish and rebuilding the city. Federal troops and militia kept ruthless order, many looters being shot on sight. Tent cities for shelter, pavement kitchens for the distribution of food and emergency hospitals for the sick and injured, such as the one in Golden Gate Park, were in operation by the time the *Ventura* arrived.

The city was working again. The railroads were operational and money and supplies were pouring in from all over America. The San Francisco *Chronicle* of 30 April even complained that life was dull because of the curfew. The pleasure-loving citizenry was looking for entertainment once more. On the night of the earthquake, only hours before the blast, Caruso had taken nine curtain calls at the Grand Opera House, then capped that performance, after the shock, by rendering an aria from a window of the Palace Hotel before escaping in his pyjamas. Now the equally spirited Sarah Bernhardt opened her San Francisco season in Oakland on 15 May, and was applauded royally.

There was still an enormous amount of work to do in restoring the city and caring for refugees. The camps needed clerks, labourers, nurses. The two young women pitched in to help by working with Seventh Day Adventist relief. Even in all the extraordinary circumstances Franklin had not forgotten her ultimate purpose. Jack London had been reporting the earthquake for *Colliers'* magazine. Three weeks after landing, no doubt banking on the successful Henry Lawson precedent, she wrote to him about her work. He replied courteously but firmly on 28 May that he did not recommend books or writers to publishers, and wished her well in playing Mary Anne in the United States.[2]

Lovelorn Edwin still wrote and Linda, from far away Talbingo, reprimanded her for leaving so many broken hearts behind. The girls moved on from San Francisco to Los Angeles and stayed in a girls' home there for a time before Stella went on to a missionary sanitarium called Loma Linda, in the beautiful rural San Bernardino valley, some thirty-eight kilometres from the city. Here a Sister Burden took her under her wing.

News came from home — Linda was awaiting her first baby, and even her sweet nature was a little soured at the way she was given small credit for the coming child. She resented the fact that relatives referred to the baby-to-be as little Charlie and she was missing her sister badly, and fearful that she might be lost to her by marriage.

Stella had enjoyed her stay with the missionaries but now it was time to move on. The period in California had been an exciting and reviving break, a time to recover from the hurts of the last few years and to gather strength for the renewed attack she must make on the citadel of success. Initially her destination in the United States had been New York, for she had an introduction to Carrie Catt there. But since Catt had gone overseas for a long stay the Whelan sisters wrote to another outstanding woman, Jane Addams of Hull House, Chicago, introducing the new arrival.[3] It was to Chicago that Franklin now began to make her leisurely way, across deserts, mountains and prairies, travelling by the great railroads then at the peak of their renown.

Leaving California and "the sweet peas and opulence of the Redlands", she crossed to the Wasatch Mountains and Salt Lake City, where she spent some of the summer at the modish Kenyon Hotel, probably earning her keep by waitressing there. Edwin marked her trail with his love letters though the postal service scattered obstacles, and the letter he received from Salt Lake City in September was very dilapidated. She stayed at a big hotel in the Colorado mountains and in September visited Hanging Lake in the Rockies where her riding and shooting exploits won an invitation to join a circus and a proposal from its strong man. Then on she went across the vast plains of the Middle West to the centre of the continent, to the huge and lively city of Chicago.

Here Stella Franklin spent some of the most vigorous years of her life. Here she built a new and different career, amid the freezing winds off Lake Michigan and the clatter of the Loop. The skyscrapers of State Street towering under a smoky sky supplanted the clear, still ranges of her childhood and the energy and drive of one of the world's most bustling cities replaced the dull placidity of her dairy-farming community.

It was a stimulating place. Almost twenty years before Stella took her train there, another writer from the empire, a young man of twenty-five, had visited "the city among the shambles" and having seen it never wanted to see it again. He acknowledged it was a real city, the first American city he had struck, but he thought its inhabitants were savages.

A young American genius, coming to the city at about the same time as Kipling, saw it in a totally different aspect. To Theodore Dreiser its youth and vigour suggested romance. Lyrically he compared it to Florence in its best days and to Venice in its youth for he thought that like the fabled cities of the Renaissance it was without traditions but absorbed in creating them.

Dreiser rejoiced in the rawness, the robustness, the newness, but to Kipling these qualities were only part of barbarism, materialism and money worship. Kipling loathed the ugliness, the look of the city with its long, flat streets, maze of telegraph wires overhead and dirty pavements underfoot. To him the Palmer Hotel, for the people of Chicago a great, proud symbol of their wealth and elegance, was a gilded and mirrored rabbit-warren where people spat on the marble floors while talking about money. In the equally powerful artistic imagination of Dreiser the squalor, the meretriciousness and the materialism were part of the strange grandeur of the city. However pretentious, however bad, Chicago was vibrant and eager and exciting.

Both writers saw part of the truth. There was ugliness, brutality and sordidness, but there was also immense energy, daring and creativeness. It was a tough city. The men who had built its wealth, Marshall Field, Pullman, Swift, Armour, Palmer and their like were of a type — iron-hard, self-made, giving no quarter to competitors or employees. In the short run they were heartless and ruthless, but in the long run they had turned a prairie village into a great city, and had produced for its inhabitants in general a material standard of living surpassing anything in previous cultures. Stella Franklin later paid tribute to this.

> The good old USA spoiled me for all the other countries physically. If the US never contributed anything else to civilisation I always hold that to have made warmth available to all by its way of life is one of the greatest pieces of culture experiences since history began.[4]

There speaks the child, rising in an unheated, draughty house on a morning of black frost to milk with frozen fingers.

It was a vital, polyglot city. Drawn by the magnet of work, immigrants had flooded in as the iron men built their empires in lumber, railroads, machinery, in grain and stock markets, in food packing and in real estate and retailing. By 1890 Chicago, with 2,000,000 residents, was the second city of the United States in population, and also second in wealth. In its style it had become a symbol of the republic.

New York was sneered at by Chicagoans as too English, for their city was a true melting pot, with Slovaks in the lumberyards, Irish on the railroads, Germans, Greeks, Poles, Italians, Croats, Serbs, Russian Jews and the freed Negroes from the south flowing into its thousand and one industries.

It was a proud city. Already it had a place in world history for it had sent Abraham Lincoln to the US Senate, and the Republican Convention in Chicago in 1860 had given him the presidential nomination. It had welcomed back its dead hero on May 1, 1865 when his bier was brought home on a train whose engine boilers were draped with the black blankets trimmed by silver stars usually worn as mourning by horses drawing hearses. In typical Chicago fashion, George M. Pullman had managed to attach the first Pullman car, the Pioneer, to the train.

It was a city acquiring a reputation for wickedness and wildness, with vice districts an accepted part of society, paying their regular cash tributes to political bosses. Mickey Finn had dispensed his extraordinary drinks at the Lone Star Saloon, and in the notorious Levee district two young women from Kentucky, the Everleigh sisters, had established their flashy and world-famous brothel, and were honoured guests at the annual First Ward orgy, where vice paid homage to Aldermen "Bathhouse John" Coglin and "Hinky Dink" Kenna, while "ten thousand joyless, reveling pickpockets, bartenders, prostitutes and police captains celebrated the reign of graft."[5]

It was a turbulent and often angry city. Power, money worship, hard-dealing, enterprise, daring, vulgarity and materialism were becoming mingled with the rising rage of part of the working class. Some European migrants, especially some from Germany, had brought with them a new and ruthless doctrine, anarchism, advocating violence and dynamite to change society. In the Haymarket riots of 1886 between workers from the shut-down McCormick plant and the police, a bomb had been thrown, resulting in the deaths of six people and injuries to hundreds. Who was to blame was never clear but three anarchists, Parsons, Spies and Engel, who were not even present at the disturbance, were hanged along with a man named Fischer. Others were sentenced to prison and there was great bitterness among German workers particularly. There were other explosions of labour unrest including the paralysing Pullman strike of 1894, led by Eugene Debs, and the Stockyard strike and the Teamsters' strike of 1905. By the early years of the twentieth century Chicago had become the most radical of American cities.

Yet in this most materialistic of cities, "the only city in the world to which all its citizens have come for the avowed object of making money",[6] the very wealth of the rich led to a concern with culture and the arts. Thorstein Veblen, lecturing at the University of Chicago from 1892 to 1906, in a masterly phrase labelled the pride in magnificence and in the owning of beautiful things "conspicuous consumption". The money-men spent where it could be seen, on grand homes, on jewellery and precious objects, and also on great public buildings such as the Art Institute (1879) with its magnificent Ryerson collection of Renoirs and Impressionists, on the Field Museum of Natural History, on the grandiose buildings of the White City for the World Fair in honour of Columbus in 1893, and on the new architecture of skyscrapers being evolved by Daniel Burnham Root and Louis Sullivan and his pupil Frank Lloyd Wright. Millionaires funded the Chicago Symphony Orchestra (1891) under Theodore Thomas, and the Chicago University under the deeply religious and broadly tolerant President William Harper.

The tycoons' wives mainly expressed their need for conspicuous consumption in clothes, balls, concerts and grand dinners, though acknowledged society leader Mrs Potter Palmer had the wit to collect Impressionist paintings. Edith McCormick, wife of the reaper-king and daughter of John D. Rockefeller, gave dinner parties (which were teetotal) on a gilded silver service which had belonged to Napoleon's brother-in-law,

Prince Camillo Borghese. (Later she was an early patron of James Joyce— until she read the manuscript of *Ulysses*.)

But in many women in this milieu the work ethic was as strong as it was in their striving husbands. Chicago-born novelist Henry B. Fuller examined the new skyscraper society and portrayed as a type Mrs Granger Bates (rumoured to be an ex-washerwoman), who is happiest in a small, shabby room buried in the midst of the grand mansion which her husband has crammed with pictures and treasures. ''I'd sooner have a boy of mine dead than a mere gentleman,''[7] she says in a pugnacious exposition of the work ethic. The themes of the leaders of this city were enterprise and energy, not idleness and soft luxury, despite their devotion to wealth and show.

By the early years of the twentieth century, when Stella Miles Franklin first saw it, a tide of criticism was beginning to run against the fundamental assumptions of Chicago's traditional leaders. Chicago University economist, Thorstein Veblen, though not a social activist, had rejected the popular socio-economic idea of the survival of the fittest on which the thinking of Chicago's builders was based. He warned that small scale competitive capitalism was being replaced by large scale monopolies which attempted to limit production and raise prices. Novelists Frank Norris, Henry B. Fuller and Robert Merrick criticised the business obsessions and crude materialism of many of the leading citizens, and Dreiser in *The Titan* dealt with the unabashed bribery and corruption, linking some businessmen and politicians. The critical mood extended to areas other than those of economics and politics.

Kipling had written an unforgettable description of the cruelty to animals involved in the stockyards, of the blood-covered workers, the blood-sodden floors and the blood in the killer's eye, but in 1905 the simmering scandal of the squalor of the stockyards, with its threat to public health, was brought to a full boil by a series of articles in the medical journal *The Lancet* and by the serial version of Upton Sinclair's *The Jungle*, which was published in book form the following year. A new breed of muck-raking journalist, such as Lincoln Steffens, flourished in the magazines *Colliers'*, *Harper's*, *McClure's* and *Everybody's*.

The Prohibition movement also gained strength, for the openness of the link between saloons, brothels, gambling dens and certain police and politicians aroused the disgust of many, and the Temperance Reform movement, which had been given a boost by Englishman William T. Stead's polemic against vice and political corruption, ''If Christ Came to Chicago'' (1893), gained supporters. Chicago became almost as well known for its evangelists such as Gipsy Smith and in later years Billy Sunday as for its gamblers and gangsters. ''America then was still puritanical and the soberest place I have ever seen in the world,''[8] noted Stella Franklin.

The movement for social change was growing when Franklin reached Chicago in 1906. More concerned people were becoming aware of the dark side of the glittering coin, of the depressed state of much of the working class — particularly of migrant women. They, isolated by language and custom, bore children, cooked and cleaned in shabby cold-water tenements lacking sinks and sewerage, adequate light and air, overcrowded in the stifling summer and underheated in the harsh winter. Such women also formed part of the workforce in ''sweat-shops'' and unpoliced home industries.

The near destitution of so many blotched the admitted achievements of the city, and stirred the consciences of a number of more favourably placed citizens, who centred their benevolent activities around the social settlements of Chicago University and Hull House. These humanitarian idealists compared the huge fortunes and magnificent mansions of the few with the near-starvation wages and slum-shanty dwellings of a neglected world, and felt that changes were necessary to save the soul of this vital city.

Stella Franklin, stepping off her train, clutching around for support, carried with her a passport into this world of liberal idealism and reform — a letter of introduction from Carrie Whelan to magnificent Jane Addams of famous Hull House. Such a letter was a lifeline in this surging, tempestuous metropolis.

Stella had left her secluded, protected station in the ranges for the narrow little farming communities around Goulburn, and then, full of hope, had swept into the small and friendly city of Sydney to become for a brief time a medium-sized fish in a modest-sized pool. Now, with the Pacific behind her, she was a tiny minnow in a gigantic lake. She had exchanged an isolated, almost unknown country on the edges of civilisation for a giant about to take its place, centre-stage, in world affairs. From a people, then of almost totally British Isles descent, owing allegiance to the British Crown and often looking to England as home, she had come to join a complex, multi-racial, multi-cultural, multi-lingual society with a proud tradition of fought-for independence and republicanism. The daughter of quiet, frugal, conservative farming folk, she was now in the centre of money-making, money worship and display, and of the flaming radical passions which these provoked. She came from a breezy, cheerful city of temperate climate and easygoing lifestyle, to one of hard dealing and no quarter, of smashing cold and smothering blizzards, to the struggle for survival of one migrant among hundreds of thousands, in this gilded, smoking, mid-west colossus.

She came too from the security of a supportive network of family and friends to an immense loneliness. Clarence Darrow, the famous radical lawyer, recalled in his memoirs that such was his loneliness when he first came to Chicago in 1888 that he would stand at the corner of Madison and State, watching for a familiar face, but felt he might as well have hunted in the depths of a Brazilian forest. And he was from nearby Ohio!

Since Darrow's time many more thousands of people had been swept into that ferocious loneliness. Of these many Stella Franklin was one of the luckiest, for her destination was, temporarily, Hull House, a refuge, a meeting place, a starting point for the adventures ahead and the residence and life-work of one of America's most famous women, Jane Addams.

10 Jane Addams, Hull House and Alice Henry

The plain red-brick building of three storeys and an attic floor, to which Stella Franklin made her way, had been in earlier years the mansion of Chicago pioneer, Charles Hull. Situated in the rundown West Side, only a few blocks from the O'Leary house where the Great Fire of 1871 supposedly started, its surroundings were stark and unattractive. No garden separated the building from the pavement, and the street car ran a few metres from its entrance. Straggling Halsted Street (the longest street in the world was its boast) must have been a dispiriting sight in a "winter dreary with blackened, bedraggled snow and all the ugliness of this season in a soot-ridden city".[1] October, by the calendar, was autumn, but October of the year of Stella's arrival was icy cold. "In 1906," she wrote later, "the natives of Illinois assured me that snow in October was a freak."[2]

The Chicago climate came as a physical assault after the mildness of California, where at Loma Linda, in the rural peace of the San Bernardino Valley, Stella had been surrounded by the balmy air and the citrus, olive and apricot trees of that temperate region. Summer in the mountains had been fresh and invigorating. But as she described Chicago later:

> The damp, ungracious rawness, laden with fine snow as sharp as salt, and rising vastly from Lake Michigan like an Arctic dragon's breath was sucked so furiously through the artificial canyons formed by the skyscrapers that pedestrians handicapped by women's garments could not hold a footing against it. In many instances on the lake front they were blown along like ice boats.[3]

At this stage, however, to Stella Miles Franklin, surging with vitality after her months of liberation and relaxation, Chicago was new and exciting, a challenge to her courage and talent. Hull House was not just a square, severe-looking edifice in a long and slushy street. It was a symbol of the goodness, charity and concern for others which had made its foremost resident already a legend, even in distant Australia. A visiting actress from Australia admitted that she had never heard of Lake Michigan or the Chicago stockyards, "but there is a hospital ward in Sydney," she said, "to furnish which we all helped

top: Jane Addams' Hull House, Chicago, 1910.
bottom: Jane Addams.

in a benefit, which is dedicated to Jane Addams. Is she really the only woman in America?''[4]

A month after Stella's arrival, the *Chicago Tribune* ran, in November, a "Who is the best woman in Chicago?" feature. The overwhelming first choice of voters was Jane Addams of Hull House.

The inspiration and founder of this first social settlement in the United States was born in Cedarville, Illinois, on 6 September, 1860. Her Quaker father, who had risen from lowly beginnings to business success, was a close friend of Lincoln, an admirer of Mazzini, and a State Senator from 1854 to 1870. Jane, whose mother died young, was brought up by this honest, idealistic man, whom she adored, in an atmosphere of moral seriousness and conscientious thought for others.

At seventeen she entered Rockford College, Illinois, an institution of high standards in learning and of an almost missionary spirit in the pursuit of higher education for women. There Jane studied Latin, Greek, philosophy, history and literature and found a serious like-minded group with which to discuss everything under the sun. After Rockford, Jane enrolled in the Women's Medical College of Philadelphia, but an old spinal trouble put a stop to her studies, and as her beloved father had died, leaving her a modest fortune, she went abroad in 1883 to drink in the arts and history of Europe, in the manner of rich American girls of her day. A fellow passenger on her Atlantic crossing, surrounded by a bevy of Daisy Millers, was Henry James.

Overcome by the sight of the wretchedness of the East End of London in November, 1883, Jane began to question her feverish search for culture as a waste of time and money. She felt that girls of her generation had been given too much to study, and that what they really needed was the opportunity to be practical, to learn from life as their mothers had.

On a second trip to Europe in 1888 she formed a plan with Ellen Starr, who had been a freshman with her at Rockford, to rent a house in Chicago, where they, and young women like them, might work for the good of the community. On 18 September, 1889, just after her twenty-ninth birthday, Jane Addams opened Hull House, modelled on London's Toynbee Hall. The event marked the beginning of modern social work in the United States.

On the migrant-flooded West Side, Hull House became a rock to which to cling amid the tempestuous uncertainties of life in a new country. Here there were help and counsel for the needy, the confused, the desperate. As a neighbourhood centre it offered practical help, but it also provided a range of services for the enrichment of the lives of families of the district, such as a boys' club, a men's club, a women's club, a music school for children, a drama group, a science club and a resident Jane club for working girls. It held classes on many subjects, but it provided entertainment too, with concerts, dances, debates and discussions. There was even a nursery for the children of working mothers, funded by puritan millionaire Richard T. Crane, who said:

"We cannot close our eyes to the fact that in many cases the wealth of the rich has been wrung from the poor."[5] Miss Addams, bereft of her mother at two, thought it part of the stupidity of life that mothers should have to leave young children for the coarser work of the world.

Jane Addams, in her life of service, was nurse, midwife, friend and counsellor to the community around Hull House, as well as inspiration and guiding star. She was also an important member of a number of boards and committees, including the Chicago Board of Education, 1905-1908, the National Child Labor Committee, the Playground Association (which she founded) and the National Women's Suffrage Association. She was a prominent member of the Progressive Party, led by Theodore Roosevelt, and her lifelong devotion to the pacifist cause culminated in her being awarded the Nobel Peace Prize in 1931.

Rose Scott, in Sydney, had introduced Stella Franklin to the world of good causes. Jane Addams was Rose Scott writ large, on the grand Chicagoan scale. Stella said of her that she "was one of the biggest single influences for good of her time . . . she was not only the most famous social worker of America but also a world figure."[6] Stella Franklin's letter of introduction took her into Jane Addams' circle, and into the atmosphere of dedication and service of the Hull House group.

The institution, though half the residents were men in 1906, had built a reputation as a feminist centre as well as a social settlement, largely because Jane Addams' warm genius had attracted a group of talented women to work there. Most of these associates shared Addams' social and educational background and, like her, wished to use their abilities for the good of society. Many left their mark.

In earlier days Hull House resident Florence Kelley, both a socialist and a divorcee in an era when to be either raised eyebrows, had become Illinois State's first factory inspector. When she moved to New York she became general secretary of the powerful Consumer League and one of the founders, in 1909, of the National Association for the Advancement of Coloured People. Julia Lathrop, who had been at Rockford with Jane Addams, had gone on to the prestigious women's university, Vassar, and in time became the first Head of the Children's Bureau. Alice Hamilton, a distinguished medical graduate, had investigated the Chicago typhoid epidemic of 1902, and specialised in industrial diseases. She became a member of the conservative Harvard Medical School Faculty in 1919, and first Professor of Industrial Medicine. Chicago University academics Edith Abbott and Sophonisba Breckenridge investigated and exposed housing conditions in the tenements of Chicago. Other brilliant women in this circle which Stella Franklin was now to enter included sociologist Mary McDowell, "the angel of the stockyards" in the 1905 strike, academic Grace Abbott (sister of Edith) and art critic and poet, Harriet Monroe.

While to those at the bottom of the ladder of life Hull House was a refuge and source of encouragement, to a number of upper crust Chicago citizens, like society leader, Louise de Kouen, who became president of the women's club, and the wealthy Lloyds, Jane Addams and her band of able, dedicated disciples were worthy of warm regard and firm support in their efforts to assuage the city's social problems.

But, understandably, there was as well a certain distrust of Jane Addams and her work in the Chicago establishment. She had visited Tolstoy, and had welcomed as guests revolutionist Prince Peter Propotkin and socialist economist, Henry George. She had been a friend of Governor Altgeld, who had pardoned the anarchists imprisoned after the Haymarket riot of 1886, and she had spoken at his funeral when no "liberal" clergyman dared to do so. She had supported the workers in the Pullman railway strike, though she liked and admired George Pullman. Her friends Professor Graham Taylor and Professor John Dewey of the University of Chicago were suspected of advanced ideas, and the Social Science Club at Hull House had gained a reputation for radicalism by reason of its vigorous discussions on socialism, economics and anarchism. In addition, Hull House was suspected by many worthy burghers of being a hot-bed of rampant feminism. Active suffrage groups and the National Women's Trade Union League centred there.

Jane Addams' tolerance of this broad range of ideas might cause chills to run down the spines of some of Chicago's civic leaders, but to Stella Franklin, coming from the narrowness of an Australian bush community, and from the limitations of a small, provincial city, such freedom was welcome. After her early lonely struggles, to find such a group was a joy.

But what were respectable business and professional men, who prided themselves on being good fathers, to make of all these distinguished women of good background and upbringing, pursuing unladylike careers and causes from a house in the slums? How would it all affect their daughters?

> . . . a place so big with life as Hull House could not be ignored, and a mere mention of it over dinner tables anywhere started argument. Girls were 'thrilled' but men of the 'everywoman's place-is-in-the-home' type called it queer and dangerous.[7]

One of the girls thrilled was Stella Franklin. Here was what she had dreamed about: women doing fine things, using their abilities, being acknowledged by the world. Here she could meet people of like mind and give vent to her ideas without being thought weird and unnatural. Though she was but one of many in the Hull House ambience, Jane Addams was kind and welcoming and put her on the guest roster, while the talented women in the group, making their own way in the world, by their example reinforced Stella's determination to succeed again. The place itself enchanted her. In her words:

> Hull House was a delightful place to visit, its accumulation of buildings, including theatre, class rooms, gymnasiums, a creche, meeting halls and so on rose off a street dusty and dishevelled in summer, or in winter deep in snow or slush, and dark under the confined smoke of a great industrial city. Then one entered to meet some of the most interesting people in the world in a home of such warmth and comfort as the United States alone provides for ordinary mortals.[8]

It was a far cry from the drab threadbareness of the selector's rough home to these old-fashioned, high-ceilinged reception rooms with their white mantelpieces and French windows. The guests in the long dining room, which was wood panelled and lit by Spanish-iron chandeliers, could range from famous names to shy girls, and could include social reformers, socialists, millionaires, muck-rakers, singers, writers and overseas visitors. Grander guests might gather for a formal dinner, but on Sunday afternoon many of the guests at tea were working girls.

Among the ''most interesting people in the world'' there on an autumn day Stella Franklin met a middle-aged fellow Australian, journalist and feminist Alice Henry. As fellow countrywomen and writers they had much to talk about. So began a friendship, at times filled with exasperation on both sides, which lasted life long. The chance meeting affected the course of Stella's life for some years, for, adrift and perhaps just a little afraid, she clung to this new and kindly acquaintance, and veered further into the activist stream.

They were an odd pair. Miss Henry, forty-nine years of age, prim, serious, absent-minded, had risen above any personal emotional storms to become totally dedicated to the cause of women's rights, including industrial rights, and was the very picture of the ''new woman'' of caricature. In contrast, Stella Franklin was the ''modern girl'', pretty, flirtatious, pleasure-loving, spirited, very keen on the cause, but largely as it related to her, and still tossed hither and thither by emotion and ambition.

Alice Henry, like Stella, was born in the bush, on a selection in Gippsland, Victoria. But her Scottish-born accountant father left farming and moved to Melbourne, where the girl lived a city life. She attended a Swedenborgian Church, imbibing a liberal draught of high ideals and its philosophy of social service, then, after school, taught for a while before becoming a feature writer from home, for the Melbourne *Argus* and *The Australian*. Henry interviewed South Australian electoral reformer Catherine Spence in 1893 when that outstanding woman was on her way to the World Fair in Chicago. The meeting aroused in Alice Henry an intense admiration of Catherine Spence, to the extent that she, in turn, became an expert on the theory of proportional representation. She became also a rock-solid feminist, and supporter of women's suffrage. She moved in pacifist and reformist groups and among her friends was novelist Sumner Locke, mother of novelist and dramatist Sumner Locke Eliot, of *Rusty Bugles* fame.

Franklin with Alice Henry.

Alice Henry represented Melbourne charities at an English conference in 1905 and was present at the renowned women's suffrage protest at the meeting in the Manchester Free Trade Hall in October that year. Finding it difficult to obtain employment in England, she left for the United States, arriving on 8 January, 1906, with introductions to feminist leaders, including Susan Anthony. She toured, lecturing on Australia's approach to women's suffrage. When the earthquake struck San Francisco she was in Boston. Then she visited Washington, and from there was summoned to Chicago by Jane Addams and Anna Nicholes to assist them in securing the municipal vote for the women of that city. She arrived on a warm summer morning in 1906 and stayed at Hull House for several weeks before taking more permanent lodgings. One Sunday fellow guests at the tea-table included wealthy social workers Margaret and Raymond Robins, who also were staying at Hull House while looking for somewhere to live. Alice Henry made an excellent impression, for next day Margaret Robins offered her a job as office secretary of the Chicago branch of the newly-formed Woman's Trade Union League. Alice had been living a somewhat hazardous existence, but with this stroke of luck acquired a steadier foothold on American soil. It marked too the start of her career as a labour leader in the United States.

For Stella Franklin the meeting with Alice Henry seemed a piece of rare good fortune. Here was a link with the homeland which she missed so much, a ready-made friend, a surrogate mother (though she remarked later that she thought of Alice more as a father and always called her by the nickname of Pops), and, most importantly, someone who shared her views on the position of women. Here was someone who had been in Chicago only a matter of weeks, yet, already, had managed to secure an interesting job. Edwin Bridle in a September letter had asked if Stella had started negotiations with publishers yet, and how long would it be before she reached New York. However, there had been no encouragement from the tooth and claw publishing tribe there. Why push on to that alarming metropolis when in Chicago she had a centre of feminism and thought at welcoming Hull House, an enormous, exciting city to explore, and a heaven-sent guide and friend in Alice Henry? Here Stella could take stock and plan her further campaigns. She settled for Chicago, at least for a while, and took lodgings in the same house as Alice Henry, at Dr Young's home, 71 Park Avenue,[9] after a brief period at Miss Wood's, 268 South Wood Street.

Edwin Bridle wrote to her in December 1906 to say that the letter he had received from Chicago was a beautiful one. He felt more hopeful about their future happiness, though he agreed that they should not rush into anything until she was ready. But Stella was never to be ready for generous, loving Edwin. As she wrote: "Alice Henry led me into the Trade Union movement."[10] Stella Miles Franklin, would-be novelist, was to be "diverted to sociology and swallowed up by the social movement in U.S.A. and London''.[11]

Her pressing need for the moment, however, having decided to settle, was to find employment. Grandma had been most upset in September 1906 to hear that her favourite had been working as a barmaid, and had exhorted her impious granddaughter to read her Bible and to remember that disobedience is punished. It is hard to say whether the barmaid story was true or not. It would have been the kind of teasing joke Stella Franklin would have enjoyed playing on her severely respectable Grannie. But possibly she helped out in some capacity at the Kenyon Hotel in the summer, and a photograph taken in the grounds of the Colorado Hotel, Glenwood Springs, in early September shows her with a group of girls in black skirts and white blouses, in the company of a solitary man, a group which looks very much like a restaurant staff.

What is clear is that in Chicago Franklin obtained work in one of the big department stores. For an untrained girl, who was none too keen on domestic labour and too finicky for factory employment, this was the most likely way of earning a living. Historian Eleanor Flexner has written that in 1907 new leaders began to emerge from the ranks of working women, and listed among them Stella Franklin of the department store clerks. Stella may have clerked literally, or possibly sold shoes or waitressed in one of the emporiums. Some personal experience seems reflected in her remark: ''There is no work, not even selling shoes which is a sizzling little job in its way—which is so surrounded by irritation as serving people with their food.''[12] There are some barbed comments on department stores and their clientele in the novel she set in Chicago, *The Net of Circumstance*, in which she labelled conditions in that trade as a danger to morality.

> Many another young girl has been similarly lured by the department store and has discovered to her sorrow that it is a mighty semi-charitable institution supported by that part of the public which through ignorance gives a long day's work for a third of a day's pay. Many a girl had graduated to the brothel by way of the department store and its starvation wages.

And those served are not spared. ''Harrow's patrons were drawn from that insolent, well-fed, expensively and smartly dressed, aggressive type of American woman who usually comes into Chicago from the suburbs.''

Stella Franklin certainly had some background in this trade for in 1909 she represented the department store girls during the struggle for the Eight Hour Bill, the ''Girls' Bill'', in the State legislature at Springfield, Illinois, though by that time she was anchored safely in an office job. Her experiences, though, were such that an antipathy to emporiums and their ways lingered long in her writings. She described one such as ''a cheapjack drapery enterprise'', which ''throve on the labour of girls who worked for a nominal

Stella Franklin (No. 11) with a group of staff at the Colorado Hotel, Glenwood Springs, 1906.

wage under the classification of apprentices and were replaced by a new crop at intervals.''[13]

As the first warmth of excitement at being in an exhilarating new city faded, reality became clearer and chillier. It was a punishing experience, physically and emotionally, that first winter, battling cold, exhaustion and homesickness, eating in cheap, sleazy cafeterias, travelling by bumpy street car back to a lonely room after a long and arduous working day to mope over the thwarting of her hopes. She caught something of this physical atmosphere when she wrote of ''the fetid air in the ill-ventilated conveyances, the barbarous overcrowding resulting in being jostled and bashed against large, tired men more addicted to beer and tobacco than the bath'',[14] and when she described a girl like herself, who ''turned sickly from cheap food and frowsy eating places, shuddering to contemplate how many thousands of undainty mouths must have manipulated the half-washed cups and cutlery that she was daily forced to use''.[15]

Like poet Dick Mazere in the novel *Back to Bool Bool*, Stella Miles Franklin had left her country ''undismayed, nay unconscious that [she] was equipped with nothing but youth and handicapped with a hypersensitive soul and body''. From being the darling of Sydney's élite only five years past, she was now just one more insignificant migrant in a mass of 2,000,000 citizens. Her naive vanity about the quick recognition of her literary abilities in the US having been shattered, it was essential that she equip herself for less taxing and more profitable work. Like her heroine Ignez, of *Cockatoos*, who also migrated to the United States, Stella must have taken one of the cheap night courses in typewriting ($4-10 a term) in which Chicago abounded, for she escaped from her initial drudgery into office work. But the severe climate, the long hours, the strenuous labour for poor wages depleted her energies.

Edwin Bridle worried about her health that winter. In March 1907 he wrote that life could not be too pleasant for her, working all day and part of the night. He feared that she would break down completely if she kept it up, and then would not be fit for her great work. He hoped that it would not take too long for her to try her literary wings and that she might come back home with him if he came to America.

Separation from her family grieved her, and ''the aroma of the gumleaf and the perfume of the wattle blossom''[16] haunted her, but as yet there was no progress in her literary career, and return would be an admission of failure, a monstrous blow to her pride and ambition. Marriage was not what she sought, but fame. In any case despite the fatigue of her work, the harshness of the climate and the cheerlessness of her lifestyle, Chicago was far away from the boredom of Possum Gully. ''The thunder of the Loop is sweetest music to me,'' says a girl in one of Franklin's Chicago stories. ''It tells me that the day is to be full of motion and people.''[17] So Stella must have felt on the good days, when in spite of all the hardships, her ambition and vigour and gaiety flared again. Life continued to surge about her in a nonstop tide of crimes of passion, race clashes, strikes and social and cultural occasions. However hard the great city might be, it was never dull. Its zest matched her own lively nature.

In December 1906 the annual First Ward Ball took place, as the underworld paid its regular tribute to the Democratic Club, while Mrs Potter Palmer queened it at a grand charity function. For citizens of more urbane tastes there were concerts, plays, operas. At Hull House there were meetings and discussions for the serious-minded, and as a friend of Alice Henry, Stella Franklin was caught up in a number of edifying activities. In February 1907 there was a Grand Suffrage Meeting at the Arts Institute, and an industrial exhibition was held at Fullerton Hall. Alice Henry spoke on the ballot, and from England came women's labour leader, Mary Macarthur, to say in *Tribune* that the greatest curse of England's workers was the spirit of class. "You can have no idea here what that is." To balance these worthy interests, in March there was for Franklin a special pleasure. Madame Melba sang at the Grand Auditorium.

Sweltering warmth in time replaced the slushy cold. The heat of the summer of 1907 was so intense that free ice was distributed. In July the fervour of emotions, on both sides, about the trial of union leader Haywood for the assassination of the Governor of Colorado matched the temperature. In that month the Woman's Trade Union League, which employed Alice Henry, conducted an interstate conference at Hull House. No doubt Stella Franklin was there with her friend, and she was most likely among the audience when Henry spoke, in August, at Brand's Hall, in support of striking women telegraphists, who alleged discrimination against women by officials of the Western Union Company. The kaleidoscope of Chicago life kept revolving as citizens, Stella among them, concerned themselves with problems of transport, gambling, Sunday trading, fire hazards, water supply and white slavery, as they sweated for their daily bread.

By summer, 1907, Edwin Bridle stopped writing, for it seemed clear that his love was not returned, and even Linda complained in June, when thanking Stella for a pretty cup sent to her baby son, that her sister had not written. Linda and her husband were about to move to Warwick, Queensland, where Charles Graham had bought a house of seventeen rooms, the State Governor's summer residence. Linda urged her sister to look after her health as the main thing in life, and invited her to make Warwick her home, whenever she returned to Australia. To weary Stella it must have seemed an idyllic prospect, to be with Linda again, for, whatever the fever of her aspirations, whatever the excitements of Chicago, she was cut off from the family affections which meant so much to her. Perhaps in Warwick, jaded and strained though she now was, with her idolising sister to sustain her, she would find the peace needed to concentrate on writing. It was an impossibility

at the moment, with her ambitions not yet sated, but a dream for the future — to be again with Linda and Charles and their little son in her own land.

Then early in October 1907, when she was living at Miss Staller's at 1522 Edgecombe Place, where she had moved in order to be closer to freelance typing work, a bombshell exploded in her life, blowing her fragile new world to bits. Her mother wrote: ''Our dear little Linda died in her new home on 24th August, nine days after reaching it [of pneumonia, after flu] . . . the poor child suffered so since her baby was born . . . Why was not I taken who is scarred with the battle of life.''[18]

Linda the golden, the gentle, the loved and the envied, at twenty-five years of age, had left Stella forever. Her memory is recorded by her sister in the counter-heroine to Ignez in *Cockatoos*, in happy-natured Silvia, who accepted love and marriage, and who, ''Beautiful as a fairy and kind as an angel, upon the advent of her first baby one glorious spring day when all the birds were singing and the world was a sea of wattle gold, had left a fair prospect of life and a devoted young husband.''[19]

The result for Stella Franklin was complete collapse. Alice Henry and the other friends she had made were concerned and kind, taking her to the beautiful garden suburb of Winnetka, about twenty-five kilometres out of Chicago, to the mansion of the wealthy and hospitable Lloyd family, friends of Jane Addams and Hull House. In these tranquil surroundings she began to mend and by 14 November had recovered some of her vigour and impatience, for she sent a postcard home from there saying: ''I am staying with the Lloyds in the big red house. They own all the land down to the Lake and as far as you can see on this side. There is no talk of me being fit for work for months yet. I'm getting jolly sick of it.''[20] Consoling her friend Kate Baker on a similar collapse years later, Stella wrote from America: ''I hope you have recovered from your nervous breakdown . . . I was put to bed for that reason for three solid months the first year I was over here.''[21]

The kindly care and comfort of the Lloyd household soothed her sadness and revived her spirit and courage. Ironically, the months which brought the tragic news about Linda, brought as an antidote the offer of a stimulating and challenging position. After a battering year, emotionally and physically, when it had taken all her energies merely to survive, a new prospect opened up before her, a new and important friend took a special interest in her. Margaret Robins, Alice Henry's employer, who had become acquainted with Franklin through Hull House and Woman's Trade Union League activities, thought she had a place that the girl would fill very well.

> I am very anxious to have someone to take care of what I term my correspondence and work as national president of the Woman's Trade Union League . . . I have been wondering if you care to undertake this work for me. The salary for the beginning would have to be a small one, but neither would the work be very heavy.[22]

It was the beginning, after a year of strenuous marking time, of a move forward in her career in the United States. Stella Franklin, labour leader, was about to emerge, somewhat hardened in temper, for the year of hard grind, in dreary circumstances for little pay, had left an ineradicable bitterness towards the idle rich, "that infinitesimal and insolent section of humanity which believes it has the right to patronise even genius",[23] and a lasting empathy with fellow working girls in their hardships.

11 Margaret Dreier Robins, the National Women's Trade Union League and the Group

Of the people around Stella Franklin during her American years the most important and most able was Margaret Dreier Robins who was the mainspring of the activities of the National Women's Trade Union League in that organisation's difficult early period of growth. The relationship between the two was important personally and in its achievements.

This emotional, strong-willed crusader for the under-privileged in general and for working women in particular was born at 36 Monroe Place, Brooklyn, New York in 1868, of German migrant parents. Her father was a prosperous businessman and community leader, being a trustee of the Brooklyn Hospital, a member of the Chamber of Commerce and an elder of the German Evangelical Church. Like Stella Franklin's Grandfather Lampe, he came from Bremen.

There were four daughters, of whom Margaret was the eldest, and a son. The family led a contented and comfortable life with holidays often spent with relatives in Germany. Though Margaret did not go to college she studied history and philosophy at home and her obvious natural abilities resulted in her being invited to join, at nineteen, the Women's Auxiliary of the Brooklyn Hospital, of which she became secretary-treasurer. This service first aroused her interest in industrial questions. She was appalled by the sight of little boys crippled as a result of working conditions and of small girls who had lost the use of their legs from the endless treading of printing presses. Like Jane Addams, she felt a call to practical service to alleviate suffering.

In 1902 she was asked to become a member of the Visiting Committee for the State Institution for the Insane, and in 1903 she was chairman of a committee of the Women's Municipal League which successfully lobbied for a Bill to control exploitative employment agencies. In 1904 she was influenced by Leonora O'Reilly of the Garment Workers' Union to join the New York Branch of the recently-formed Woman's Trade Union League, later known as The National Women's Trade Union League. She was then

Margaret Robins.

Raymond Robins.

thirty-six years old and unmarried. In 1905 she was elected president of the branch and, with an eye for talent and dedication, recruited brilliant young orator Rose Schneiderman of the Cap Makers' Union to the group. Helen Marot, a thoughtful socialist and librarian of Philadelphian Quaker background became secretary.

Brave, forceful, handsome, a commanding figure on the platform with her flashing brown eyes, high colour and smoothly-parted brown hair, Margaret won the attention of an equally dashing visitor to New York when he first saw her at a meeting of the Woman's Trade Union League in April 1905. Raymond Robins, born in Staten Island in 1873, raised on a Florida plantation, ex-farmer, ex-surveyor, ex-goldminer in the Klondike where he had made a lucky strike in 1897, now millionaire lawyer, preacher and settlement worker, had come from Chicago to Brooklyn's Plymouth Church to preach on the social gospel of Jesus. Within three months this pair of handsome, rich idealists was married, on 21 June, 1905 and after a honeymoon at Robins' estate near Brooksville in Florida, returned to Chicago to spend a few weeks at Hull House before settling into a cold-water apartment, four flights up, in a grimy tenement on the West Side in West Ohio Street.

The Robins' neighbours were mainly Italian garment workers, while the turbulent district had gained the name the Bloody Seventeenth, because of riots and violence there on election days. But both these romantic reformers wished to share, as far as possible, the life of the workers whom they hoped to aid. High-minded and independently wealthy, Margaret Robins also felt deeply the responsibility of inheritance for, unlike Raymond, she had never earned a dollar of her comfortable income. In the Woman's Trade Union League, she found an outlet for her great abilities and a cause to support emotionally and financially.

Though women had been in the workforce for many years there were few unionists among them at the beginning of the twentieth century. The idea of a movement to aim at the organisation of women workers had sprung from the co-operative efforts of two very different people, both of whom had been influenced by Hull House.

An Irish working woman from the West Side, Mary Kenney (later O'Sullivan), who almost single-handedly had organised the first women's bookbinders' union in Chicago in the 1880s, joined forces with a wealthy graduate of Chicago University and Harvard Law School, William English Walling, when they met at the annual convention of the American Federation of Labor in 1903. Walling, a settlement worker at New York University, had studied the British Women's Trade Union League (founded 1874) in England that year. He and Mary Kenney O'Sullivan together drew up plans for a similar body in the United States. Samuel Gompers, president of the American Federation of Labor, and a number of union leaders gave their

NWTUL medallion, 1903.

blessing and small branches of the Woman's Trade Union League were formed in New York, Boston and Chicago.

In New York, Walling, O'Sullivan and Leonora O'Reilly of the Garment Workers' Union turned for support not just to women in industry but also to a group of capable, sympathetic, wealthy wellwishers, including Margaret Dreier and her sister Mary, women who had the position and time and money to help influence opinion. There was some suspicion of this aspect of the league among many union leaders who thought it a dilettantish, rich women's hobby. So the league invited Samuel Gompers to address its first national conference, held in New York in the spring of 1905, in the hope of forging bonds with the trade unions. Gompers' speech backed the league as being a useful part of the labour movement, not just some kind of charity. Still, relations between the basically male American Federation of Labor and this new women's organisation were often prickly.

In Chicago Margaret Robins made her mark quickly. Raymond Robins became involved in city politics and Margaret took an indignant interest in a school board dispute, which meant conflict with the Chicago *Tribune*. She wrote to muck-raker Lincoln Steffens (that "pillar of the Stalinist church in America", as Max Eastman later called him) on the subject in November 1906 and had made such an impression in a short time that she was an also-ran in the *Tribune*'s "Best Woman in Chicago" feature of that month.

The Woman's Trade Union League was, as yet, very weak. There was a national organiser, Gertrude Barnum of Hull House, a graduate of the University of Wisconsin and the daughter of a Chicago judge; but the very brief, handwritten report of the second national meeting held at Hull House on 5 January, 1906 shows the frailty of the system at that time. No doubt when Margaret Robins swept up Alice Henry from the table at Hull House, she was convinced that Henry's competence and dedication would help to build up the league. The Chicago branch had begun to progress in 1906. *The Union Labor Advocate* offered space in its columns and Anna Nicholes, the secretary, became editor of a women's department, which covered such stories as suffrage, equal pay and the experiences of women in various industries. Alice Henry, as well as assisting Margaret Robins and working as office secretary for the Chicago league, also helped with this journalistic section in 1907.

The idea of a strong national organisation, not merely a collection of branches, was part of Margaret Robins' thinking when she approached Stella Franklin in October 1907, but it had been raised a year previously when Sophonisba Breckenridge of Chicago University suggested to Mary McDowell that Miss Abbott, a highly qualified graduate of Chicago University and of the London School of Economics, might be employed in a central research office to organise the work of the league, at a salary of $800—$1,500, with an office assistant at $500. This was far beyond the resources available at the time.

However the dynamism of Margaret Robins forced the league forward in public attention during 1907. She drew to herself firstly the working women. The Robins' little apartment in West Ohio Street became a meeting place, a centre of many supper parties with girls overflowing from chairs and settees on to the floor, talking of their lives, their work, their weariness. No doubt lively Stella, accompanying serious Alice, told there the tale of Mary Anne, for on 13 March, 1907 Margaret Robins gave a lecture at Hull House on "A Domestic in a Democracy".

In New York in April 1907 Gertrude Barnum resigned as national organiser and Margaret Robins was elected national president on the same day. The idea of a central office was discussed and a committee appointed to look into it.

Margaret Robins' passionate, impetuous nature led her to take strong stands on controversial issues and she was soon good copy for the Chicago press. The *cause célèbre* of unionism in 1906 had been the Haywood case. Haywood, Pettibone and Moyer of the militant Federation of Miners in Colorado had been leaders in a bitter strike involving violence and deaths. Governor Steunenderg had called in troops and arrested 800 miners. Feeling among the miners had blazed. Then the Governor had been assassinated. Radical lawyer Clarence Darrow appeared as defence lawyer for Haywood on a murder charge.

Many unionists, like young Rose Schneiderman, felt that unionism itself was on trial. Giving witness to her almost religious belief in organised labour, in May 1907 Margaret Robins, president of WTUL, marched in a pro-Haywood procession, shocking many admirers. In May also she rallied striking bakers in the Jewish district, in company with Emma Steghagen, and addressed them in German. Such activities, while publicising the league, led to her being black-balled by the Chicago Women's Club.

In July she recorded her happiness at the not guilty verdict for Haywood and was elected president of the Chicago branch of the league, with Emma Steghagen as secretary, Agnes Nestor as treasurer and Alice Henry as office secretary.

Ambitious, vigorous Margaret Robins looked ahead to further expansion and activity. As national president and Chicago president she needed competent help in carrying out her plans. Alice Henry was busy with the Chicago office, so, recognising Stella Franklin's ability, Robins wrote on 29 October, 1907, the letter which was to so cheer Stella's convalescence. She had consulted Franklin's physician, Doctor Young, who had not opposed the idea of the job, as the duties were not heavy. It was to be a part-time and private position and Mrs Robins would pay the salary of $12 a week herself with Stella free to take some other work. She wanted someone who would be thinking of the league nationally and who could co-ordinate the work of the local branches. (Inevitably, while the duties became full-time, the salary remained the same.)

While Mrs Robins' need for such help was genuine, Alice Henry's concern for her little friend and Margaret Robins' own kind-hearted nature probably played their part in the offer. Shocked and saddened by the death of Linda, her health already undermined by overwork and the testing climate, her romance with Edwin over and her ambitions unfulfilled, Stella needed a fillip. Here was the chance to work with a leader in a great city, in the cause of women. To be sought after by such an outstanding figure — "Dear lady, you do not know what a help you would be, if you felt that you could and would undertake this work."[1] — brought new strength. She accepted gladly. Like Ignez in *Cockatoos*:

> When she found that two of her outlets, family life and the arts, had been firmly cut off as by water-tight bulkheads, she opened up other holds in her cargo of general capability and intelligence. She was soon in the dizzying rhythm of social service effort with its stimulating contacts and colleagues of international renown.

So, when the constitution of the National Women's Trade Union League, adopted at the convention at Norfolk, Virginia, in November 1907, was printed, the name of Miss S. M. Franklin appeared on it as office secretary. After a pleasant period of indulged convalescence at the Lloyds' lakeside mansion in Winnetka, the new office secretary moved back to Doctor Young's in Park Avenue, ready to begin duty with Mrs Robins on 1 January, 1908.

The league had an active year in Chicago in 1907 with regular meetings at Hull House, where speakers included Professor John Commons and English parliamentarian John Hodge. The first convention had been held to coincide with the American Federation of Labor convention, with only seven delegates. The name of the league had been slightly changed from the Woman's Trade Union League to the National Women's Trade Union League and the constitution amended to include, among other provisions, the stipulation that a majority of each of the executive boards should be trade unionists in good standing, in the hope that control of league affairs would pass quickly to working women.

The enthusiastic presidency of Margaret Robins, whose magnetic personality drew talent like filings to a loadstone, began to make an impact. Her generous donations were equally important. The annual financial report read at the meeting in January 1908 showed she had given $2,000 of the $3,500 total receipts. Labour historian Allen Davis has written: "More than any other single person Margaret Robins was responsible for making the Woman's (*sic*) Trade Union League an effective force for the organisation and protection of the women wage earners ... Under her leadership the

Agnes Nestor.

organisation established branches in several other cities, lobbied for a federal investigation of the problems of women in industry, agitated for the restriction of hours and conditions of labour among women and perhaps most important trained a large number of working women to become leaders in the struggle."[2] He listed among those leaders Stella Franklin. Also listed are a number of women with whom she worked closely in the league, including Agnes Nestor, Mary Anderson, Elizabeth Maloney, Elizabeth Christman, Emma Steghagen and Rose Schneiderman.

Of the leaders the closest to Franklin in Chicago days was "dear little Agnes" of the Glovemakers' Union, small and sweet-faced, who was the daughter of an Irish Catholic member of the Knights of Labor and had been raised in an atmosphere of unionism and ward politics. In 1897, when she was fourteen, the family moved from her native Grand Rapids to Chicago and she found work first as a shop girl and then as a glovemaker. The petty rules and long hours of the industry aroused her ire and drove her to seek advice from the Chicago Federation of Labor where President John Fitzpatrick befriended and guided her. She became vice president of the International Union of Glovemakers when barely into her twenties, and through Hull House met Margaret Robins who drew her into the league with her "radiant personality". Agnes, a fine public speaker whose delicate looks belied her strength in cool, logical argument, forged ahead in the union movement and became secretary-treasurer of her union, treasurer of the Chicago league and a delegate to the Illinois State Federation of Labor, as well as a league delegate to the American Federation of Labor.

Elizabeth Christman, another member of the Glovemakers' Union, became a close friend of Stella, and eventually became secretary of the national league. Another friend, Elizabeth Maloney, the founder and leader of the Waitress' Union in Chicago, fought to raise the standards in her industry, "to make it a real trade by which any girl might be proud to earn her living,"[3] and became an influential member of this group of young leaders.

Another colleague attracted first to Hull House was Mary Anderson, who had arrived in the US as a sixteen-year-old in 1888, had found work in the boot and shoe industry and become an officer of that union. "Hull House and Jane Addams opened a door to a larger life," she observed, and "then Margaret Robins became a friend. We used to go there [Ohio Street] and talk things over with Mrs Robins."[4] Emma Steghagen, also a boot and shoe worker, became secretary to the Chicago branch of the league, sharing a desk in the office of the *Union Labor Advocate*, first with Anna Nicholes and then with Alice Henry. Plain and stolid in appearance, in character she was steadfast and devotedly loyal to Margaret Robins, their German parentage being an emotional link. But she did not win Stella Franklin's affection, and Stella referred to her always, somewhat acidly, as "Sister Emma".

But of all the working girls who served the organisation the most outstanding was Rose Schneiderman of the New York branch. She was certainly the most effective orator. Alice Henry, usually as dry-as-dust, almost gushed in paying her tribute:

> Russia in America is embodied in Rose Schneiderman. She is the living representative of the gifts that the Slavic races and especially the Russian Jew have contributed to American life . . . Penetrated with the profound sadness of her people and passionately alive to the workers' wrongs Rose Schneiderman can stir immense audiences and move them to tears, as readily as to indignation.[5]

Rose Schneiderman, born in Russian Poland in 1882, came to New York as a child of six. When her tailor father died in 1892 he left a pregnant wife and three small children. Rose spent a period in an orphanage, then at thirteen began work as a cash girl in a department store. To earn more money she turned to cap-making and in 1903, aged twenty-one, formed her own branch of the union, called in the American idiom Local 23, with tiny Rose as delegate to the Central Labor Union of New York.

In the stabbing cold of the winter of 1904 she picketed during a strike by her union, and wooed other unions for funds with her oratory. Margaret Robins called on her to offer help and the two became friends, Schneiderman being a guest at the Robins' wedding. In 1906 she was elected a vice-president of the New York branch of the league. A policeman in one of her audiences, condensing her effect, commented: "One of them furriners, but she can make you weep." The emotion that might have turned inwards in self-pity flowed outwards in compassion for others. Beneath her rousing rhetoric on behalf of the insulted and the injured lay a profound personal stoicism. She remarked once that when people talked about being happy or miserable in childhood she was puzzled. She did not remember being either. In a similar abnegation of ego she accepted calmly that the work of the league would keep her from marriage and a family.

There were other leaders in the group which enclosed Stella Franklin who were not unionists but "allies". In New York were Mary Dreier, quieter in manner than her flamboyant sister but just as dedicated, spending her life and money in the cause, and Helen Marot, Quaker intellectual who was more radical in thought than most of the others and eventually became a socialist. In Chicago there were Jane Addams, Gertrude Barnum, Mary McDowell, the Abbott sisters and Sophonisba Breckenridge. In its earliest years the league had drawn heavily on the talents of these "allies", concerned, educated upper-class women. But 1907, as Eleanor Flexner noted in her history of the women's rights movement in the United States, saw the emergence of the new leaders grouped around Margaret Robins, coming from the ranks of trade unionists.

Alice Henry and Stella Franklin, though paid-up union members, fell somewhere between the two types. They had not the background and

Rose Schneiderman.

independent means of the "allies", but boot and shoe worker Mary Anderson classed them with the "allies", probably because they worked with their minds and were highly literate. Though they were just as dependent as any factory worker for their livelihood on an employer, they came from middle-class backgrounds in egalitarian Australia and had never known the pressures of the factory or the mill. Their interests were those of a more leisured class — music, books, the arts, ideas. As Australians who were also intellectual and artistic, they drew the attention and friendship of a notable Chicago family which had a special tie with their homeland.

William Bross Lloyd, at whose home Stella had recuperated after her breakdown, had spent some months in New Zealand and some weeks in Australia when he toured the southern democracies in 1899 with his father Henry Demarest Lloyd. It is likely that through an acquaintance with the leading NSW politician Bernie Wise they had been present at one of Rose Scott's soirées. As a result of the trip the senior Lloyd wrote two books, *A Country Without Strikes* (New Zealand) and *Newest England*.

The Lloyds were one of the most outstanding and most interesting families in Chicago, and had a reputation among their wealthy set as reformers and nonconformists. Henry Demarest Lloyd had come to Chicago from New York in 1872 to write for the *Tribune* and had married in 1873 Jessie Bross, only child of William Bross, one of the founders of the Chicago *Tribune*. William Bross Lloyd, who with his wife Lola had played Good Samaritan to Stella in her breakdown, was the eldest son of this marriage.

The father, Henry Demarest Lloyd, born in 1847, had come of a dissenting tradition, being the son of a minister of the Dutch Reformed Church. After taking his degree from Columbia and being admitted to the New York bar he became involved in the Young Men's Municipal Reform Association whose aim was to expose and eradicate the corruption of Tammany Hall.

He took his political interests further in opposing Horace Greeley's nomination at the Liberal Republican Convention in 1872, on free trade principles. That extraordinary character Greeley, publicist, anti-slavery leader, dabbler in a variety of causes and a trenchant advocate of protective tariffs, won the Republican nomination, then, weirdly, won the Democratic one as well. This did not simplify the matter of the presidency, since many of his former supporters were so enraged that they transferred their allegiance, and after a tense campaign General Grant defeated Greeley.

But Henry Demarest Lloyd's hopes in politics had been dashed too, and he turned to journalism, becoming financial editor and editorial writer for the *Tribune*. He represented a new kind of journalism in his attacks on monopolies particularly in railroads and oil. "The first as he perhaps remains the greatest of the new muck-rakers",[6] left the *Tribune* in 1885 to freelance and moved towards a more radical stance. After the Haymarket riot of 1886, though he was not in sympathy with anarchism or violence, he spoke up for the accused men, took a petition to Governor Oglesby, who commuted the death sentence on two of them, and wrote some verses for the funeral of the four who were hanged. His enraged father-in-law cut him out of his will and left his fortune to Lloyd's children.

Henry Demarest Lloyd was, of course, a friend of Jane Addams and his home at Winnetka, The Wayside, was almost an extension of Hull House, a gathering place for thinkers and workers in social services, the arts and the labour movement. Like Hull House it was a refuge. Professor Vida Scudder of Wellesley said: ''To pass from an atmosphere charged with incredulous perplexity to one full of friendly tranquil comradeship is an experience one does not forget; the Lloyds' home must, I should think, have afforded such haven to many a solitary spirit.''[7] Lloyd championed the miners' strike of 1902 along with Clarence Darrow and John Mitchell, and finally joined the socialist party in the year of his death, 1903.

William Bross Lloyd and his bride, Lola Maverick, carried on the tradition of Lloyd hospitality to writers, artists and intellectuals at their home in Winnetka, The Halfway Side. There, from time to time, gathered the Lloyd clan, the four brothers, William, Demarest, Henry and John, handsome, young and tolerant, blessed with enough worldly goods to enjoy the pleasures of fine living and beautiful surroundings, but enough their father's sons to take an interest in advanced thought and social change. There, too, feminism found some favour, for Henry Demarest Lloyd had taken this phenomenon seriously, saying that Rome fell because the Romans were only half reformers, and that ''we will all be women someday''.

Such was the interesting group of diverse talents, backgrounds and personalities in which Stella Franklin took her place as she launched into the new career and the new year of 1908. It was a group largely composed of women, and mainly young; a collection of idealistic enthusiasts ready to do battle for their cause, with a phalanx of maidens determined to slay the dragons themselves, without relying on St George. Most of these dedicated young women did not marry, for the job was not only hard and demanding but involved sudden travel, odd hours and unconventional work; but they found friendship and sisterhood together and satisfaction in the gradual achievements of the league. Largely through their efforts the league grew in standing. Helen Marot has said that it had been tolerated in its early years as a passing whim. But in 1914 she wrote: ''It is not so regarded today . . . The league has been persistent, strenuous, militant.''[8]

12 Early days

The new recruit set to work enthusiastically:

> ... the union work was done in holes and corners. The offices were Mrs
> Robins' flat and my bedroom ... [we] rose to small offices at the end of the
> suite of the CF of L ... And oh, the fervour and self-sacrifice and belief in
> those days ... We had mapped out our code of behaviour — mere females as
> we were with some rich outsiders as associates — those specially awakened
> among the privileged, incented and impetused by Theo Roosevelt's muck-
> raking and very suspect by the genuine working men trade unionists ... we
> were doubly suspect in those days of raging suffragettes in England, so we were
> to be circumspect and refined in dress and action, and to keep to ourselves,
> never by any chance must we intrude upon the men. We were as quiet as mice
> and as chaste as dedicated nuns ... Editha Phelps ... used to talk about Miss
> Henry going to tour the different parishes of her diocese.[1]

The work was done on a shoe-string budget yet "there was hardly a strike
of women workers from 1905 on in which the WTUL was not to be found
taking an active part in organising the strikers or picketing, raising bail or
strike funds, mobilising public opinion or running relief kitchens and welfare
committees."[2] In the thick of the fight, at Mrs Robins' elbow, stood
"Lieutenant Franklin",[3] as Raymond Robins styled her. Her admiration for
Margaret Robins was great. Recalling that period she wrote: "She was the
pivot on which we all revolved ... her warm, vivid personality, her courage
and resourcefulness were never dismayed but always full of energy and plans
to transcend difficulties and banish melancholy."[4]

Margaret, in a happy marriage, was childless and her "little girls" of the
league were almost daughters to her, though she was barely ten years older
than many of them. She was thoughtful about their needs. Stella Franklin
wrote: "I recall Mrs R said I was with too many older serious people and had
the right to friends of my own age and she picked you [Louise and Arnold
Dresden].''[5] Arnold Dresden, then of Chicago University, later professor of
music at Madison, was making a name as a musician and conductor, working
with the league on a plan for concerts in Chicago parks. He and his wife were

stalwart and loving friends to Stella during her years in Chicago. In these first months Margaret Robins was a mother figure to her new employee. "She was particularly near and dear to me as she supplied the loss of relatives (so far away) and had me with her so much at her home and when travelling, even to sharing her sleeper on those sorties when we went two in a berth to save funds."[6] Yet, in spite of this closeness of association Stella Franklin always adressed Margaret Robins in her letters as Mrs Robins and used the same polite mannerism of the day in all her extant references to her. Similarly in the American years she used the formal Miss Henry for Alice Henry, though in later Australian years, she called her by a nickname.

With Stella Franklin's energy and intelligence as a back-up to Margaret Robins' dynamism the league got off to a quick start in the New Year, deciding in February to quit Hull House and seek a more labour-oriented atmosphere for its meetings at 275 La Salle. Mary McDowell was miffed: "We have been as free to express ourselves at Hull House as anywhere," she told *Tribune* though practical little Agnes Nestor voted for the move as the Halsted street-car service was awful.

It was a grim winter with banker Malcolm McDowell feeding hundreds of waifs from a cart in the street. Fear of violence gripped the city as socialist Mother Jones addressed the restless unemployed and a young man, Doctor Reitman, was arrested by Police Chief Skippy for leading an unauthorised march of the out-of-work. On 2 February in Portugal the King and Crown Prince were assassinated by anarchists and on 4 February in Chicago the anarchists held a big meeting on the West Side. In March there was a sensational attempt to assassinate Police Chief Skippy, which ended in the death of a twenty-year-old Russian Jew, Lazarus Overbach. No political plot was ever discovered and it seemed that Overbach was mentally deranged by worry and poverty. But there were arrests of Jewish workers and the police checked on Emma Steghagen. Hull House came under fire— "the social settlements are first cousins to the anarchists" said *Tribune*. The Robins, Jane Addams and others arranged for an autopsy on Overbach's body. The coroner's verdict was justifiable homicide but there was still some suspicion among league members that Overbach had been unarmed and that his death had been a panicky murder by Skippy or his driver. As Margaret Robins' personal assistant Stella Franklin had been involved in the dramatic episode.

Meanwhile, anarchist Emma Goldman, after an initial ban on her talk, "Why emancipation has not freed women", spoke at a crowded meeting, and on the night of the release of the coroner's report the "Red Queen" dined with the now-freed Doctor Reitman at one table in the fashionable Bismarck Restaurant while Police Chief Skippy and his wife occupied another. Turbulent Chicago life rushed on, past the death of unhappy young Lazarus, just one more incident in the quota of disasters, murders and extravaganzas which Chicagoans swallowed with their morning coffee. The league continued to progress. Alice Henry took over the editorship of the women's department in the *Union Labor Advocate*. Margaret Robins was elected to the executive board of the Chicago Federation of Labor in 1908. Dazzling Rose Schneiderman secured a scholarship from Irene Lewisohn which meant she could go to school for a year, league women formed a regular chorus ''to sing for the eight-hour day''—to publicise their campaign for a shorter working day by recitals—and Franklin became an enthusiastic chorister. Arnold Dresden helped greatly in this cultural propaganda effort. Though Margaret Robins was depressed for a time at how necessary her money was for carrying out any plans, feeling that her intelligence and character would be useless without money, by November she was writing as the work of the league expanded of ''these great but packed days'' to Stella who by this time had new lodgings at the Harvard Hotel, 5714 Washington, a four-storeyed stone building with bay windows overlooking willow trees. Robins had been elected a fraternal delegate to the American Federation of Labor, and attended its convention in Denver that November. She had been involved also in the interstate conference of women's trade unions held in Chicago in September and chaired weekly staff meetings to plan the work ahead.

During 1908 Edwin Bridle married Australian Wentworth Little and, with that romance sealed off, Stella's quiet personal life centred around the Robins and Alice Henry, her time being spent between her room, the apartment on West Ohio Street, and the league offices at 275 La Salle Street. It had been a year devoted to coming to grips with a new career, a year for acquainting herself with her duties, for making contact with other league branches and their officers, for getting to know the Robins as friends, for seeing a little more of America, in Margaret's company, and for settling into the routines of her position.

From 1909 on the story of Stella Miles Franklin in America can be read, in abbreviated form, in the tiny pocket diaries, with their brief daily entries, which she kept painstakingly, however busy or tired or ill she might be. These record only a sliver of her life, with a packed day reduced to one or two short lines, but they give an outline of her main activities, a good deal of detail on minor matters, and throw a strong light on her most intimate feelings. There is little about her friends, her relatives and other people, of a personal kind; practically no comment on the general issues of the day; but a great deal about her own sufferings, physical and mental, in the stressful Chicago environment, and an exposé of her growing disappointments and despairs as the years flew past.

But the diary for 1909 began in a quiet and cheerful vein. Stella dined often with Alice Henry and the Robins, attended meetings of her Stenographers' Local (trade union branch), practised with the League Choir, visited the Dresdens and the Lloyds occasionally, and lunched with Agnes Nestor and Editha Phelps, librarian for the league. One of the highlights of early 1909

Edwin Bridle, 1909.

was the NWTUL ball on 22 February, where dressed in Norwegian costume Stella sang in the spinning wheel scene. It appeared a busy and reasonably interesting life, if lacking in excitement and rather spinsterish.

But Stella Franklin kept her counsel on one matter. When the door closed on her in her room at the Harvard, after her day's work, she set herself to another task. In spite of her new friends, new job, new city, new concerns, her determination remained the same—to succeed again as a writer, to grasp that fame and glory that Joseph Furphy was so sure were awaiting her. Though she earned her bread energetically promoting causes in which she sincerely believed, that did not satisfy her appetite for creative expression and fame. During 1908 and early 1909, while seemingly as devoted as any other servant of the cause, she worked on a play "The Survivors", and on some short stories, polished up *Some Everyday Folk and Dawn* and added a glossary of American and English equivalents of Australianisms used. She despatched the novel to Blackwood on 15 April, 1909.

She used the name Miles Franklin as she had done before but very few of her colleagues knew of her literary past. She did not blazon her career as an author. Mary McDowell, one of the outstanding women in the Hull House group and in the early days of the league, was amazed when she heard of it in Geneva in 1923, though she was a friend of Stella's. Franklin was reserved, even secretive, about that part of her life. She had suffered too much already from the burden of "promise".

A few days after she posted off her novel she was in the state capital, Springfield, Illinois, to attend a great suffrage rally and to do some lobbying for the league's eight-hour day Bill for women. Speakers from the suffrage special train addressed crowds along the line and suffragists, wearing their symbol of the yellow jonquil, descended upon the legislature. Stella wrote later:

> I recall one big time when we were let loose on Springfield and had a governor's reception where Octavia Roberts took me with her to be one of the young ladies pouring tea . . . a combination raid for woman suffrage and the ten hour bill [as it later became] . . . That was the time Dr Blount nearly made an earthquake by bawling from the rear platform (of the train) that women wanted the vote to make the home as important as the brothel . . . Agnes was our one special speaker (from the pulpit addressing the House) . . . the manufacturers were defaming Agnes as a disruptor of the home and virtue etc . . . Hollywood couldn't have planned a better scene as Agnes' dear little face appeared . . . with its plaits of hair and her white collar and cuffs and her disarming and charming face and manner like a little Priscilla schoolgirl.[7]

The *Tribune* reported that protesting manufacturers were backed out of the State House by fair lobbyists Elizabeth Maloney, Anna Willard and Agnes Nestor. Stella Franklin had played her part in the campaign too.

Although for nine weeks Agnes Nestor, Elizabeth Maloney, Anna Willard and Lulu Holley had done most of the lobbying in Springfield, "others who went down in relays were Mary McEnerney of the binders, Mary Hurley and Emma Steghagen of the boot and shoe workers, Lena Buchwerts of the garment workers and Stella Franklin of the dept store girls'', and ''every elevator man in the state capitol, every janitor, page-boy, clerk and stenographer did all they could to push 'The Girls' Bill'.''⁸

The opposition of manufacturers who feared they would be forced out of the state brought changes to the Bill, and the NWTUL finally supported a compromise Bill for a ten-hour day which passed both houses by 30 May. John Fitzpatrick of the Chicago Federation of Labor belittled the result, saying that the women should have stuck out for eight hours, but league officers took the view that it established a principle of limitation of work, thus aiming a heavy blow at the unregulated sweat-shops. They thought it a great victory for women.

Stella Franklin could claim some small part in this victory but she was not jubilant. She had suffered from bad colds for some months and by May, her diary reveals, she was ''depressed and weary'', ''damnably unhappy'', ''dreary and miserable'', ''miserable! miserable!'', ''too miserable for words'', ''feeling feeble and played out''. In a very short time she had become exhausted and unhappy in her new role.

Some Everyday Folk and Dawn had been accepted by Blackwood, but still she was dispirited. In June she went to Madison and registered for a summer school at the University of Wisconsin to study French and Tennyson. She stayed at Kappa Kappa Gamma Lodge, corrected proofs of her novel and made friends with some young men who took her to the circus, to dinner, and picnicking and canoeing. They serenaded her in the glee club and when they left on 6 August her diary entry for the next day was ''desolation, desolation''. One of them left his handkerchief to mop up her tears. The loss of their friendly, youthful companionship left her ''lonely & dispirited'' and ''horribly homesick''. She went riding, and had some singing lessons from a pupil of Marchesi, but still felt ''very poorly''. Her thirtieth birthday was looming and youth was draining away.

When she went back to Chicago on 14 September, she saw the procession of Republican President, William Taft and worked with Margaret Robins preparing reports for the 1909 convention of the league which opened in the Fine Arts Building on 27 September. She read the reports at the opening, feeling ''very tired'', and dismissed the whole thing as a ''routine convention''. The convention ended on 2 October and on the sixth she moved to the Eleanor Club at 3111 Indiana Avenue, but found life there impossible. The pinch-penny drabness of this semi-charitable hostel offended her fastidiousness and her pride. ''Exhausted'', ''very tired'' was her constant theme.

The Times Literary Supplement's review of *Some Everyday Folk and Dawn* on 7 October, 1909, was brief, amiable, and, like other notices, very lukewarm compared with the reception accorded *My Brilliant Career*. On 15 November Stella was "feeling as if I couldn't struggle any longer".

On 20 November she moved again, to 123 Indiana Avenue. She was still trying to write, but was in poor health and the Chicago winter was closing in around her. As her last diary entry for 1909, on 31 December, she noted: " . . . thus endeth the old year's record to the accompaniment of a violin played by Miss Burroughs in Mrs Moorhouse's room opposite. Hoping the coming one will be more eventful, less futile and more lucrative."

On the other hand the league had had a good year. The convention had been successful, with sixty-nine delegates from eighteen trades and eight states. Mary MacArthur, Secretary of the British Women's Trade Union League, had come from England and Margaret Schweichler of the largest union of women workers in Germany from Hamburg. It had produced a legislative code as well as an interesting and informative handbook on conditions in various trades, an excellent piece of propaganda guaranteed to arouse sympathy and indignation in readers. Though it is unsigned, there is the smack of Stella Franklin's racy, fresh, attacking style in many of the pieces, on trades such as sewing, dressmaking, boot and shoe and glovemaking and textiles.

In New York the league branch there became involved as the year drew to a close in the historic shirtmakers' strike. This conflict brought the league into the news, for its members took the strikers' case to the public and enlisted the aid of society leaders. The "allies" came to the front when picketers in the freezing streets included Ann Morgan, daughter of banker J.P. Morgan, and when Mrs Henry Morgenthau Snr, Helen Taft, daughter of the President, and a Bryn Mawr graduate, wealthy young Carola Woershoeffer furnished bail for those arrested. This was something new and startling, the "mink brigade" joining in the struggle for the improvement of conditions for working girls. This first picket corps from outside labour's own ranks raised the standing of the league in the eyes of union leaders. The strike ended in February 1910 and Rose Schneiderman was offered a job as full-time organiser with the league at $25 a week.

In Chicago Stella, though still only a simple office assistant, had been appointed to the Constitution Committee by Margaret Robins, and was editing the convention proceedings with Alice Henry. Two years of hectic activity for little pay ($48 a month compared with Alice Henry's $78),[9] combined with her obsessive literary endeavours had drained her body and soul. Even the simple exertion of moving between home and office was distressing. "The half hour on the [street] car at the end of the day reduced her to a low level of exhaustion . . . [she] found that late hours reading or at the theatre had to be paid for in painful lassitude next day."[10] The words are those of one of her characters describing a Chicago life, but the fetid air and overcrowding would have fretted Stella in much the same way, as would have the cheap lodgings and tasteless meals, the "sloppy mess of codfish or chipped beef with some lumpy cereal and poisonous tea or coffee slapped before her at breakfast, the cheap beef and badly cooked potatoes ... with something such as ... cornstarch pudding for dinner."[11] Hot-tempered Margaret Robins was now sometimes "cross and unreasonable" and the strains in her assistant between the outer shell of altruistic reformer and the inner core of determined, self-absorbed creative writer were causing suffering and confusion. The sheer physical burden of coping with two careers, combined with the weight of loneliness and homesickness, was crushing. Perhaps 1910 would be better.

But 1910 began badly with cruel weather. Her diary records that on Thursday the sixth she stayed in bed all day and next day was still completely exhausted with the cold. On Sunday 8 January she kept to her bed again until dinner-time, when duty called and she went to the annual meeting of the Chicago league. Yet despite chronic fatigue she kept busy with work and outings. On the fourteenth she was elected to the executive committee at her stenographers' meeting. She heard Emma Goldman speak, went to *La Boheme* with the Lloyds, to a matinee of *Madam Butterfly* — "... of course Miss Henry kept us late getting in" she noted irritably — to an exhibition of Charles Haag's sculpture at Hull House, to a meeting of socialist women and to hear Tetrazzinni sing — "supreme delight". She also began taking music lessons again at the Kimball Hall on 8 February, although at thirty it was too late for the once longed-for musical career.

She visited St Louis in February on league business, and again in May when an executive board meeting there made two decisions which were of significance to her personally. Her salary was more than doubled (to $25 a week) and it was to be paid by the national treasurer not by Margaret Robins. This put her financial affairs on a firmer base, easing bonds of personal obligation and freeing her from the worst of niggling economies. The board decided also, encouraged by the success of the women's section in the *Union Labor Advocate*, that the league should have its own magazine, a resolution that was to culminate in *Life & Labor* in January 1911, with Alice Henry as editor and S.M. Franklin as assistant editor.

As she chronicled in her tiny journal, in the summer of 1910 Stella saw a good deal of her wealthy friends the Lloyds, including the younger brother Demarest at times, and they took her automobiling, and canoeing on the lake. But these pleasures and the improvement in her finances did not cure her melancholy. In a sense it deepened it, for "the contrast illustrated in a glaring manner the unattractiveness of her life, its barrenness and haphazard ungraciousness".[12] Once more, the reflections are those of one of her characters, but they seem close to her mood at this time, for she was, day after day, exhausted and gloomy. During a holiday at Harbour Springs in

August with Editha Phelps she moaned about the bad weather and bad food as she assaulted her hired typewriter.

Stella was not making her fortune by her literary endeavours. In March 1910 Blackwood informed her that royalties on her two books amounted to £18-15-0 (£17-13-5 being for *Some Everyday Folk and Dawn*). They had stopped the sale of *My Brilliant Career* as she had directed. She replied that she had no objection to the remaining copies going to Australia as long as no more were printed. Those days of early glory were as dust, and pain outweighed the pride she had felt in her first success. But doggedly she offered the publisher the manuscript of a ''most inimitable sequel'', no doubt *The End of My Career*, adding that she had intended to give it to an Australian firm when she returned home in 1911.[13] About this time she also sent *When Cupid Tarried* to the Lothian Publishing Company in Melbourne. This was obviously the same story as *The Love Machine*, on which she had worked in November 1909, for this flat and whimsical romance, set in an unnamed harbour city in the South Seas, involves a ''love machine'', an absent-minded scientist and an inheritance which depends on four girls marrying in order of seniority. This tedious fantasy has nothing in common with the realism of her previous work, and, though a slight thread of feminism winds through it, seems a desperate attempt to write a pot-boiler for the happy-ending market.

It was a gloomy time. *Some Everyday Folk and Dawn* had not been a success, colds plagued her, the office work was often ''fearfully heavy'' with long hours, and, she noted in her diary, Margaret Robins was at times very stormy. Happiness, even modest comfort and contentment, escaped her. She was over-stretched physically, and her tiny diary for 1910 is flecked with entries such as, ''weak, sick, depressed, worn out'', ''crawled out to office'', ''too exhausted for anything'', and, on 16 October, the entry is ''stayed in bed all day . . . trying to get up steam for coming work''. She needed that steam, for the Chicago league was about to embark on its biggest adventure, the Garment Workers' Strike of 1910-11, and she was to play a major part in that historic industrial conflict.

Somehow the fight called up reserves of energy in her. She threw herself into the struggle, using all her intelligence and talents, particularly her gift for communication. The sympathetic story of the strike, as told in the newspapers, owed a good deal to what is known today as PR, to Stella's ability, in her role as publicity officer for the league's Strike Committee, to interest the press in the strikers' case in human terms. The condition of girl migrant strikers kindled her particular indignation, and putting aside her own woes, reinvigorated, she dashed into battle.

13 The strike

Coming into Chicago today by the freeway from O'Hare Airport one cannot miss a tall building downtown, lettered on its side in mighty capitals, Hart, Schaffner and Marx. In September 1910 one of this firm's manufacturing shops reduced its rate on certain work by a quarter of a cent, and a number of girls walked off the job. Though the clothing industry was growing rapidly it was still largely unorganised in the first decade of the century. Yet almost immediately another 1,200 un-unionised garment workers struck.

The strike spread quickly and spontaneously and on 26 October the United Garment Workers' Union called a general strike of the trade in Chicago. Remarkably, indicating the unrest and discontent with conditions, 41,000 workers, mainly migrants and including 10,000 women, came out, paralysing the industry in the city.

The union was very weak, most of the strikers were non-unionists, and strike funds were almost nonexistent. The National Women's Trade Union League came to the fore, using the experience it had gained in the New York garment workers' strike. ''To keep so many under discipline and to supply them with the necessaries of life was a herculean task. The WTUL came to the union's assistance. Prominent settlement workers also enlisted in the strikers' cause. The two groups helped strikers to gain favorable publicity, furnished speakers and helped raise funds.''[1]

At Hull House a citizens' committee was formed under society leader Mrs Henrotin, and a strike committee under Dr Hirsch (''Mrs Hen-rotten'' and ''Rabbit Hirsch'' to impertinent Stella Franklin). Margaret Robins organised the league's own strike committee, with herself as chairman-treasurer, Miss Steghagen in charge of pickets, Miss Potter responsible for co-operation, Miss Carr and Miss Emma Pischel in charge of individual relief, Miss Coman in charge of grievances, Miss Agnes Nestor responsible for organisation, and, perhaps, in the long run, the most important of all, Miss S.M. Franklin in charge of publicity. Strike headquarters was at 275 La Salle, where a number of the stronger women's unions had their offices.

Miss Franklin proved to be very good at obtaining press notice. The *Tribune* of 2 November reported riots and arrests and an attack on a tailor's shop by strikers. It also reported the confrontation between the police and "aristocratic" pickets, led by elderly gentlewoman Miss Ellen Starr of Hull House, and Miss S.M. Franklin and Miss Emma Steghagen. The women were convoying a marching group of about fifty strikers when the police swooped, using clubs vigorously. Miss Franklin was grabbed and shoved along, the police ignoring proffered cards and explanations. One told Miss Franklin, "I don't care who you are or what you are, you have to get out of here," while another advised patrician Miss Starr to go home and wash the dishes. Undeterred, Miss Starr demanded that the peaceful procession be let pass. The result was two arrests. Stella noted in her diary, "went picketing . . . saw police brutality".

No doubt the police had reason to fear the passions of the crowds. Next day a fourteen-year-old girl, leading a crudely armed mob, yelled "Get together men . . . go for the police"—the police reserve was attacked and there was a violent riot opposite Margaret Robins' apartment. In retaliation the police charged with clubs and drawn revolvers, and there were many arrests. Stella, on the picket line again, complained to a *Tribune* reporter that the "police were brutal, talked real gruff to her and clubbed some inoffensive boys".

In the face of the growing violence, prominent citizens began moves to end the strike on 3 November, though the *Tribune* of 4 November pictured Margaret Robins and her "cabinet", Agnes Nestor, Clara Masilotti, Emma Steghagen, Stella Franklin and Lillian Carr, devising ways and means of raising funds for the relief of destitute strikers, and hot-tempered Ellen Starr had another verbal spar with the police.

Conditions among the strikers were becoming chaotic with thousands in desperate circumstances. The head of the Chicago Garment Workers' Union, feeling matters were hopeless, came to an agreement with Hart, Schaffner and Marx on 5 November. At a mass meeting the strikers rejected the terms and President Rickert and other officials were forced to flee from the hall to cries of graft and sell-out. The strikers invited the Chicago Federation of Labor and the WTUL to form a new strike committee. Franklin recorded it in her diary: "At office all day. Great slump when we heard of agreement. Tremendous excitement when it was repudiated. Went to see Fritzi Schifft in *Mikado*."

On Sunday, 6 November, she worked all day with Margaret Robins and was "just dead exhausted". But on Monday she felt there was nothing special to do on the strike and went to the theatre again, this time to see *The Sorceress*—and she was near the heart of the storm! Small wonder that many Chicagoans were more interested in *The Chocolate Soldier*, Sarah Bernhardt, *Aida* and the November mid-term elections, which the Democrats won, than in a run-of-the-mill strike. In terms of world history the start of a meteoric

top: Mrs Robins' ''cabinet''.
bottom: Emma Steghagen.

political career for fifty-four-year-old professor, Woodrow Wilson, new Governor of New Jersey, was certainly more important than a dispute over piece work.

But for those involved, particularly for Margaret Robins, it was engulfing, "became part of her very being . . . and burned into her soul",[2] and Stella Franklin, notwithstanding her seeming nonchalance, did an excellent job with publicity.

The account of the grievances in the industry, by professor of history at Wellesley College, Katherine Comans, together with the simple stories of the girls involved, as told by themselves, but perhaps with a little assistance from Miss Franklin, was printed and distributed, and brought thousands of dollars. "The girls' own stories" appeared in *Life & Labor* in February, 1911. Stella kept seventeen halls filled with speakers, including English visitors Sylvia Pankhurst, Margaret Bondfield, the MacMillan sisters and Mrs Philip Snowden, who stressed the fine quality of the girls on strike. Stella managed to work well with the reporters covering the story. The journalists probably included Carl Sandburg, whom Mary Anderson recollected as being one of the most helpful of the labour reporters. Parlour discussions in society homes where allies like Gertrude Barnum and Professor Comans spoke, gave the strike "social recognition". There were touching pictures in the papers of 12 November of famished garment workers, some with infants in arms, waiting in line for strike benefits which did not come. Another sympathy-winning picture in the *Tribune* depicted several girl strikers, scarcely more than children, their pretty faces crowned with large hats, demure and neatly dressed, accepting the Art Institute's invitation to earn a few dollars for food by working as models. The strike headquarters was besieged by as many as 700 men, women and children a day, according to the league's official report of the strike committee, with stories of hardship and privation—police brutality while on picket duty, grievances in their shops. Sudden wage cuts, petty fines and fear of the hard-driving foremen were some of the complaints of the rebellious workers.

Stella and Ellen Starr, who had been appointed to a committee on church co-operation, interviewed visiting evangelist Dr Wilbur Chapman on 15 November. He averred that it was the duty of every Christian citizen to aid and encourage the strikers, and took 6,000 circulars to hand out at his meetings.

The league engaged women speaking Yiddish, Polish, Italian and Bohemian to work among the predominantly migrant strikers, and opened commissary stations where the hungry could obtain a ration of bread, meat, beans, coffee, sugar and oatmeal, for lack of food was weakening resolution. At a public meeting called by the league on 13 November it decided that the fighting propaganda basis would be "food, fuel and milk for babies". On 16 November a special appeal for milk for the innocents in the struggle, the babies, was launched. Many society women, led by Mrs Henrotin, supported this cause. Ironically the *Tribune* that same day ran a special issue on Chicago's prosperity and greatness.

All this league activity provoked Noren, the head of the national union body, to state that the United Garment Workers' Union was running the strike and not anybody else who might be seeking notoriety in the newspapers. However, John Fitzpatrick of the Chicago Federation of Labor knew an effective weapon when he saw one and began talking about babies dying for want of milk and of mothers starving. He was not exaggerating. The *Tribune* reported on 24 November that men and women fought for relief tickets at food stations, which prompted merchants to distribute free Thanksgiving baskets of food on the twenty-fifth.

In the midst of her efforts to win publicity, Franklin found time on 25 November to hear *Salome* with Mary Garden. This portrayal caused a greater sensation than any strike riot, being assailed as immoral, bestial and perverted. Stella made no comment on it in her diary, but perhaps brought back to his original purpose by this scandal, evangelist Wilbur Chapman invaded the red light district with his disciples and pleaded with the women there to lead better lives.

On 29 and 30 November Stella Franklin went to court to appear as a witness of alleged police brutality to strikers but the case did not come up. As the league's magazine *Life & Labor* was due to make its first appearance in January, the assistant editor had a great deal of work to fit in between her strike duties. The pace was telling and she spent each Sunday in bed with visits to Doctor Walker wedged between her activities.

The first outright killing of the strike occurred on 2 December when a special policeman, escorting two workers home, was attacked. In retaliation he shot and killed one of his assailants. On 7 December there was a grand parade of 60,000 strikers, ending in a meeting, addressed by Raymond and Margaret Robins and Agnes Nestor in the bleak weather.

The city government had intervened in the strike on 28 November with Mayor Busse initiating talks in an effort to end the deadlock. A peace plan had been worked out, and the Chicago Federation of Labor had endorsed a proposed agreement with Hart, Schaffner and Marx. But the radicals opposed the settlement and on 14 December, in a secret ballot, the strikers rejected it.

The violence increased as conditions worsened in the winter cold. There were more deaths. Funds were running low and some strikers, losing heart, returned to work. Officers of the union were criticised for lukewarmness by the Chicago Federation of Labor and Margaret Robins wanted to know from Samuel Landers of GWU what had happened to strike funds collected by the league and the federation. The strike dragged on but the Chicago public had other interests. Mary Baker Eddy, founder of Christian Science, had died on 3 December and the *Tribune* ran a full special front page on the fifth, Fire

top: on the campaign trail.
bottom: Stella in Chicago in evening dress.

Chief Horan and twenty-four of his men lost their lives in a stockyard fire on 23 December, focusing the *Tribune*'s sympathy on the bereaved families and its indignation on the state of the city's water supply.

In an effort to keep spirits up and interest alive John Fitzpatrick played Santa Claus at a Christmas tree party for the strikers' children and league members distributed toys. Among the donors to this event was William Bross Lloyd with $100. A new giant parade was planned and a little more money collected.

The strike claimed more lives. One nineteen-year-old boy was killed by a special policeman, and a special policeman was shot in the back. Another nineteen-year-old, a girl, died as a result of exposure in the picket line in the sleety weather, and a hero emerged among the strikers when young Sidney Hillman seized a revolver from a strike-breaker. More appeals were made for babies in danger of starvation. At last there was some action from the state capital at Springfield and the Senate started an enquiry on 6 January.

Margaret Robins was still in the front line of the battle, planning a house-to-house canvass for 22 January, to be labelled 'Sweat-shop Sunday'', but the weeks of hunger and cold endured by the strikers had quenched their fire. There were more peace talks and on 14 January, 1911, Hart, Schaffner and Marx reached an agreement with strikers' representatives John Fitzpatrick, Margaret Robins and unionists Rickert and Harris. Though the radicals opposed the solution Fitzpatrick and Robins were cheered at the Hod Carriers' Hall.

Little seemed to have been gained. The agreement provided for the return of the Hart, Schaffner and Marx workers without discrimination and for the formation of an arbitration council of three, one member to be chosen by the firm, one by the workers, and a third by both parties. Clarence Darrow was selected as the employees' representative. But workers from other firms were still on strike, and so they remained until on 4 February, without consulting John Fitzpatrick or Margaret Robins, President Rickert made peace. Samuel Landers and other officials said to meetings: ''Men and women, the strike is called off. We have lost and the best thing for you to do is to go back to work as fast as you can.'' Robins suspected they had been double-crossed and said: ''We are defeated but not conquered.''

Strike funds and the milk fund were exhausted. After twenty-two weeks, five deaths, $4,000,000 lost by employers and $3,000,000 by the workers, matters were almost the same as when the strike had begun. It was a flat end to what had seemed an heroic struggle. In the March issue of *Life & Labor* Alice Henry and S.M. Franklin summed up: ''The hunger bargain has been struck and Chicago has permitted it.''

Though many had suffered and some had died the great city had not changed. Most of its citizens prospered, being more interested in the big show of the latest invention, the ''auto'', in February and in coping with blizzards, than in the outcome of a strike. The *Tribune* tried to cheer up half-frozen readers with a supplement on sunny Florida.

But, though it was small, the concession in the Hart, Schaffner and Marx settlement was significant. "The limited recognition accorded the union by HS & M was of outstanding importance for it marked the beginning of the most highly elaborated industrial government in America based on the equal participation of employer and union."[3] Editors Alice Henry and S.M. Franklin in the January issue of *Life & Labor* saw the strike as having a far-reaching result: "Whatever the nominal result the tremendous protest that the strike has embodied will have an incalculable educational effect upon the strikers themselves, while the general public has been awakened to a far deeper understanding of the industrial problem at its door." Trade union historian Gladys Boone thought the garment strikes put the league "on the map" between 1909 and 1913 and another consequence was that the Senate committee proposed that the deplorable sanitary conditions in some shops be regulated by law.

Apart from her enormously forceful president, Stella Franklin had worked as hard as anybody in the league during the course of the strike. The defeated radical group might sneer at columns of interviews bearing directly on the sufferings of the strikers given out by Margaret Robins to the capitalist press, but its resentment was a form of tribute to the ability of the league and Stella Franklin in winning the press notice it would have dearly loved to have obtained for its own views. The propaganda had been effective in gaining sympathy, winning funds and friends enough to prevent the workers from being completely defeated. The strike had also produced a hero and a new leader of labour in a cutter from a Hart, Schaffner and Marx factory, Sidney Hillman, a future president of the Amalgamated Clothing Workers of America. Both Bessie and Sidney Hillman became Stella's friends.

Stella Franklin had every reason to take pride in the part she had taken in this important industrial action. But it was as though she lived on two planes, led two existences. As the enthusiastic, energetic, innovative propagandist, though she was dispirited about the outcome of the strike she must have recognised that she had done a fine job. But as the discontented, lonely seeker for she knew not what, it may all have seemed a futile, draining endeavour. She had been ill and tired when it began. The excitement of the fight had carried her through but was the precious vitality lost in the cause worth the small gain? For her, all had to be weighed against her ultimate goal.

The war had not been lost completely and the peace had been honourable, but weary Lieutenant Franklin spent the first weeks of the New Year mainly in bed, and the tone of her diary in the first few months appears to be of withdrawal from the effort of reform and return to the solace of the arts. On 17 January, the very day that Margaret Robins was cheered at the Hod

Carriers' Hall, Franklin noted tartly in her journal: "went to 275 La Salle, grabbed by Mrs R and missed music lesson." There is no record of either exultation or dismay at the outcome of the strike into which she had put so much, while the missed music lesson rankles.

An irritable fatigue shows in her comment in a postcard home on suffragette Sylvia Pankhurst (who had given a lecture in Chicago in January on life in a London prison): "Of all the dowds she beats them. All the English look like dish-cloth frumps."[4] She was exhausted and disgruntled after the damp squib ending to the fireworks of the preceding weeks. But work continued. She must earn her living while she practised her music and invoked her hard-pressed literary muse.

14 The league

Whatever the shifting sands of her attitude to the league, a large part of the production and writing of its new magazine fell to Stella Franklin as assistant editor (unpaid), while she coped at the same time with the general office work of the league and with the organisation of the national convention to be held in Boston in July 1911, a difficult task in itself since the Boston members were very testy about the expense involved.

Her first pieces for *Life & Labor* were articles on the strike, written in collaboration with Alice Henry and signed by the editors. The feeling and energy of "Chicago at the Front" in the January issue, written before the settlement, contrasts with the depressed tone of the March report "The End of the Strike". The mood of dejection among league members gave place to outrage in April when 143 women and girls died in a Triangle Factory fire in New York because of poor safety precautions. Rose Schneiderman, at her melting best, addressed a mass meeting at the Metropolitan Opera House on 2 May, and 120,000 people took part in the funeral procession.

Chicago branch members, including Franklin, threw themselves into working for the pearl button strike in Muscatine, Iowa. Then in March there was another suffrage special train to Springfield for a governor's reception and a league banquet. Margaret Robins and her woman Friday shared a berth on the trip back. In April Stella worked on "convention publicity stuff" and attempted to write creatively as well, sending off some short stories—"Mrs Mulvaney's Moccasins," "Not at all a Coward", and "The Mystery of her Parentage"—to a New York agent[1] with the hope that he would have better luck than to date. She also tried them on an English agent and tinkered with *The End of My Career* for Blackwood.

The doctor and the dentist saw her often, for her health was poor and her concern about it obsessive. In April to her horror her eyesight deteriorated. "Ye Gods she ordered glasses." It seemed a final blow. Franklin entered her reaction in her diary: "My life has been one series of forcing against the grain. I feel I have no more forcing material left for this last straw." On 1

May she was, ''in such horror over prospect of glasses'' that she went to bed ''in despair''. But there was a reprieve the next day. ''So happy that I practised for two hours.'' It was a brief respite, for the journal entry for 15 May is ''got specs''. On the twenty-seventh she was ''more rational about glasses'', but vanity prevailed on 28 May, for at the Garrick Theatre she ''fell down steps because I couldn't see them''. Though her health had certainly been undermined by her extensive activities, general unhappiness had apparently induced a somewhat hypochondriacal state, and Linda's early death must have added to this anxiety.

While Stella was being devastated by the doctors and plagued by the printers and bothered by the Bostonians, her tempestuous leader, after the rush of battle, was recovering her calm in Chinsegut, on a high hill twenty-five kilometres from the Gulf of Mexico. From Florida on 18 April she thanked her dearest little Stella girl and most imperial and efficient secretary for putting her ragged statement so finely together. She wished that Stella could be at Chinsegut too, with the roses, magnolia, lilies, honeysuckle and glorious sunshine and moonlight. For all her virtues of courage and generosity, Robins lacked the imagination to project herself into her overworked secretary's soul. But when she returned to West Ohio Street she gave her blessing happily to a plan for Editha Phelps and Stella Franklin to share a summer holiday in England, and as well offered to assist with one month's vacation with pay and a second month without pay. But first, before the pleasures of the summer, there was the Boston convention to be carried through.

On 6 June the league group of delegates took the train to Boston. There is a lively account of this trip in the August 1911 issue of *Life & Labor* under the title of ''How Chicago went to Boston'', and again the free-wheeling style, the evocation of atmosphere and the light play of humour indicate the Franklin hand.

> At the station 'There's a man in our car' shouted everybody in one voice, even the heat forgotten as this new calamity faced us. Now let it be understood that we, individually or as a body, have absolutely nothing against a man (provided it's the right man) but to have the railroad company foist a strange man upon twenty-nine helpless women, it was an outrage and more than we could stand. Apparently there had been some mistake, which the man himself didn't seem a bit averse to having rectified (hateful thing) for very soon he had vanished and we were left in complete possession of our Pullman car, where we proceeded to make ourselves at home.

The Third Biennial Convention of the National Women's Trade Union League which opened on 12 June was very busy. There were now five more branches: Springfield, Illinois; Cleveland; Kansas City, Missouri; Baltimore; and Denver. In an attempt to tighten the bonds with the American Federation of Labor, two of its leaders, John Mitchell and James Duncan, had been listed as speakers, but at the last moment they had urgent business elsewhere, which would not have endeared them to a chagrined organiser. But all else went smoothly. As well as the business sessions there were committee meetings, parties and excursions, including one to Nantucket Beach where the seventeenth birthday of the heroine of the button workers' strike, happily named Pearl McGill, was celebrated. At the convention a platform was adopted calling for organisation of all workers into trade unions, equal pay for equal work, the eight-hour day, a minimum wage scale, full citizenship for women, and all the principles involved in the economic programme of the AF of L.

The election of officers resulted in the return of Margaret Robins as president, Melinda Scott of the New York branch as treasurer, and as the new national secretary, Miss S.M. Franklin of Chicago. No longer a mere office assistant, Stella Franklin now took her place as a top officer of the league, a recognition of the organising work she had done already and of her contributions to the garment workers' and other strikes, and to *Life & Labor*. The convention finished on 18 June, but Alice Henry and Stella Franklin stayed on a few days to get the proceedings in order.

Shortly afterwards a postcard was despatched home from New York: "Miss Phelps is taking me to London to see if it will set me on my feet." [2] And on 30 June, after five trying years in the New World, Stella left from the port of Quebec on the *Empress of Ireland* for that unknown setting of her first naive literary attempts, for that land as yet still of hope and glory and magnet for British colonials, England.

They docked at Liverpool and called at Chester, Stratford, and Oxford before reaching London, where Stella saw the sights, the art galleries and the British Museum and looked up old friends. She met Vida Goldstein, who had been speaking at suffragette meetings, on 22 July and had tea with Molly David at Fullers on the twenty-ninth. Lord Tennyson, the former governor-general, who had taken an interest in her career, proposed lunch at his home at Haslemere and recommended a Harley Street dentist. At Harfield, home of Elizabeth Robins, actress, writer and sister of Raymond, she met Christabel Pankhurst on 3 August.

From the fourth to the tenth of August she was in Paris but did not take to France, finding the climate taxing, the food not to her taste and her summer school French very inadequate, though she enjoyed *Rigoletto* at the Opera House and *Coppelia*. Helen Marot who was in Paris about the same time felt that Stella had not stayed long enough to discover its charms. But Stella answered:

> I could not wrestle with a foreign language in my tired state so I hied me back to the heart of my British empire and you could not believe what a rest and joy it was to me. I think it eased some of the strain of my homesickness or something as I have returned very much stronger and very happy indeed to have my work. [3]

Whatever the charms of England, she sailed back to the United States on the *Empress of Britain* on 20 August, feeling that her future lay in America. After the disappointments in Australia she had spent five difficult years in a huge and strange land climbing to a position of some standing, with reasonable pay and prospects of further achievement. Love of her British empire did not tempt her to start over again in England, to throw away the doggedly won gains and the friends she had made.

The unromantic office stool was to be her base. She wrote to Helen Marot after her return:

> Everyone else in this league can public speak and do the greater things which are entirely beyond me so I see it behoves me to hang on to my office stool and round up about the details which everyone despises but which if neglected soon bring any organisation on the shoals.[1]

The grand gestures of Margaret Robins, the spellbinding eloquence of Rose Schneiderman, the cool logic of Agnes Nestor, the whole-hearted dedication of Alice Henry were not in her style. Like her heroine Ignez in *Cockatoos* she was working hard among reputable people, "holding a wonderful position for a girl. She'd never have had it if she'd stayed and rusted at Oswald's Ridges." She was using her intelligence and literary talent in the work loaded on to her except that perhaps like Ignez again she felt:

> She had fallen among reformers, and that for an artist is more fatal than for a merchant to fall among bandits. Her heart was frozen by her secret tragedy . . . She suffered no personal neglect but lovers were never permitted to become paramours or husbands, and perhaps she was no more unhappy while the fever of self-sacrifice lasted than she would have been on any other track. The days were a turmoil of high-geared living and hard work.

However dangerous it may be to see the story of the author in the created character, the paragraph could certainly fit Stella's mood at this time.

It was a necessary and sensible return to duty but not a happy one. Within a week she was so irritable that she noted on 14 September, "Miss Henry took a day at home—thank God." The noise and mosquitoes at her new apartment were so unbearable that she was forced to abandon it and found refuge with Margaret Robins for the night on the twenty-fourth. Outwardly she had returned to the security and fervour of the league. At home she turned with even greater determination to her writing, working again on *The End of My Career* and on a new novel, the title of which caught the sense of imprisonment she felt, *The Net of Circumstance*.

Work was ever pressing. The button workers had risen again at Muscatine and for the first time the AF of L asked for league help in the person of Miss Steghagen. The president and secretary were glad to co-operate, and while Sister Emma went to Muscatine Robins and Franklin set off on 24 October for Pittsburgh and Irwin, where they visited the miners in their shacks and were shocked by the utter lack of sanitation, the choked drains and the general desolation. Franklin was touched particularly by the plight of the children. Going straight from the night train to the office on their return to Chicago she "worked like a horse" getting out the reports on Pittsburgh and Muscatine. That expert on soul-stirring, Rose Schneiderman, thought the Pittsburgh report "splendid".

With work on "*L & L* stuff" and on convention proceedings, with visits to doctors, with league meetings and stenographers' meetings, with *Net of Circumstance* to be finished, and with some struggling with a new project, *In the Business of Cupid*, probably a re-working of *While Cupid Tarried*, she dragged through the rest of 1911, about the only bright spots noted in her journal being a Single Tax Banquet — "very jolly" — and a lunch with Demarest Lloyd on 12 December — "very pleasant".

In December she helped Margaret Robins write "pars" on the Kansas City Child Welfare League, the AF of L report and on the McNamara case, the outcome of which had stunned many in the labour movement. February *Life & Labor* reported: "The McNamaras have pleaded guilty. Out of the night on December first these words flashed across the horizon and burned themselves into the hearts of thousands of men & women with a great and nameless grief." John McNamara had pleaded guilty to the conspiracy charge in the blowing up of the Llewllyn Iron Works and J.B. McNamara had pleaded guilty to the blowing up of the *Los Angeles Times* building killing twenty-one people. The case had been a *cause célèbre* for unionists, like that of Haywood. The guilty plea from attorney Clarence Darrow sent reeling many who had believed in their innocence, among them Rose Schneiderman who wrote: "It was a great blow to me personally from which I took a long time to recover, for my youth and confidence in the labour movement would not let me believe that trade unionists would do such a thing."[5] Was Stella Franklin more cynical or just less emotionally stirred? On the day following the guilty plea she worked on *In the Business of Cupid*, and next day on *Net of Circumstance*. She made no comment in her diary on the case but then neither did she note there the return of *The End of My Career*, by Blackwood on 13 November, 1911, saying they did not think it strong enough to follow her other books. This must have been a devastating blow.

Christmas was happy enough, spent with the Dresdens at Madison playing with their baby, but when Stella returned to the office on 29 December she found it in turmoil, and on 1 January she was so cold and weak and ailing that she stayed in bed next day, "feeling terrible". Good Alice Henry came to the rescue and stayed all night. The diagnosis next day was measles, serious in the patient's weakened condition, and Docter Young ordered a nurse. After ten days in bed the invalid was shepherded to the Resthaven Sanitarium, where under its blissful routine she managed to finish the first draft of *Net of Circumstance* and read *Anna Karenina*. Meanwhile Margaret Robins cancelled all out-of-town engagements, as she had no help, and had to refuse a request from the Kansas City league for Miss Franklin's services. Sara Conboy wrote on behalf of the Boston league, "I very much regret Miss F's illness. She is a wonderful worker."[6]

By 5 February it was back to all the old pressures, back to the office, to routine league work, *Life & Labor*, suffrage meetings, visits to doctors and dentists. There was no pause in the pell-mell pace as the pocket diary for 1912 confirms. On 13 February Stella made up the March issue of the magazine, on the fourteenth and fifteenth dealt with the printers, and on the sixteenth took the night train to Springfield for some ten-hour business. There was "snow up to the neck" in some places that month and on the twenty-third Stella "had a real tiff" with Margaret Robins. The dismal record of "sick from overwork", "too tired even to sleep", "sick with cold and pain", "great pain at night" continued through March, accompanied by the typing out of *Net of Circumstance*.

Then came April and spring, and a new friend, Guido Mariotti who was teaching Editha Phelps Italian. Franklin, Agnes Nestor and Margaret Robins made a quick and exhausting trip to New York for a board meeting. There they heard of the terrible disaster of the *Titanic*, with the loss of 1,513 lives, including that of W.T. Stead. On her return Franklin moved again ("horrors, moving day. Sat in a filthy muddle all day") and sent off *Net of Circumstance* to an "American" agent on 6 May.

Life was "busy but futile and without zest", brightened by the friendship of the Lloyds, meetings in June with the Burley Griffins and by talks, walks, picnics, lunches, dinners, five cent shows and late night chats on her porch with Guido. It was some six years since her romance with Edwin Bridle, and, oddly, she had made no male friends since then except with married men — Arnold Dresden, Raymond Robins, and W.B. Lloyd. She had a slight acquaintanceship with the other Lloyd brothers, and occasionally had lunch or dinner with a man, but Guido Mariotti was the first admirer with whom she had spent so much time. Given the fact of her undoubted charm she may have deliberately kept away from any entanglement in the early years in America. Now, as the diary entries indicate, she and Guido were for some months inseparable, and another man came into her life also, Fred Pischel, brother of Hull House supporter and league "ally" Emma Pischel. Franklin was now thirty-two. Possibly she felt it time to consider more seriously the questions of marriage and a family which she had put aside during her twenties in favour of her ambitions.

In June she was busy with the Republican convention but life was not pleasant, with Margaret Robins becoming enraged by the costs of the magazine, and after working all day on "*L & L* hacking" on 25 June, Stella got home tired the next day to find that the unskilled help had thrown out many of her papers.

Her diary reveals that her sleeplessness during the summer of 1912 was so bad that she had to resort to veronal and other sleeping draughts. Her friend Helen Marot was in town for a few days in July, otherwise she spent her spare time with Guido. But the highlight of the season was the "great and glorious day" that she marched in escort to the women delegates to Theodore Roosevelt's "Bull Moose Convention" at the Coliseum.

The six-week-old Progressive Party had split from the Republican Party and had gained the support of many women's groups when its leader Roosevelt gave his approval to women's suffrage. Raymond Robins was prominent in the convention, heading a group which included in its platform eight hour days for women, protection for child workers and elimination of night work for women. The big feature of the opening reported in detail by the *Tribune* on 6 August was the grand suffrage parade. The procession formed up at 10.30 outside the Arts Institute and included academics in cap and gown, society women like Mrs Medill McCormick, league personalities including Margaret Robins, Agnes Nestor, Stella Franklin, Alice Henry and Mary Anderson. The *Tribune* wrote:

> Women whose fortunes ran into millions walked with schoolma'ams who haven't a cent in the world except next month's salary, and society girls, social settlement workers, professional nurses, factory girls, leaders in civic, social and moral reform organisations and the officers of labour unions whose membership is exclusively feminine made up the rank and file.

Led by a squad of mounted police, waving 500 yellow suffrage banners and accompanied by a band, with Jane Addams, the Illinois delegate, and other women delegates in "the triumphant automobile" they set off through the streets of Chicago, Mrs Kellog Fairbank and other society leaders marching past the conservative Chicago Club in the company of trade unionists and "four methodist deaconesses in bonnets and black dresses".

There was only one incident, when the band caused some indignation by playing before the parade "Darling, I Am Growing Old". Dr Anna Blount was there to speak up. "What do they mean?" she asked. "This is the birth of our rights and the birth of a new party ... We are certainly not growing old." The peak of felicity was reached when Jane Addams was the first woman to speak as a delegate seconding a presidential nomination.

Stella revelled in the atmosphere from a good press seat: "Never enjoyed myself so much for years." The convention satisfied her appetite for the grand and dramatic, so much so that she had to take a sleeping draught at night "to quiet down". Reporting on the convention she wrote: "(It) was marked with distinct religious fervour. It opened with the Lord's prayer and closed with the doxology," and Roosevelt's appearance on 6 August "caused a storm of cheering which lasted fifty-five minutes without cessation."[7]

After all that high politics her own defeat in the contest for the vice-presidency of her Stenographers' Local, even if it stung, was a minor matter.

What were of more concern were the illness from which she suffered, causing persistent pain and fatigue, and the sorrow she felt at the death of her adored Grandma Lampe in June. The physical affliction was mysterious. Her journal records that she consulted doctors again and again. On 5 September she was "examined inside and out". On the twenty-first she was in bed all day with pain. On the twenty-ninth she saw Dr B. van Hoosen and "received a terrible verdict"—which did not stop her beginning final corrections on the manuscript of *The Net of Circumstance* that day, or attending the Single Tax Banquet the next, though that night she "took panic over the diagnosis" and "spent ghastly night".

Franklin had good reason to be concerned over her health. Her three sisters and one of her brothers had died young, and rather suddenly. On the *Ventura* on 12 April, 1906, she had sent a postcard home complaining that the vibration of the ship had made her heart bad, for a couple of days. The stress of her Chicago life had eroded her natural stamina. But, after dealing with the threatened defection of the league's star organiser, Rose Schneiderman on 1 October, later that day she saw the doctor again, and her fears were quietened. Her journal shows that she had painful manipulative treatments during October and November, possibly for the spinal problem that had troubled her since childhood.

It also attests that she attended vice hearings at City Hall, and, on the personal side, ended her relationship with Guido Mariotti. She summed him up, on 13 November, rather unkindly, as "the most vacuous specimen of humanity". Guido had been a constant and comforting companion during the six months of their friendship, but did not measure up, apparently, to her exacting standards. Perhaps her illness accounted in part for her rancour towards him; perhaps her change of heart was the result of a native fickleness, a tendency to become bored with the too devoted. Perhaps news of the death of Joseph Furphy in September had brought back to her an image of a "beau ideal".

But, having disposed of poor Guido, Stella swung back to a more pronounced interest in feminism, to more concern with politics and ideas as shown by her writing to Keir Hardie and to Bernard Shaw, and reading *Advance of Women*. She continued work on the second half of *Net of Circumstance*, helped Mary Anderson write an AF of L report and began to feel more cheerful. The twenty-fourth of December was "a very lovely day beginning with Christmas celebration in office", and ending with a party at the opera to see Mary Garden. Christmas Day was spent with the Pischel family but on the eve of the New Year of 1913 with no replies from the post office she was again "tired, worn-out and without zest".

Though she carried out her duties zealously, though each day was filled with incident, it was as though she were on a treadmill leading nowhere. Sleeplessness, fatigue, illness, irritability and overwork chained her down. The years were flying past and the grandeur she had longed for still escaped her. No heroic prince came to free her, and for all her efforts, there were no great acclaim, no applauding multitudes, no liberating wealth, no luxury, none of the daydreams of her tempestuous girlhood fulfilled. In bondage now to service and routine, ''feeling as if life was beyond endurance'', she entered another year.

15 *"Life & Labor"*

By the end of 1912 Stella Franklin had been assistant editor of *Life & Labor* for two years, had been secretary of the expanding national league for eighteen months, had taken an active and important part in a major strike, had finished another novel and had made her first acquaintance with Europe. That would seem to be a fairly satisfactory record, except that the rush of all these activities, combined with a none-too-strong constitution and a workaholic nature, meant that she lived on a plane of intense fatigue, neurasthenia and unhappiness, working against the grain most of the time, snatching hours for the writing and music which meant so much.

Her tiny pocket diaries are a brief account of this period, an indication of how she felt at her lowest ebb, but they must be seen in perspective. It cannot be emphasised too strongly that one would learn nothing of this misery and despair from the public record. Her writings for the magazine were vigorous and optimistic, full of affection for the working girls she met and of unswerving dedication to women's causes. People don't want a wet blanket about them but people of all kinds sought her company, the sophisticated and cultured Lloyds and Dresdens, the glamorous Robins, the girls at the office, Ethel Mason, Editha Phelps and Mary Galvin, her fellow officers and "allies" of the league, Agnes Nestor, Mary Anderson, Pauline Newman and Helen Marot. Jane Addams kept her on her roster of dinner guests, and she was a friend of Harold Ickes and his wife, of Floyd and Margery Dell, the Pischels and many other leading Chicagoans. The testimony of the ceaseless string of dinners, lunches, outings, concerts, plays is that she was sought after as a witty, lively and amusing companion. Little Billy Lloyd retains today, as William Bross Lloyd, Jnr, the memory of tales of a very interesting, vivacious and intelligent Australian lady, a friend of his father and uncle.[1] Her easy and attractive manner was useful in her work also, and Margaret Robins praised her as specially helpful in bringing about co-operation. Intensely proud and reserved about her inner self, her sometimes waspish irritability was one of the few outward signs of the hidden inner tensions. The armour of humour protected and disguised also. However sad at heart, she could still laugh. She recalled almost falling off her chair in a fit of giggles at a luncheon for some "allies": "Mrs Fairbanks beside whom I was wanted to know what was the joke and I had to say I was English and thought of something that happened six months before."[2] Elizabeth Christman, who was later national secretary wrote to her: "Every now and then I get a good laugh when I refer to the old records and come across one of your letters to the Board. I wish I could be as philanthropic and entertaining a secretary."[3]

Stella Franklin was a very capable secretary in a time of growth. Her reports about various critical situations kept branches in touch with the total of the league's activities. The league advised branches and unions on such practical matters as how to run a meeting, how to write a letter, how to keep books, and on picketing and strike organisation and rights. It educated and encouraged. Margaret Robins in 1922 paid a tribute to secretaries Emma Steghagen and Elizabeth Christman which applied equally to Stella Franklin: "It is your secretaries who bear the brunt and burden of the day and it is through their never failing devotion and work that the league has held its own so valiantly."[4] Alice Henry has recorded that between 1904 and 1909 work was very slow and results insignificant. The dynamic leadership of Margaret Robins, backed by the painstaking organising ability of Stella Franklin and the talents of Agnes Nestor, Rose Schneiderman, Mary Anderson, Elizabeth Christman and other leaders combined to set the new organisation on a firm basis. Historians of the women's movement have recognised the place of the league. "It proved no less a spur to the women's movement than to the labour movement . . . the work of the league may be viewed as in the tradition of a reform movement of a distinctly concrete nature."[5] It produced leaders among women. "The opportunity afforded by the league to such women for growth through action and the exercise of responsibility, both largely denied them within the AF of L, can hardly be overestimated."[6] In 1914 Helen Marot wrote: "In the ten years of its existence the league has functioned as a woman's as well as a labour organisation,"[7] and even Samuel Gompers observed of it in 1913:

> The popular attitude toward women's work has changed completely . . . This woman's movement is a movement for liberty, freedom of action and thought tending toward a condition when women shall be accorded equal independence and responsibility with men, equal freedom of work and self expression, equal legal protection and right.[8]

One of the main weapons in furthering the aims of the league was its little magazine *Life & Labor*, edited by Alice Henry with Stella Franklin as associate editor and Frances Squire Potter as departmental editor. Small in format, thirty pages, run on a shoe-string, always in financial difficulties in the manner of most little magazines, nevertheless it played an important part in the early years of the women's labour movement.

Issued monthly it contained articles of concern for working women, notices of trade union meetings, descriptions of different kinds of women's work, strike reports, poems and general news stories. The paper also excerpted government reports and made them readable and interesting to a working women's audience. *Life & Labor* is one of the most valuable sources we have for the history of working class women.[9]

How the credit for its success in the years when Alice Henry and Stella Franklin collaborated should be shared is a perplexing problem though in later years the junior partner had no doubts about the solution:

Miss Henry would never have gotten out *Life & Labor* if I hadn't done it all behind the scenes. I always had to fill in her gaps and squandered my own opportunities. She had the most marvellous memory and mind for sifting things but there was some strange break that prevented her from ever doing anything complete on her own.[10]

She also claimed that she had started Alice Henry on two of her books and that "the task of extracting them from her was monumental".[11]

Alice Henry in her *Trade Union Woman*, published in 1915, does not mention her fellow countrywoman in connection with the magazine, though Francis Potter is acknowledged as departmental editor. She merely states that Stella Franklin for long held the reins in the national office in Chicago. In her *Memoirs* she was more generous, acknowledging the able assistance of fellow Australian Miles Franklin, who had a sound reputation in the literary field. "Besides giving yeoman service to the president on the national side of the work she acted as assistant editor and often filled in gaps."

Stella Franklin certainly did her share, handling the printers, Sauls (always a demanding job), editing, rewriting, commissioning, chasing up stories, filling up spaces. The offices were at first at 79 Dearborn Street, then later at 137 Dearborn Street. In the first two years there was little signed Stella Franklin though she collaborated with the editor on the garment strike articles "Chicago at the Front" (January), "Holding the Fort" (February) and "The End of the Struggle" (March) in 1911. She must have worked as well on the separately published "WTUL Official Report of the Strike Committee, Chicago Garment Workers' Strike, 1911".

She was probably responsible for many of the unsigned pieces over the years that she spent with the magazine. She certainly worked on the unsigned articles on the Muscatine button makers' strike of 1911, and "Button-Pearl Buttons" in May shows her typical intimate style. "We all use them. What would shirt or shirt-waist be without the handy fastening and neat finish of the pearl button. We buy them by the card. We lose and break them by the dozen . . ." The detailed, unsigned account in August of the Third Biennial Convention at Boston is also very much in her manner. "Of course the convention had to be photographed . . . Did some shadow of a coming event cast before, of future secretarial responsibilities, efface the familiar features of S.M. Franklin who is to be imagined as somewhere in the background just beside the sympathetic Leonora's hat.'' This photograph of the Convention is so crowded and indistinct that it is difficult to tell whether Franklin's face is obscured by one of the many hats, or even if she is there at all.

The colour frontispiece of the December 1911 issue from a drawing by Katherine Dreier drew the fire of some ardent anti-monarchists with its title ''The Woman's Coronation Parade in London''. The assistant editor had to explain to her president.

> Oh, My, O, me, oh, My, oh, My!!! To think of the messes we can get into with our editorial stunts. I suppose I should have put Coronation Suffrage Parade. Suffrage parade is not its true name as there have been countless suffrage parades and only one woman's coronation parade in the history of England, if I know. This foolish idea of some of our friends that we must not even mention royalty — which after all does still exist as an integral part of our civilisation, is just as asinine as the attitude of very pure modest people who are shocked at the mention of our fallen sisters which also exist as an integral part of our civilisation in its present state. It is a good thing we were pretty well seasoned before we started running a magazine or we surely could never have survived the strain, could we?[12]

This matter of lingering affection for her empire was to cause more bitter problems in the future.

The magazine was informative, practical and entertaining, with league news, book notices, a votes for women department, a jokes section called ''In Merry Mood'', a letter-box, reports from overseas, and verse. In the early issues Australian poets Bernard O'Dowd (''On Duty'' and ''The Working Folk'') and Victor Daley (''The Woman at the Washtub'') appeared.

The first article signed by Stella Franklin appeared in August 1912. It dealt with Republicans Florence Porter and Isabella Blaney, the first two women delegates to a national convention called to elect a presidential candidate. The author was somewhat carried away:

> The joy of the great world movement for a fuller, more efficient citizenship is that all the brainiest, most truly motherly and totally womanly women are in the thick of the fight in one branch or another so that those still afflicted with the antiquated notion that women should essay nothing but a domestically restricted motherhood will soon have to keep themselves company on a sequestered billabong dedicated to antediluvian craft.

In September 1912 she paid tribute to the Lloyd family in her enthusiastic review of Caro Lloyd's biography of Henry Demarest Lloyd:

> It is a slice of what might be called the delicate underlining of American history, the history of thought which shapes the deed, and which all those who wish to understand the underlying significance of this great republic during the last three or four decades cannot afford to leave unread.

She praised him for his brilliant journalistic crusades against monopoly and for his fearlessness in explosive situations, and quoted his enigmatically blunt motto: ''In all issues the principle of but one side can be right. The working man is often wrong, but he is always the right side.'' The legendary Lloyd hospitality from which she had benefited in time of crisis received its due praise.

In December 1912 there was an announcement about *Life & Labor* policies which stated also:

> When space permits the assistant editor ·S.M. Franklin will review books that are analogous to our story, from the sociological point of view, and will continue to adjure all in the struggle for industrial justice to keep up their spirits, to preserve and enlarge their sense of humour and to beware of making contributions too long or dismal.

In the tradition of the clown, whatever her private woes, the public face was cheerful.

Though the magazine by this time seemed well established the three women most involved were at odds in character and style, and difficulties were increasing in its production. Commanding Margaret Robins was a woman of the grand gesture and the broad sweep, not to be bothered too much with petty detail. She enjoyed being centre stage, and was not the least dazzled by the limelight. The women's club rostrum, the convention hall platform, even the street soap box were where she shone. Though she wrote well enough she often called on Stella Franklin for assistance as her intense, dramatic personality found action and oratory her real weapons.

Alice Henry was a competent, if dullish journalist, a researcher rather than a creative writer, a nervous and serious lecturer and of a rather disorganised and haphazard manner in general, which was noticeable particularly in dress, so much so that Margaret Robins conspired with Stella to devise a straggle-proof costume for her. ''Miss Henry never could keep those shirt-waists, skirts and belts together and with her eccentricity about hat pins presented a weird and derelict appearance not to be endured by the efficient and gadget intoxicated Americans.'' So Miss Henry appeared in a new outfit, made by Mrs Robins' own expensive dressmaker, of black transparent stuff over gorgeous black silk, but she outwitted the schemers by adding touches of her own — a rosy lace collar ''as crumpled as if it had been used for stuffing a shoe'', or metres of flaring yellow ribbon wrapped around her neat black dress when she addressed a socialite suffragette meeting (''those pampered over fed, over rich birds in their Parisian loot'',[13] as Stella bitingly described them).

The youngest of the trio was neat in appearance and deft in organisation, but basically she was a person who, though frank and free in private manner, was terrified of public speaking. ''You may remember there *was* one thing in which I was clever,'' she wrote to Elizabeth Christman, ''and that was in escaping platform speaking. I have got over some of my deadly stage fright now ... but I am still not a speaker.''[14] Naturally enough to the crisp, efficient junior partner fell a large share of the detailed production of the magazine.

Inevitably, under the increasing rush and pressure as the league expanded, temperamental differences were expressed more openly. There was the complicating factor of money. Both Margaret Robins and her younger protégée felt badly used. Robins financed the venture largely from her own pocket and felt the editors had a cavalier attitude to her money. As early as September 1911 Robins complained to Alice Henry that two additional workers had been added to the *Life & Labor* staff without any consultation with her. Stella, of course, thought herself overworked and underpaid. Then there was the matter of the assistant editor's curious and complicated personality. Margaret Robins had total confidence in Alice Henry's devotion and loyalty to the cause, for though her hair might be loosely pinned, her hat awry, her platform manner nervous and her routine disorganised, Alice Henry's belief in the movement she served was calm and deep and simple: "It is the girls who must ever be the movement."[15] As Stella said, "She never seemed to be afflicted by weakness and doubts."[16] Margaret Robins could depend on Alice Henry's utter dedication, but was uneasy about the more obscure attitudes of the brilliant, egotistical younger woman, so restless and striving, with her quicksilver impatience and hesitations.

Their relationship had begun very well. Childless Margaret had mothered the girl, signing her Christmas postcard of 1908, depicting a plump four-year-old eating her porridge, "with a whole heartful of love to one of my dearest little girls".[17] She had at one stage "carried off Miss Franklin bodily"[18] from her lodgings with Alice Henry at 71 Park Avenue, expressing the view that Miss Franklin would have more chance of getting extra work in rooms near the university. There had been many lunches and dinners together and the flat at West Ohio Street had been a refuge. During her secretary's illness in January Margaret Robins was most concerned that she should not rush back to work, urging: "Remember we need you greatly a little later and remember some of us love you very dearly."[19] Stella on her part had a need of her employer's strength and abounding confidence. Writing to her in Europe as late as June 1913 she expressed this dependence: "Dear me. It felt as if my rock of refuge had walked off when the train pulled out and took you out of sight, but I expect I've got to learn to get along by myself,"[20] and 25 July: "Dear me, what on earth would we do — some of us — if the Lord hadn't given us you to put us together and keep us held that way for a while now and again."[21]

In dealing with any Franklin letters there is the problem of how much is playing to an audience, how much genuine feeling, how much the writer's art, how much spontaneous. But the long correspondence with Margaret Robins seems proof of real feeling and closeness. Yet the friendship began to split under the stresses of *Life & Labor*, and the differences in their backgrounds and characters became more apparent and more dividing. Robins was rich, happily married, the admired elder sister in a close and loving family. Franklin was poor, alone and far from relatives and native land. Robins was totally involved in the struggles of the league. Rose Schneiderman said of her, "There never was a better trade unionist anywhere than Margaret Dreier Robins ... She was the best public relations person the trade union movement ever had."[22] Franklin, though a feminist through and through, was cynical about the miracles expected from the vote by American women, and a streak of pessimism underlay her league mask of optimism as far as political action was concerned. As she said in *Cockatoos*, "Woman suffrage and Federation made no perceptible difference in virtue, prosperity or living for either sex."

She yearned for freedom but was the prisoner of her office stool, and she saw herself as a creative artist writing *Life & Labor* "stuff" to earn her bread and butter. No Boadicean warrior figure leading her people into battle with the panache of Margaret Robins, no passionate idealist in the mood of Old Russia like Rose Schneiderman, not even a pious, true believer with the faith of Alice Henry, Stella Franklin, something of a literary cuckoo in an activist nest, was finding that lodging more and more confining.

There seemed little chance of escape. She wrote more and more for the magazine in 1913. The anonymous piece on organising department store clerks in the January issue was probably from her pen and "The High Calling of the Waitress" in the February number certainly was. She was sympathetic and relaxed, dealing with the work of her friend Elizabeth Maloney. "The waitress's role is far more arduous and exacting than drawing room deportment, as any drawing room belle would quickly discover upon practical investigation . . . it might well be compared with a long stiff part in a comedy repeated five or six times a day."

In March she reviewed *My Little Sister*, subtitled "a story of white slavery", by Raymond Robins' sister Elizabeth. The book dealt with prostitution, always an emotional subject to Stella Franklin, and she brusquely attacked the view that art was for art's sake. "We are achieving a degree of civilisation wherein we have small tolerance for the art for art's sake driveller . . . It is art for life's sake, art attuned to the service of humanity."

An article written jointly with Ethel Mason, "Low Wages and Vice", published in May, gave her an opportunity to lash two of her favourite hobby horses, prostitution again and the department stores. "It was clearly brought out by the testimony that the department store is in many cases an institution in a great degree dependent for its fabulous profits on the charity of parents who help pay the wages of a large percentage of employees." The Illinois State Senate had held public hearings at La Salle Hotel on the connection between the low wages of women and girl workers in department stores particularly and the white slave traffic, the euphemism of the day for prostitution. "There was a dramatic contrast between the witnesses — the merchant princes of State Street and the mailing houses on one hand, the lowly paid girl workers and the inmates of a certain class of house on the other." The word prostitution is not used, the tale being told in terms of "going wrong" and immorality.

In June Stella reviewed the prolific Elizabeth Robins again, this time a book dealing with the contemporary militant suffragette movement in England, *Way Stations*, which was dedicated to Margaret Robins. Franklin quoted Elizabeth Robins' statement that among women leaders of reform the majority did not assume "that men have consciously and deliberately initiated all the injustices from which women suffer", then commented in the preaching style that (sentiments aside) marred a number of her novels:

> For this statement from a high source we give hearty thanks, having the infelicity to flourish in a civilisation extensively blighted with the superstition that the feministic ideal of race regeneration is nothing more than a revengeful determination on the part of women to subjugate men, compel them to be virtuous and unselfish, even to wear skirts and high-heeled shoes, while women themselves usurp male privileges prominently the right to be respectable though licentious.

Here her future preoccupation with moralistic "eugenics" is mixed with her contempt for the double sexual standards of her era.

Her feminist passions had their head in this review:

> Any movement for social justice can count on the resistance of such organised forces as the whisky trust, and the vice trust and the money trust, but the women's struggle has additional opposition. Even publications that have stood true to democracy in other controversies ... have become vitriolic about militant actions in London. Such reformers can go far enough to understand the rebellion (no matter how violent) of every enslaved section of the human family excepting women.

She ended in revolutionary defiance: "In militancy (acting as we are the first to admit in conjunction with a world wide tendency) a force was set to work six years ago which needed only counter force, needed only ruthless expression, to develop an explosive power which should crack the crust of ages."

In a tribute to the militant suffragette, "Mrs Pankhurst in the United States" published in December 1913's *Life & Labor*, she defended militant methods:

> Bitter necessity of keeping the cause before the stupid, lethargic British public at any cost then would seem to be one reason for militancy with the responsibility on the British public. It must be borne in mind all the time by those who would be just that militancy is the smallest part of the vast activities of Mrs Pankhurst's followers.

A notice of Arnold Bennett's "Your United States", in June 1913 struck a more generally evangelistic note: "A person who sits down content or hopeless in a new republic is a fool or a coward — he is worse — he is an inefficient nincompoop." There was a long unsigned report on the Fourth Biennial Convention of the league held in St Louis in the July issue and, on a more personal level, her last "par" for the year dealt with a new fashion which mitigated an old irritation, for the slit skirt "while not an entirely satisfactory garment may be hailed with hope as letting a little light into that dark prudery which has assumed that women are built solidly like a tree-trunk or a post office pillar''. A critique of the Little Theatre's *Trojan Women* in March showed her as pacifist and a gentle, down-to-earth article on Agnes Nestor of the glove workers as affectionate friend. ''To think of the glove workers without Agnes Nestor would be like contemplating the AF of L without President Gompers.''

In the pages of *Life & Labor* she had a platform for her league personality, but 1913 was not entirely devoted to business. In January, never disheartened at her lack of literary success to the point of surrender, Stella began on a new book, ''wrote a little of Sybyl'', which probably turned into her unpublished novel of Chicago life, *On Dearborn Street*, for its heroine is Sybyl. In the early months of the year she also wrote a three-act comedy, *Sophia*, ''dawdled'' over a short story, about which she wrote to Doubleday & Co, began to dramatise a novel by Charlotte Perkins Gilman, *Mag-Majorie*, took French lessons, attended performances of the Irish Players and of *Lohengrin* with W.B. Lloyd, chatted with Demarest Lloyd and even Guido Mariotti, lunched with society leader Mrs Medill McCormick, and with her special favourite, ''my sweet Ethel Mason'', and spent a large part of her time and money with the medical profession.

So the year progressed, logged in her tiny notebook, with league meetings, stenographers' meetings, doctor's treatments, balanced by more frivolous outings. Meanwhile her friendship with W.B. Lloyd burgeoned. And all the time she was ''feeling utterly defeated and worn out''. She saw brilliant Nazimova in *Bella Donna*, Mary Garden of the *Salome* scandal in *Jongleur*, and a number of other shows, all with Bill Lloyd in attendance. She saw *Hindle Wakes* with trusty Fred Pischel, and heard Clara Butt sing, ''a great treat''. As a change from theatregoing, after lunching with W.B. Lloyd at the Athletic Club on 13 March, they went on together to the Cubist and Futurist Art Exhibition, then the talk of artistic and fashionable Chicago. During these months she continued to revise *The Net of Circumstance* in her free time.

In spite of these diversions with such personable escorts she was ''ill and ghastly depressed'' on 11 April, and she received a shock when at Dr Young's on the fourteenth she ''got the old familiar death sentence''. One can only speculate in a number of directions as to the nature of this verdict. There is no doubt that her once extraordinary vitality had been dissipated. It could be that ''the doctors spoke of a strained heart and hinted at T.B.'', as they did to artist Bernice Gaylord, heroine of a later novel of Franklin's, *Gentlemen at Gyang Gyang,* for the nature of Stella's life in Chicago could have laid the basis for such illnesses. It is conceivable that the ''doom'' was of a more psychologically distressing kind, that her voice had been damaged beyond mending, or that her constitution was such that children were out of the question. She had suffered from a twist of the spine since childhood, and perhaps this verdict was that this pain would be lifelong. Whatever the

The jacket of *Gentlemen at Gyang Gyang,* first published in 1956.

"sentence" it did not put a stop to her activities. Though she suffered insomnia and a "hell" of depression, even after a comforting night at Winnetka with the Lloyds on 24 April, though she had terrible nightmares about an operation and "having to be handled" on the twenty-seventh, by the beginning of June she was "as busy as an ant" again as the Fourth Biennial Convention of the NWTUL opened in St Louis on 2 June, 1913.

Here there were fifty-five voting delegates, representing twenty trades and professions, evidence of continued growth. The need for a training school for women union organisers and the importance of the ballot as a practical necessity to protect women were emphasised. The value of publicity was stressed too in Margaret Robins' presidential address, with the work of *Life & Labor* in this area underlined, as she urged all to strive to extend its circulation. S.M. Franklin, Mary Anderson, Leonora O'Reilly and Melinda Scott were among those appointed to a committee for formulating plans for training organisations and other educational work.

The faith of members in the ability of Stella Franklin was expressed when she was elected unanimously to the combined post of secretary-treasurer. She was now entrusted with a triple-faceted league job, and, though she was probably gratified to have achieved such a level of responsibility, it was to prove more than she could handle, given her other interest.

In the summer of 1913 Margaret Robins went abroad, leaving Franklin in charge of the office. She sent the secretary a gift of yellow roses on departure and Stella, in her thanks, let flow a little from the well of her deepest feelings, for the flowers reminded her of the garden fence of her childhood, "tho I was so wild to get away from that lonely monotony at the same time I don't suppose that I'll ever get over the homesick craving that comes at intervals."[1] Raymond Robins, on a visit to Australia that year, courteously visited her family and became a favourite with her stern mother. He joined his wife in Europe, while in Chicago "every person in this office is running on top of me", reported Franklin, as she straightened the files with Olive Sullivan, wrote letters to "various dear sirs and brothers" and worried about getting something moving in the school for organisers.

The friendship with the Lloyds waxed strong, and she spent a number of summer weekends at Winnetka, going sometimes alone, sometimes accompanied to that pleasant retreat by Ethel Mason, her "joy and delusion", her closest friend at the time.

The diary for this period is almost a potted case history of nervous collapse. In Chicago Stella was "sick for want of sleep", tormented by "beastly sparrows", "no rest infernal sparrows", "frantic from want of sleep owing to sparrows". At Winnetka on 14 August sympathetic Lola Lloyd (expecting her third child) read to her and she had a wonderful sleep. But by 11 September she was feeling so ill that she had a blood test. The personal tensions she was experiencing were building to an explosive point, and on 24

September she was violently sick and vomiting. The next day she met Margaret Robins on her return from Europe, and on 1 October went out to Winnetka again to see the Lloyds' new baby.

There is a calmer mood in her tiny journal in the early weeks of October. She "did over" Emma Steghagen's article on Cincinnati which appeared in *Life & Labor* in November, and heard Melba, "enchanted". W.B. Lloyd resumed his calls, and on the seventeenth she bought some dancing slippers. Stella had never learned to dance in her backblocks home and Lloyd kindly offered to teach her. Lessons began at the Powers Building on 20 October, and the Lloyd children, little Billy and Mary with their nurse Miss Russel, came to look on a couple of days later. The lessons paid off, for on the following Sunday Stella, Fred Pischel, Ethel and T. Bishop danced all afternoon and evening at the Lloyds. It was an escape into a little frivolity, away from the solemnity of the office.

W.B. Lloyd continued to act as escort, for on 1 November she went to a Trade Union Hallowe'en Ball at La Salle with him. The next day they went together to a packed Pankhurst meeting, moved on to a dinner for the suffragettes at the City Club and ended the evening hearing Pankhurst again at Hull House. That lady must have been quite stirring, for at midnight abstemious Stella took a mixture of veronal, aspirin and brandy and "thank God went to sleep". The torture of sleeplessness often made her nights a misery but these nights of late October and early November seemed the worst ever.

As she noted, she was seeing Bill Lloyd almost every day, at dinner at Henrici's, at lunch at the College Inn or the Automobile Club. He went to Boston on 5 November, but on his return on the twenty-fourth the pattern was resumed with a spate of dinners, lunches, visits to the opera and the theatre. He said he had rarely had such a treat as seeing her laugh at Bernard Shaw's *Press Cuttings*, though he missed a lot of the points himself.[2] They lunched at Bismarck Gardens, and dined at the elegant Blackstone, with its pillars and palms, flowers and flunkies. But on 23 December, 1913, after dinner at the Congress followed by Pagliacci, they "had a warm controversy" for some unrecorded reason. Next day she reached home after Christmas Eve dinner with the Robins to find a peace offering, a big basket of provisions from Bill Lloyd.

On Christmas Day, thanks to this gift, she had a fine day's work and never stirred out. The tiff seemed settled for they lunched together two days later, went driving, to dinner and to the opera.

It was certainly in retrospect a perplexing friendship. If W.B. Lloyd had not been married, it would look like a courtship. If Stella Franklin had not been so rigidly puritanical it might appear to be an affair. But raised in the strict monogamy of the bush, sexually disgusted by "loose" conduct, she undoubtedly shared Sybylla's sentiment: "No man living could have tempted

me outside a wedding ring.'' Obviously they enjoyed each other's company.
He was handsome, wealthy, intelligent and interested in reform causes and
the arts, yet also light-hearted and pleasure loving. He could shower on her
little luxuries of fine dinners and good seats, easing the narrowness of her
circumstances. She was pretty, lively and amusing, intelligent and unusual.
He was four years older, and much more sophisticated and worldly, for
Franklin in spite of her sharp mind and tongue was still something of a bush
innocent, entertaining but puzzling. ''I remember,'' she wrote to Alice
Henry, ''Will Lloyd once saying that I was the most complex mortal he had
ever 'contacted', that I could not do the slightest action without more
convolutions than a diplomat.''[3]

To Franklin, with her uncompromising attitude towards extramarital sex,
her coolness in sexual matters, the relationship had to be that simply of one
intelligent, attractive human being to another, an affection of the spirit. And
yet the sleeplessness, the unhappiness, the illness of the months when she was
seeing W.B. Lloyd most would appear to indicate even more intense strain
than usual in her pain-racked nature. Amiable Lola Lloyd, preoccupied with
her young children, seemed unworried and was also a friend. Stella, in her
loneliness, must have envied the Lloyds their marriage, their family and the
freedom and expansiveness of the life which their money provided. The rich
and happy Lloyds, the wealthy and dedicated Robins, were not trapped like her
in a prison of isolation and poverty.

As another year ended she was deeply, almost suicidally, depressed, as she
confided to her diary:

> Looking back over the year I cannot recall one thing that I have accomplished
> for another nor one of pleasure or satisfaction for myself. The futility of my
> existence, my weakness in effort—my failure in accomplishment fill me with a
> creeping melancholy that grows more impenetrable. I will fight against it once
> more by hard work and if in two years the results are no better than in the past
> I shall die by my own volition.

Perhaps it was only a literary threat but certainly she was in the grip of a
morbid and romantic self-pity, close to breakdown and out of touch with any
true assessment of her real accomplishments. She survived and battled
through this unhappy time because she was always a fighter and a lover of
life, and because she found relief in giving vent to her choking self-pity in the
novels she worked on during these years, *Net of Circumstance* and *On
Dearborn Street*.

17 "The Net of Circumstance" and Demarest Lloyd

By 18 January, 1914 the novel *The Net of Circumstance* was ready to be submitted again to a publisher. This time, Franklin decided to try an English agent.

Sybylla Melvyn had said in *My Career Goes Bung* after the publication of her book, "In future I could have a nom-de-plume carefully guarded so that my attempts could be taken on their merits without scandal." Stella Franklin had hurt and been hurt in her openness and simplicity in *My Brilliant Career*. For this new book she went far beyond just "Miles" as a cover, and chose a rather odd pseudonym, "Mr and Mrs Ogniblat L'Artsau". This was not just one of those fancy names, popular with romantic writers of the day, such as Mrs G. de Horne Vaizey, Mrs Champion de Crespigny or Marmaduke Pickstall. It was a meaningful choice, for if you turn this remarkable name about, with a slight juggle of the surname, it becomes Talbingo, Austral(ia). It probably amused her immensely that nobody would have the slightest notion of the name's significance, as a symbol of home, a little salve for her sickness. What the "Mr and Mrs" indicates, except doubling the deception and further confusing the trail, is mystifying. The pseudonym might have betokened a desire on her part for the married state. On the other hand it could have symbolised her independence and self sufficiency. Or possibly it was just a gimmick to catch the attention of the book-buying public.

This novel, her only published work set in Chicago, had engulfed her private hours while she "hacked" for *Life & Labor*. Sad to say, while much of the "hack work" in the magazine has vigour and warmth, this creative endeavour is pallid and artificial, its life being drained away in the gush of pity from the author for her poor little heroine. There are some good parts but even the backbone of feminism is sunk in the self-absorption of the leading character, Constance Roberts.

About thirty years old, no longer a girl, a stenographer and amateur singer and pianist to whom music is a passion, Constance is employed as an investigator of the conditions of women and children in industry, but does not enjoy her work as "it seemed an impertinence". She is submerged in gloom, for "struggle during the springtime of life" has robbed her of life's fulfilment for all time. (Perhaps this refers to her ability to bear a child, perhaps to general ill health.) She feels herself "merely a machine for earning food, shelter and clothes of a cheap quality". "She saw the past, colourless, uneventful—a dull commonplace struggle unrelieved by romance; but once there had been the anticipation of something more desirable to come . . . Ah the curse of lovelessness, of failure, the terror of years."

She lives at a Sarah Ann Club (which probably has a lot in common with Stella's loathed Eleanor Club), a philanthropic institution for working girls in Chicago. "They were run on the responsibility of a board of thirty-five ladies of the class which enjoys luxury produced by the class for which the places were run." Though embittered by the drabness of her life and burdened with feelings of failure, Constance is no simple revolutionary. She dislikes the frowsiness of most socialists and has no wish to be addressed as comrade or wage slave. Through an upper crust socialist friend she becomes friendly with wealthy reformer Hastings Howes of Highland Park, and while on summer holiday on Lake Michigan with these glamorous acquaintances meets their handsome young cousin, Tony Hastings. Mournfully she contrasts the barrenness of her life with the grace and plenty of her hosts' existence. Tony is attracted to Constance and her ideas, though another female guest dismisses her as some creature Hastings has picked out of the gutter since he went off his head about socialism.

Both Tony and an elderly uncle propose but feminist Constance has no wish to be immured in domesticity even though psychologically she is at rock-bottom, and life is flat and dreary and full of nothing. The tone is certainly reminiscent of the plaints of the author's diaries, even to the morbid suicidal feelings about which she consults a sympathetic doctor. The doctor understands her sensitive soul, too delicate to withstand "the crude grind of her environment" but can offer only kindly advice. Terrified of old age and seeking to escape her prison of dismal circumstance, Constance decides, in spite of her hankering for complete freedom, to accept wealthy Tony, but the grating mechanism of the plot moves him out of her life.

Constance is thrown further into the pit of depression and consults the doctor again. She asks him would it be wise to form a union based on friendship, if her great love was hopeless? Some metamorphosis is worked, and Constance, reinvigorated by the challenge of work, avoiding "the love that is not free", accepts Osborne Lewis, writer and feminist supporter, who has been waiting in the wings since the first scene. Constance soldiers on "full of the courage of the discovery that life held new and splendid possibilities".

Net of Circumstance, like *My Brilliant Career*, is a cry against fate. But the humour, the bubbling life, the poignant or loving descriptions of setting are absent, for the characters are puppet-like and the backdrop of Chicago pasteboard except for a sentence or so. The passion of her first work, which gave it strength, had become a wistful sentimentality. The parallels with her life are again obvious—the feminism, the independence, the illness, depression, feelings of failure and uncertainty, the lack of grace and colour in her existence, the kind and wealthy friends living in another world and the perplexity about the problems of love and marriage.

But the sympathy with the oppressed and disadvantaged which turned outward in Franklin's work for the league and *Life & Labor* is turned inward to one person, and that a pale shadow of herself lacking her animation and humour.

It is as if, her vital energies having been expended in the daily hurly-burly of her work, a frail ghost had sat typing in her desolate room. Too proud for the pity of her friends, she had conjured up the spirits of Mr and Mrs Ogniblat L'Artsau to pity her twin soul Constance.

The Lloyd family, in their chic and affluent way of life and their modish advanced thinking, had given her background material for this novel. They had also given her, perhaps, a model for Tony Hastings in Demarest Lloyd, "glorious Demy". While Stella dined and danced and lunched with W.B. Lloyd during 1913 she carried on a playful correspondence with his younger brother. The acquaintance went back some years, for on a visit to Winnetka in June 1910, she noted "Demy also there", and in December 1912 he thanked her for a copy of her review of his grandfather's biography. From time to time he dropped in at the office when in Chicago.

Demarest Lloyd, born in Chicago in February 1883, was three years younger than Stella. He took his Bachelor of Arts degree at Harvard in 1904, attended the Harvard Law School, and was very much the establishment clubman, being a member of the Eastern Yacht Club, the Boston Athletic Association and the Boston Art Club. He was also handsome, wealthy, unattached and full of the delight of living, and at that stage one of the idle rich. He spent the late winter of 1913 at the Hotel Poinciana in Palm Beach, Florida, and wrote to Stella from there on 26 February, 1913 of the joys of the latest dance craze, the turkey trot. He reported happily that John Fitzgerald, Mayor of Boston, who in his home city was a veritable puritan, threatening to close down Mary Garden at the Opera House for her passionate love scenes in "Tosca", and banning the turkey trot from Boston dance halls, was to be seen trotting animatedly with a lovely lady in one part of the hotel ballroom while his beautiful young daughter (Rose perhaps?) danced this latest fad with a college boy in another.

The correspondence developed into a light literary flirtation. He was full of high spirits, addressing her as dear, fascinating little rascal, or starlight, starbright, while he signed himself Sinbad the Sailor, a reference to his pleasure in yachting. When he bought a new car while staying at the Hotel Majestic in Paris in April 1913 he thought it would look its best with her in it, and he threatened a flying machine next. The letters were sporadic and on 17 September, 1913 he apologised for not having written for some time, though he was full of concern for her and on the twenty-second felt she was in some kind of trouble. This was the time of her great tension and sleep-lessness before the birth of Lola's baby. Demarest had recently become an earnest and fervent convert to Christian Science and on 6 October warned her against the materialism of the labour and socialist people with whom she was involved. He confided that he had had a narrow escape from being a ne'er-do-well but that Christian Science had helped him and he urged her to consult a practitioner, to tell the whole story of her unhappiness and get it off her mind. He comforted her in her depression, suggesting that she come to Boston for a vacation and see the most thrilling sport in the world at its best. He was convinced that football would get rid of her blues.

Stella invited him to a dance in October (probably the hallow-e'en ball to which his brother William escorted her), but he could not come though he hoped to spend Christmas in Chicago. He continued to urge Christian Science as a remedy for her ills and thought her unhappiness was somehow associated with the cynicism of his brother, and that his brother had transmitted his turbulence to her. He was glad that her affections were well spread out between the members of William's family. Demarest stayed at Winnetka over the 1914 New Year period and took Stella to dinner; to Shaw's *Fanny's First Play*, and to lunch at the Blackstone. In the same month his elder brother escorted her to lunch, to dinner and to the operas *Parsifal* and *Manon*.

She had her public duties to perform despite the tangled confusion of her private emotional life. On 21 January, 1914 she was in Indianapolis for a miners' convention, the only woman on the platform. Though sick with a nervous headache at the thought of speaking to an audience she struggled through, and sat on the stage beside the president. "He is a true man." She loved the miners: "They are dear—so many British and they sing songs every now and again like the shearers and diggers at home."[1] In her *Memoirs* Alice Henry commented on Franklin's rapport with working men: "With the labour men she was always popular and could be depended on to draw them out and obtain from them opinions and information which they could never have put so attractively themselves." There seems no doubt that she was a young woman of considerable charm, to all manner of men.

When she returned to Chicago on 24 January, Demarest had gone back to Boston, but she lunched with W.B. Lloyd on the twenty-sixth and put a letter to Demarest on the Twentieth Century, the grand train running between New York and Chicago, demanding an explanation of one received from him. She heard Helen Keller's lecture on 5 February, which she "wouldn't have missed for anything", and went to Winnetka on the fourteenth for a short

Demarest Lloyd, 1915.

visit. On 16 February Demy arrived back, and they had a long talk after the others had gone to bed. Two days later she parted from him in anger at midnight at the Hotel Sherman after a quarrelsome dinner and her judgment on him was cold and harsh. "He was a conceited and inexplicable boor in every way but interesting study. Shall pursue him for copy." Notwithstanding her irritability and bad temper she still fascinated. Demarest sent her a great box of spring flowers on 28 February.

Mild-mannered Fred Pischel was still attentive, offering to teach her to drive, and while she worried desperately about an illness of her brother Tal, she filled her spare moments with speech classes, singing lessons and throat treatments. She farewelled the Burley Griffins on 10 April which must have roused her homesickness, but on 13 April there was a cheering letter. She received and accepted an offer for *Net of Circumstance* from the English publisher, Mills and Boon. It was almost five years since the publication of *Some Everyday Folk and Dawn*. This was the reassurance she needed that, in spite of the years sweeping past, the road to literary success still lay open ahead.

Her 1914 pocket journal shows Stella as still continuing to juggle her set of Lloyd friendships, visiting Lola and the family at Winnetka, writing to Demarest, lunching with William B., helping him choose new suitings at Fields, with Ethel Mason, attending a music festival with him at Evanston, and she meanwhile worked on leaflets for the waitress strike, and though she had already received an offer for it revised and cut *Net of Circumstance* for her agent A.P. Watt and prepared a copy of the revised manuscript for Doubleday, as she still hoped for an American publisher.

Even so she was not happy. The cycle of hard work, personal perplexity, ill health and discontent kept rolling on. She sighed " . . . wish I had a little income so I could get off the wheel for a little while." Difficulties in the office were piling up. "Trying days in office-worry. Wish Mrs Robins would get on to her job. Oh for a little private means. How the Lord does love the rich." Both Lloyd brothers were away for the summer and Fred Pischel, who was teaching her to drive, became her squire. After the fifth driving lesson they had a talk and "Fred was very dear XXXXX". The prim and childish symbols seem to represent kisses in this context.

Though her knotty personal problems had absorbed her attention during the first half of 1914, the industrial front had not been quiet. In the early months of the year the league was involved in supporting another big strike, this time by waitresses. Stella Franklin did not picket but worked hard on publicity and leaflets. Grey-haired Ellen Starr of Hull House had taken to the streets once more in support of the strikers and had been loaded into a patrol wagon on 2 March for protesting against the arrest of a picket. The strike had begun in February, centring around Henrici's and other restaurants in the Loop. Conditions for picketers had been cold and slushy in zero temperatures; there were many arrests and charges of police brutality again, two girls claiming to have had their arms broken. Franklin listened to Margaret Robins testify in the case. Reporting the strike for the tiny socialist paper was Carl Sandburg who made daily visits to the league office.

Ellen Starr was providing plenty of material for the press, as, the picture of respectability with cameo brooch, high collar, rimless glasses and straw boater, she was charged with disorderly conduct. After being deadlocked for eight hours the jury returned a not guilty verdict on 21 March. Said Starr, in the *Tribune* on the twenty-second: "It was not little me that was involved, it was the right of free speech." Ellen Starr had won her argument but the strikers struggled on for several more months.

There were entertainers other than Ellen Starr for Chicagoans during the first months of 1914, including Harry Lauder, George Arliss, Tetrazzinni and burlesque artists. The citizens danced the latest craze, the tango, and in April began to read a new sports journalist in the *Tribune*, Ring Lardner. W.B. Yeats was guest of honour at a dinner given by the literary group The Cliff Dwellers in March, and his companions there included Vachel Lindsay, Harriet Monroe and Carl Sandburg.

While Stella Franklin ground out her daily bread and agonised over her unhappy novels other writers were finding Chicago a centre of stimulation and excitement. Playwright Ben Hecht, then working as a reporter on the *Daily News*, where he was joined at the next desk by poet Carl Sandburg in 1914 (after his stint on the tiny socialist paper *Day Book*) has said about this era: "During its quick and vivid years—there were hardly nine (1913-22) Chicago found itself mysteriously, a bride of the arts."[2] The phenomenon was not so totally puzzling for the city had its tradition of the "Little Room", an informal association of those working in the arts, had bred a new school of architecture, and, partly through Hull House, had been dosed with new social ideas and the new drama.

One of the mainstays of the Little Room, Harriet Monroe was a long-time associate of Hull House and the league. On 23 September, 1912 she published a new magazine, entitled simply, *Poetry*, devoted to the modern movement in poetry, and Ezra Pound, Richard Aldington, W.B. Yeats, Vachel Lindsay and William Carlos Williams shone in its pages. In June 1915 it scored a dazzling hit with the first publication of T.S. Eliot with "The Love Song of J. Alfred Prufrock". Margaret Anderson's *Little Review* also drew contributions from innovative writers. The newness and raw pride of Chicago rejected the urbane traditions of other cities, even in literature. In the literary set Stella Franklin, who kept her creative writing endeavours a secret, met, "in moments of recreation, people such as Theodore Dreiser, Edna Ferber, Margery and Floyd Dell, Charlotte Perkins Gilman, Susan Glaspell, Ben Hecht, Edgar Lee Masters and all the crowd of Maurice Brown's famous Little Theatre."[3] But she never became involved with the writing group. To the world at large she was a feminist and reformist journalist and organiser, even the tale of *My Brilliant Career* being hidden.

Feminism rather than general labour-orientated reformism predominated in her writings of these months. In February 1914, in her profile of Elizabeth Martini, first woman to pass the Illinois state examination for architects she wrote:

> Many people enjoy the pleasant delusion that in the United States all professions are open to both sexes equally and that here is a paradise for women . . . It is only by comparison with other countries where women are in the position of invertebrates that American women seem so free.

In June she reviewed Lady Constance Lytton's *Prison and Prisoners*. Lady Constance, an impassioned suffragette and a woman of determination, had been arrested four times, but let off prison four times because of "a heart condition". Finally she disguised herself as a working class feminist and won her prison term. Franklin describes the book as a "trenchantly human contribution to the study of penology".

The Biennial of Women's Clubs which coincided with a big suffrage festival in June provided another feminist story for the August issue:

> There were present, as hard-working and earnest delegates, grand ladies with competent staffs of servants to conduct their homes and little women who did their own cooking and had to leave their babies with a sympathetic and trustworthy neighbour while they congregated to the Auditorium to do their share towards social adjustment . . . the congress was a testimony to the tremendous force that the feminist movement has attained among the most conservative of women, for the rank and file of the membership are by no means radical; they are the 'home women'; in fact the 'women's sphere' women, while those unnatural creatures who go out into the industrial field to support themselves and others were only represented here and there.

The convention was an enormous success with a speech by President Wilson's daughter as a compelling attraction. There is a tinge of sarcastic amusement in Stella's account:

> Around 8 o'clock Congress Street and Michigan Avenue were filled with rows of automobiles as on a grand opera night . . . Troops of ladies in evening dress, with a rare attendant swain, went up and down, asking questions of attendants, begging elevator boys to take them up to higher floors and knocking on stage doors and showing badges.

Carrie Catt spoke magnificently, but Charlotte Gilman "one of the greatest speakers extant had to curtail her message owing to the verbosity of the gentlemen who had preceded her".

Justice Higgins from Australia came to afternoon tea on 8 June and on the same day Bill Lloyd came in to say goodbye before he left for summer holidays.

Then, on 5 August, 1914, the *Tribune*'s banner headline swept aside individual preoccupations whether of the heart or the mind. "England at War with Germany'' was the sombre message.. ''The unthinkable, the inconceivable has come upon us,'' declared the little magazine's editors, in their September article ''The Menace of Great Armaments''. Their pacifist message was plain if naive: ''War is inevitably the result of preparation for war.'' Stella tried to work on *While Cupid Tarried* but was ''so deadly sad about war that life does not seem worth living''. Racked by pain ('dentist tortured my lower teeth' is her entry for the twenty-sixth), so overtired that she and Ethel Mason lay down on the floor to rest in the summer heat on the twenty-eighth. Then Stella Franklin suffered a minor collapse.

> The outbreak of war was the negation of everything decent in humanity to me. Childishly I had been thinking that we were working for and moving perceptibly towards a better order. It made me sick like ptomaine poisoning. Fred Pischel found me sick [on 31 August] and took me home to his mother who nursed me out of a bout just like a gastric disturbance.[4]

The ghastly chariots of Mars had begun to roll, but, for the time being, it was business as usual, at least in America. On 6 September Stella started a new story, ''Forget It'', on the tenth she went to see the striking girl broommakers (an interesting account of this migrant girls' strike appeared in the October issue), on 26 September she went picketing with Sister Emma and the embroidery workers, and on the thirtieth gathered the story of this strike. She continued her talks with W.B. Lloyd on his return in September and drives with Fred Pischel, as well as the correspondence with Demarest. But to her disappointment a letter received on 14 September said that the war had postponed publication of *The Net of Circumstance*. And meanwhile the dissension between herself and Margaret Robins intensified, in spite of the fact, as Helen Marot noted in 1914, that: ''In the face of all difficulties the organisation of women in the last five years has advanced at an unprecedented rate.''[5]

18 War and love and "On Dearborn Street"

The split between Robins and Franklin, largely over the costs of the magazine, was widened by the war. Though both were professed and ardent pacifists emotionally they were drawn to opposing sides. Margaret Robins, daughter of German migrants, with happy memories of holidays spent in that country and with ties of blood there, had no particular love for England. She was one of many Chicagoans to feel this way and the large German population of the city reacted strongly to the news of war. On 6 August patriotic German-Americans marched through the streets of the Loop district, singing songs of their homeland and the "Star Spangled Banner", and they had support, for on 5 August the *Tribune* had said: "France is a corrupt and immoral nation. Belgium is not much better. But Germany is in the full bloom of health and power."

In *Tribune* of 8 August prominent trade unionists differed in their stands, for Agnes Nestor, an Irish American, was quite certain of her position: "Union labour has always been against war"; while John Fitzpatrick was uncertain: "It depends on the war."

Stella Franklin, though she had links with Germany through her Grandfather Lampe and had corresponded with her German cousins, had grown up in a British Empire country, and still retained some feeling for Britain. She wrote of this time later to American friend Leonora Pease: "... Life grew difficult. I was at last rendered unhappy being an alien, in my beloved America where it had not mattered previously. Persuasion was put on me to become an American."[1] Demarest Lloyd, an uncomplicated patriot interested in flying, wondered if a fighting airman might have the power to thrill her heart.

Relationships with Margaret Robins were at flash point. On 5 September Mrs Robins was very disagreeable when she came into the office, and on 29 September at a party at West Ohio Street she was angry with both Franklin and Alice Henry when they came to the front door (instead of, presumably, the back).

The various entangled threads of Franklin's life were breaking and pulling apart. Her flirtatious friendships, her health, her writing, her league career, her loyalties were all under strain. Fred Pischel was becoming more and more affectionate and the arch correspondence with Demarest Lloyd, which he continued to sign with whimsical names such as Sinbad the Sailor, or The Bull, and to address her as Dear Psyche, Hornbreaker and Her Ladyship, had reached a stage where some sort of resolution was necessary. Following a talk with Fred on the lake front on 2 October—"XXXXXX", as she coyly recorded, in her personal code—Stella packed her bags far into the night and next day took off for a holiday in Boston, staying with Octavia Sprague at 113 Gainsboro Street.

In Boston she had the happiness of seeing Aileen Goldstein again, and, during the weeks there, her friendship with Demarest reached its peak. The story is told in her little journal.

On 6 October: "Demy came at three and away we went over hill and dale at such a great rate—grand! Dinner at Ferncroft and came soaring home at 9.45. Rather cold in spite of coats." They watched the Harvard versus Washington and Jefferson football match on the tenth, on a lovely summer-like day, then went driving again. They went dancing at the Carlton on the afternoon of 14 October, then on to dinner at the Crown of Providence, Rhode Island. After more dancing they had supper at Newmans and Demy consumed too many cocktails and too much champagne from puritanical Stella's viewpoint. They reached home at 4 am with Franklin most alarmed by his driving and manner. It seems an innocent enough escapade for someone of the class and style of collegiate Demarest, but it was a turning point for Franklin. "Escaped death or tragedy by a very small margin," she noted, and when Demy asked her to tea the next day she refused. But on 16 October she relented, they went driving again, and Demy "almost retrieved himself".

Possibly she fancied herself in love with him, perhaps even marriage presented itself as a possibility. She was sleepless again and on the seventeenth, though she tried to start on "a movie-play-novel", "the muse was jealous of the other things" that occupied her mind. For his part Demarest seems to have behaved with well-bred good humour to this contrary woman. He enquired on the sixteenth whether they had quite finished the game of chess, was it her move or his, and he assured her of his sincerest good will. He told his "Dear Illusion" on the eighteenth that if he had been able to stand it this long he could still. Stella was "feeling abject, rebellious and discontented and shuddering at the thought of being compelled to go back to Chicago grind", but with her unquenchable energy set to work on a "Red Cross" story and attended a NWTUL meeting. A week later she was panicky about her future—"O miracle come and save me". Though Demy took her driving again on 3 November, and though she was to see him a few more times in Chicago it was really the end of a chapter. On 7 November she left for Philadelphia via New York to attend a national executive meeting of the NWTUL and the AF of L convention.

The friendship with the Lloyds had provided background material for *The Net of Circumstance*. The relationship with Demarest Lloyd furnished copy for the novel she had begun as a series of stories about a girl named Sybyl (later the unpublished manuscript *On Dearborn Street*)[2], another work of mediocre quality in a similar vein of self-pity to its predecessor. It deals with the romantic entanglements of Sybyl Penelo (a shade of Sybylla Penelope Melvyn), a dainty little feminist who runs a stenographic service in a building on Dearborn Street, in partnership with an even daintier young lady, Edna Maguire (some relative of Ethel Mason, perhaps?). Sybyl who has "greeny-grey-blue-brown eyes" and "an impertinent thrust to her chin" bewitches the wealthy forty-year-old hero, Cavarley, who has espoused the women's movement as his hobby. Miss Penelo also has a very remarkable literary gift and "quite a bunch of society people claim credit for books and articles that would have been terrible only for Miss Penelo". Though "richly dowered with sexual attraction", and sometimes lonely, she is very much against any plan to settle down in a dear little home. She is accustomed to having men cluttered underfoot and has come to Chicago from some distant, mysterious region . . . maybe South Africa or perhaps Australasia.

Bobby Hoyne, cousin of that Tony Hastings who disappeared into Europe in *The Net of Circumstance*, is a rich young man about town from the east coast, who comes west for a few weeks every winter. He too falls in love with Sybyl but falling in love "was an everyday affair with him like taking a bath". He is a recent convert to Christian Science but "at thirty he was as unsophisticated as a boy of ten with his first bicycle. As a roaring young blood he could be quite enlivening . . . but as a Christian-Mental Scientist he was a plague and a bore". He visits Sybyl's office frequently and they have many final partings ruminated over in letters. They dine out together and go driving wrapped in his fur coats.

But she is determined not to marry. "It is a game between men and women but the whole of life is on men's side . . ." War breaks out and Sybyl is distraught. Then Bobby is killed in a car race. To cheer her up Cavarley teaches her to dance and they caper at the Dreamland Pavilion and restaurants. But she still stands firm against marriage, though she confesses, "I nearly married [Bobby] because he was so self-sure and decided and I was all at sea and unhappy and reckless because of the war." Her distaste for men's sexual wanderings prevents any commitment: "In the feast of love women can sit down to a banquet of soiled and broken meats or go hungry. I prefer to go hungry."

But crushed by loneliness, she turns to Cavarley for comfort.

You'll be there in the night when the phantoms come, those grey ghosts of
the futility of life and the pain and the sadness and the sin and the shame and
no way out. And the fear, the horrid fear of death, nasty repulsive death which
has to be plunged through someday, and old age, creeping down the hill an
object of repulsion, no more youth or beauty.

She refuses however to "be kept in a tame hen coop to sit and wait for you
coming home at night with no entertainment but a matinee or a woman's
club or some futile fancy work . . . I escaped from the home, thank God. Ran
right away out into the world."

The book ends on an indecisive note. Perhaps she marries understanding
Cavarley and cultivates with him a garden of "sweet williams, and
pomegranate, and a magnolia tree, and jessamine and Japanese honeysuckle,
and passion flowers, and little English daisies, and anemones and gillie flowers
and wall flowers, and cowslips, and ribbon grass, and sweet scented thyme
and the sweet scented verbena tree". Like the child Stella, far away now in
time and space, Sybyl thinks seed catalogues and dictionaries the most
fascinating of all literature.

But perhaps she continues on her lonely path, for at one stage she states,
"I am never going to marry. The war has finally decided me and I have
finished experimenting." And her last word is, "I don't want to be loved or
married. I want to be left alone." Yet the manuscript ends with Sybyl,
Cavarley and his Aunt Pattie setting sail together for Jamaica to escape the
atmosphere of the war.

It would be unfair to imply that these two novels of Chicago are a kind of
historical record, but they offer an index of Stella Franklin's unhappy
indecisiveness at this stage of her life and perhaps a key to its resolution. The
war with its frightful wastage of human life seems to have been a turning
point in her position on marriage and motherhood. Late in life she expressed
her gladness that the first whiff of the 1914 war finally decided her against
being an incubator of GIs or Tommies or Poilus or any other sort of male
heroes whatever.

Both the published *Net of Circumstance* and the unpublished *On
Dearborn Street* are to a large extent feminist tracts. The heroines, while
scrupulously chaste (Sybyl's "code of relations with men was perfect chastity
of the old-fashioned sort"), are torn and questioning, seeking the answer to
the problems of sexual relationships between men and women, wrestling with
Lawrentian-like questions within the narrow limits of strict conventions.

Of the men who came within Stella Franklin's compass at this time W.B.
Lloyd, though attractive and intriguing, was out-of-bounds as a married man
and a father and exuberant, happy-go-lucky Demarest, while delighted to flirt
and fond of her stimulating company, may have had no particularly serious
intentions, and he seemed to annoy her with his collegiate complacency.
The model for faithful Osborne Lewis and kindly Cavarley was most likely
comfortable Fred Pischel—"very dear", if not exciting, a supporter of

feminism, a bachelor, well enough off, and totally devoted to her. Should she settle for a life with such a man, for companionship in her loneliness as the dreaded years advanced? Was marriage to a gentle and reasonably sympathetic man the answer or not? Could there be freedom in marriage for the woman or must it mean subservience? Was there yet a Galahad, a knight of pure romance, a perfect man who would understand and comfort and support but leave her free and independent?

And beneath the craving for liberty lay the turbid question of her sexual attitudes, formed in the years of childhood and girlhood. Something of these attitudes emerged in *My Brilliant Career*. To Sybylla it seemed that her mother's youth, freedom and strength had been lost in marriage, and that childbirth was "that most cruelly agonizing of human duties". Even when Sybylla had just accepted Harry Beecham's proposal of marriage, in a sort of hysterical rejection she then smashed a riding whip across his face. Yet, after another encounter with him, she rejoiced in "the many marks and black" which she found on her skin. Like her created character, Stella Franklin also was ambivalent in her position on marriage. She charmed many men, flirted with a number but could not accept the sexual submission then involved in marriage. Although she agonised over her loneliness, she remained disgusted at what she thought the sordidness of most sexual relationships in that era.

Ignez, in her broodings in *Cockatoos*, could reflect her creator's view: "Nothing had prepared her for one of the psychological disasters of her life. Her rearing among people who were reticent about 'the facts of life' and observed the restraints of monogamy in the isolation of the eucalyptus forests, as well as her own propensities put her on the side of the angels. Her ideal could have entered only à la Galahad as the perfect knight and true claiming the maiden undefiled." Ignez announces, "I'm never going to love at all, not in the way you mean—never," and explains, "I don't believe that the kind of love that the poets rave about is decent. How could it be . . . when *love*—she emphasised the word with distaste—can result in something cowardly and degrading, so unclean and unfair that every sense of decency and logic is revolted."

The coarse sexual double standards of her girlhood had appalled Stella. Like Ignez it was "an offence to her fastidiousness that was to affect her throughout life". When Aileen Goldstein years later dismissed *My Career Goes Bung* as not to her taste as she did not enjoy "sexy things", Stella retorted, "Your accusation is humorous because men who approached me in my nubile decades, always, when defeated, accused me of being sexless, of being not a woman but a mind."[3] Franklin had loved her father unreservedly as a child, and as a girl had been touched by the strength and tenderness of Joseph Furphy. Among women, Grandma Lampe and Linda had meant much to her, though the predominant figure of her adolescence, her mother, had aroused mixed passions. Stella had admired and respected Susannah Franklin but had raged against her asperity and coolness, and her suspected preference for Linda, to such an extent that a character, very like Stella, said in a curious story "Red Cross Nurse" which she began in November 1914: "On looking back across my life my grandmother stands out as the supreme love of my life, the one individual who never sold me out." [4] The feeling of betrayal, of being used, of not being loved for herself but for her value as an entertainer or worker, ran very deep.

In her life's journey Franklin had showered affection on many, building loyal and lasting friendships, but love, physical love, still seemed to her an illusion which could be a painful trap for women, particularly so for a talented woman. Her code in sexual matters was a simple, old-fashioned puritanism. "I loathe perversions and uncleannesses," she wrote much later. "Looking back, I know the plain things that I read (sub rosa) in my teens and earlier, never tarnished me in any way; but that lewdness that hypocritically parades as frankness still disgusts and outrages me." [5]

Beneath the sexual uneasiness lay the bed-rock of her being, her demanding and particular needs for freedom, without compromise or restriction in her personal life, for complete liberty, which she felt necessary in her struggle towards the goal of creative achievement. Her attitude might be termed narcissistic, but it was an artistic narcissism, an essential part of her being, for certainly the driving force of *My Brilliant Career* had been its unabashed egotism.

In *My Brilliant Career* Sybylla had cried: "In all the world is there never a comrade strong and true to teach me the meaning of this hollow, grim little tragedy—life? Will it always be this ghastly aloneness?" And, finally, sadly, Stella Franklin accepted that aloneness as the price of her freedom. Ten or so years after she left Chicago she epitomised her answer to Sybylla's question in the final words of *Prelude to Waking* (written in 1925 but not published until 1950):

Preservation of things
Most precious to the human soul
Sometimes lies in renunciation.

19 The end of a career

When Stella left Demy behind in Boston the matters of love and sex were put aside as she concentrated on her league work. In her report on part of the AF of L convention in the December 1914 issue of *Life & Labor* she was critical of the fact that the number of women among AF of L delegates was still alarmingly small—"... even those trades having a large proportion of women workers sent only men delegates."

Among delegates and visitors were Mary Dreier representing her sister, Agnes Nestor, Melinda Scott, Pauline Newman, Emma Steghagen, Rose Schneiderman and Helen Marot, "author of *American Labor Unions*, a book which is attracting a good deal of attention at present" and:

> ... an attractive, sprightly little woman turned out to be 'Mother Jones' the famous ventilator of the atrocities visited upon those who work in the mines in America ... Mr Furuseth (Seamen's Union) and Mrs Jones unite in facing the woman question absolutely from the wrong end; but are such picturesque and outstanding figures in labour's great struggle that they deserve a royal salaam in any case.

After Melinda Scott forthrightly declared that women were not cripples and would walk, rather than ride in the customary manner, Stella marched with other women at the end of the American Federation of Labor torchlight procession which passed through an arch of electric light bulbs to be reviewed from a specially-erected grandstand by President Gompers and other union leaders. "And that's how it goes, marching to victory in an army of peace," she concluded. The convention had its lighter moments, including the Bartenders' Banquet and Ball, then she returned to "poor old 200 E. Superior, how dirty and dreary after 1822 Pine Street, Philadelphia".

It was home again to the office, the dentist, the talks with W.B. Lloyd, to lunch with Sherwood Anderson and Margery Dell, to peace meetings at Hull House and elsewhere and to the never ending troubles of *Life & Labor*. "Billy" continued to call and take her out, to lunch at Sherman House where they had one of the "old talks", to an ostrich dinner at Midway

Gardens on 1 December and to *William Tell*. But the relationship was changing. He treated her as a confidante, discussing his marriage with her, on which she commented on the sixteenth: "I'm sorry for Lola and absolutely against Bill." Peace was the league's question of the hour, with pacifists Pethick Lawrence and Rosika Schwimiger in town. Christabel Pankhurst and Edith Lees (wife of Havelock Ellis) were visiting also and provoking discussion.

However, the financial position of *Life & Labor* and of the league in general loomed largest of the clouds in secretary-treasurer Stella Franklin's life. She had informed Melinda Scott on 16 November that she had been forced to come home early from Philadelphia because she had run out of money as her salary was six weeks overdue. She had expected Margaret Robins to talk finance in early December but Robins had gone off to Florida, and when Franklin returned from Philadelphia she reported on 16 November that "I found Miss H at breaking point with everything left on her hands and $800 owing this very minute on *Life & Labor*". She thought that the magazine was a necessity and that the convention due in June 1915 might help,

> but what are we to do to keep the wolf from the door right now . . . I have felt like pulling out more than once but since I have been talking to you [Melinda Scott] and see how hard your row is to hoe I feel that I want to stay in and help you tooth and nail till you can get someone better to put in my place. I guess the fighting never was better than it is right now.[1]

Melinda Scott replied on the twenty-seventh: "It does not seem as if we can pay the salary of another organiser if we cannot pay the secretary's salary to begin with."[2]

Alice Henry was in deep distress and did not see how they could continue to bring the magazine out as they could not meet their bills. She was particularly oppressed by the matter of rent. She did not see how Mary Galvin could continue her work as a travelling sales representative, as the board had decided, if she had no *Life & Labor* to sell. Margaret Robins was enraged by what appeared to be financial mismanagement and muddling by the secretary-treasurer, and wanted *Life & Labor* funds kept as a separate account and brought under the direction of the executive board. She suggested that the only way out was for the magazine to borrow $1,000 at six per cent. Stella Franklin thought that an appeal to affiliated groups for a $2 or $5 affiliation fee might help, but Alice Henry had become desperate and wrote to all board members and to Margaret Robins on 19 December, 1914, saying the position was critical, that the magazine owed the printers $600 and that the January issue would not appear unless some of the debt was paid. "What am I to do?" she finished.

Margaret Robins angrily telegrammed all board members, including Stella Franklin, that the letter had been sent without consultation, and in a follow-up letter on 23 December declared herself astonished and nonplussed. She reminded them that she had pledged $2,500 for only three years in 1911 to *Life & Labor* and in September 1913 had said that it would be impossible to continue contributing because of financial difficulty. She wrote that she had received no report on her proposal for a loan and that none of the letters received from Miss Henry or Miss Franklin had referred to financial difficulties (yet Henry had written to her on 7 December and on the nineteenth saying the position was critical). Possibly Robins meant she had heard nothing of it until the crisis was upon them. On 29 December she sent a telegram to Olive Sullivan at the office asking if Saul had really refused to print the January issue and saying if necessary she could borrow $500 for six months. Actually Mary Dreier finally lent the money.

The New York league also sent $100 and Saul was willing to print the January number as a loan, but Alice Henry was unwilling to go further into debt. At a *Life & Labor* staff meeting on 31 December Margaret Robins suggested that each board member might borrow $25 or $100, but those present, namely Mary Anderson, Agnes Nestor, Alice Henry and Stella Franklin, thought this no resolution of the recurrent difficulties. Margaret Robins could be justifiably angry at the way things had been allowed to drift, and yet to have overloaded one person with financial as well as organisational burdens, as well as much of the work of the magazine, had been an error of judgment in which she shared. Whatever the allotment of responsibility for the situation, passions in the office were inflamed. It did not look like a happy New Year.

But Christmas had been pleasant. W.B. Lloyd gave Stella a lovely bottle of perfume, sent the girls a big box of candy and kissed Alice Henry and Ethel Mason under the mistletoe in Alice's room. Christmas Day Franklin spent quite alone, revising "Red Cross Nurse" and "never said a word to anyone and never saw a soul all day". In the midst of the fuss about the magazine her mood became calmer, happier, perhaps because she had made some decisions. Whatever had passed between her and Demarest, it was the end of the flirtation. The friendship with W.B. Lloyd, though it is feasible that for her he was "the love that is not free", had settled into platonic affection. He took her to lunch at the Congress on Boxing Day 1914 and she invited him to lunch on Boxing Day 1915 if they were still alive. "He was to be in a position to accept or refuse as he thought fit."

After the stormy office meeting of New Year's Eve she was tranquil and content compared with previous New Year Eves. She had "a lovely hot bath while the whistles were blowing a fanfare to the New Year ... I hope I can make it a busy and therefore satisfactory division of my hitherto unsatisfactory life."

Though W.B. Lloyd discussed with her some marital troubles in the first weeks of January and though Demy, on holiday, made a brief reappearance on 26 January and sent her a ''queer missive'' on 13 February, her main preoccupations now were with the league and the magazine. ''Dismal day because of uncertainty re *L & L*,'' she recorded on 3 February, 1915. There were rows and recriminations. Alice Henry, usually submissive as far as Margaret Robins was concerned, spoke up to her on 8 February in defence of Mary Galvin, the touring sales representative for the magazine. In spite of all the drama Stella found time to go to hear Christabel Pankhurst speak. Her verdict in her diary was: ''Christabel terrible.'' Feeling was red hot between the staff and Margaret Robins. ''Another trial for our life,'' noted Stella on 23 February and she and Ethel Mason the following day considered the glorious idea of chicken farming together.

There were diversions, a peace committee meeting on 26 February— ''windy affair as usual, nothing in it''—a visit from Rose Schneiderman, a singing lesson, and work on the typing of the Sybyl stories (*On Dearborn Street*) on 12 March. Rose took her to lunch on the twenty-second and a *Life & Labor* meeting followed—''tried for our lives again. I was the one decapitated this time'', her journal reads. So next day Stella worked for the national league. ''Such a relief to be rid of *L & L*.'' Edith Wyatt of the league's ways and means commission had thought Miss Franklin's double position unfair to her strength and professional future and had recommended on 12 March that Miss Franklin be released from the associate editorship, which she had ''always generously contributed''[3]. But Alice Henry had had enough and was planning to resign, so Margaret Robins wrote quietly to the executive board on 23 March saying that Miss Henry ''owed it to her health and strength to undertake work less harassing and fatiguing''[4], and that she would ask Miss Franklin to edit.

But to Stella it must have seemed that for her the *Life & Labor* saga was over. It is a familiar story in such enterprises. The rich patron fears being exploited, the hard-working employee thinks the patron does not understand practical costs. Each thinks the other's well is inexhaustible, of money on one side, of energy and devotion on the other. The collision between the hot-tempered impetuous president and the cranky, tired secretary-treasurer was inevitable, particularly with the thrust given by emotions about the war.

The president's former fondness for her *protégée* had soured. She suspected Alice Henry was not resigning of her own accord, and she felt that though Franklin had some excellent qualities as writer and editor she was certain that she had neither Henry's devotion to the labour movement nor her fine vision. This was a reasonably accurate assessment but ungenerous in the face of the energy and effort and intelligence which Stella Franklin had put into the cause.

Alice Henry, having worked closely with her associate editor, was fairer, writing on 6 April to Margaret Robins that:

the plan of mutual co-operation that has hitherto existed between Miss Franklin and myself ... has not only been of untold benefit in the development of the league and magazine but has been the only feasible plan in these still early days of a pioneer movement such as ours and eminently practical.[5]

Margaret Robins had her own ideas. On 2 April she sent Stella some lovely red tulips as a peace offering. Demy had popped up again on 30 March but Stella had by now decided that he had no *savoir faire*, and an April fool joke of hers resulted in a ''violent'' and utterly final letter from him. So that was that. She could give all her attention to work. She spent some time with Rose in the last weeks of April and on 10 May moved offices from 127 Dearborn to 166 West Washington to save expense. It was the calm before the final storm. She noted laconically in her diary that Margaret Robins took her to lunch on 17 May and told her she wanted Emma Steghagen for national secretary, and that Franklin must stand down. A second career had collapsed around her. But not quite, for left with Alice Henry's adamant resignation, Margaret Robins needed an editor for a much diminished *Life & Labor*, and Stella Franklin was to fill the gap. In the weeks following her abrupt dismissal, Franklin tried to straighten the books and prepared for her last convention as secretary. She had expressed no opinion in her diary on Margaret Robins' decision, but a parcel she collected from the post office on 28 May should have cheered her—six copies of *The Net of Circumstance*. Perhaps after having plummeted downwards in one career, she might rise in another.

However hard Stella Franklin might work as an activist she did not fit neatly into a slot. To many of those most devoted to unionism she seemed to lack seriousness. Recalling the attitude of a unionist friend, Mr Mullenbach, she said:

> He always regarded me as more entertaining than heavyweight serious. I can remember once in the midst of an office upheaval when it seemed as if we had come to the end of funds he was most distressed about what might happen to Miss Henry. He looked at me and smiled and said there would always be a place for me because I was such a lively little flutter budget but a serious elderly woman like Miss H etc.[6]

The doubting temper that had assailed her religious faith struck at her activist beliefs. She could not turn to evangelistic Margaret Robins with her uncertainties though she could to more temperate Jane Addams. She has related that: ''In the midst of a big strike, when the controversy was heavy and bewildering I once telephoned Miss Addams and said I should like to see her, and immediately came the reply that I was to spend the night with her to give us time for discussion.''[7] Franklin had breakfasted with Miss Addams on 16 November, 1910, in the midst of the great garment strike and it is probably to this occasion that she refers. Even as she concocted her ingenious propaganda she had wavered, whereas Margaret Robins never faltered while in the field. Jane Addams was more understanding, since on the eve of that strike she had been "frightened".

Then, unlike the positive Robins who had mobile but strong links with politics (Raymond had seconded W.J. Bryan's nomination for presidential candidate at the Democratic Convention in 1908, and both Raymond and Margaret had been energetically active in the Progressive Party), independent scratchy Franklin had little faith in politics. Since she felt ill-used and over-worked she sympathised with those in a like situation, without being too theoretical about it, and since she was poor and constrained in life by lack of means she tended to be antagonistic to the rich even when they were resolutely on her side.

In her writings she could not resist the occasional thrust at the wealthy do-gooder type:

> All American cities are as rich in rich women as a Christmas cake in plums, most of them Nonconformistically industrious in good works. True, some of them accomplish little beyond the sentimental evaporation consequent upon sitting in luxurious halls or 'parlours' listening to talks about the unsavoury conditions of less efficient and less enterprising nationals.[8]

In her interview with the women delegates to the Republican Convention of 1912 she was very sympathetic to Florence Porter who "early lost the voting member of her immediate family and has had to fend for herself and three children" but dismissed in a few lines Isabella Blaney who "has always had the advantage of wealth won for her by others", a sharp and rather malicious jab which must have pained Margaret Robins.

In the midst of her falling out with her president she aimed another rancorous dart at the "ally" type in her *Life & Labor* article "Peace Ahoy", dealing with the "peace ship" in the April 1915 issue. Though she lauded the pacifist cause, she added:

> I wish to go on record as entirely free from sentimentality regarding this delegation. Instead of worshipping them as heroes, I envy them as a group of comfortable women, able to set sail on an adventurous entertaining holiday while lesser mortals are tied to the inconspicuous and monotonous grind which upholds the social fabric. But it is encouraging that Leonora O'Reilly representing the National Women's Trade Union League went to speak for the working women and that Annie E. Molloy of the telephone operators, was also aboard, for in the last, catastrophes, blunders, inefficiency all grind most devilishly on that being lower down than the lowest down—the working woman.

Her novelist's awareness that life is not cut and dried and easily arranged by theories made her sceptical of visionary plans in others. While true believers like Alice Henry and Margaret Robins saw the brightness of an approaching dawn in their ardent unionism, Franklin's perception held a spreading dark patch of pessimism about the stupidities of man and the sadness of time and decay, and with her hypersensitivity about the brutality of masculine power she reacted against that power expressed by dominating male unionists such as Samuel Gompers.

In total she lacked the whole-hearted vehemence and certainty of Margaret Robins. Joseph Furphy had said of her years before: "If only you could hate properly you would be a great man, Miles," and she later wrote, "When I got to America the fact that I did not harbour resentment but was lenient with admirer and detractor alike was again spoken of as a defect."[9] While she might zealously beat the propaganda drum she had no particular liking for the real cut and thrust. She certainly harboured resentment and bitterness about her personal situation, about her lack of means, her overwork, her dreary living conditions and her bondage to her job, but they were generally hidden in her diaries and her pseudonymous novels. To the world she was witty, high-spirited, pretty and pleasure loving, more concerned with feminism than with unionism — in short, not solid enough.

And as a final offence to Margaret Robins and Emma Steghagen there was the running sore of the British nationality of which she could not purge herself. There was the monarchy, the empire too, and all that they represented to republican unionists. But she could not throw away her childhood. When she felt unwanted in her second homeland she said: "I shall go and take up my own nationality. I have a wide empire and a wonderful new continent of my very own."[10] So she made her plans.

But first, as usual, there was a convention.

20 A last hurrah and the American Federation of Labor

The Fifth Biennial Convention of the NWTUL opened in New York on 7 June, 1915 at 43 East Twenty Second Street. There were ninety delegates, as against the seven present at the 1907 convention, about the time that Mrs Robins had hired Stella Franklin as an assistant. Los Angeles and Philadelphia now had branches. The preliminary report on the training school was presented and the decision made to start a school for working women, combining a year's classroom work with practical organising experience.

Samuel Gompers addressed the convention on trade unionism and women's suffrage and was given a standing ovation, along with Margaret Robins. In bringing fraternal greetings from the AF of L he hoped for better co-operation. The resignation of Alice Henry who was leaving her editorship to become the league's official lecturer was accepted with regret and Henry, surrounded by delegates singing ''Trade Union Girls Arise'', was presented with a purse containing $500 in gold, largely donated by Margaret Robins and her sister Mary Dreier. On the final day, 12 June, Rose Schneiderman with a pretty, affectionate speech presented Stella Franklin who was leaving the secretary-treasurership to become editor of a much diminished *Life & Labor* with a pair of opera glasses, as a little token of love ''to our sister and co-worker''. Franklin responded, ''I shall always treasure your beautiful present in memory of the ideal of the Women's Trade Union League which is to bring every little girl a chance to see the pageant of life not only from the galleries but from the grand opera boxes.''[1] Her diary reads: ''I escaped a presentation but was finally caught and given a beautiful pair of opera glasses.'' Schneiderman had had the task of nomination of Franklin's successor. Diplomatically she said: ''As a member of the executive board I know we are very desirous of having Miss Franklin as our next editor of *Life & Labor* now that Miss Henry has resigned. Therefore it is right that we nominate someone else for secretary.''[2] Miss Steghagen was elected secretary and S.M. Franklin, nominated by Miss Matthews of the telephonists, was elected to the executive board.

In her report on the magazine Alice Henry paid tribute to the co-operation of the national secretary and co-editor Miss Franklin, to her literary ability and to her work in ensuring the accuracy of national league news, so assisting *L & L* to fulfil its function. She mentioned, in assessing the influence of the magazine, that an article on broommakers had been reprinted in one of the leading Chicago dailies with a circulation of 380,000 though for months it had been impossible to get publicity in the daily press for the broommakers' strike. The proceedings do not mention that this article was by Stella Franklin, though credit is given to other reprinted writers, Rose Schneiderman and Louisa Mittelstadt. Perhaps Franklin removed her name from the report when editing, or perhaps Alice Henry did not mention it, for Henry too, in spite of their friendship, had found Franklin difficult and abrasive. Following a meeting with her years after these events Henry wrote to Margaret Robins: "We had such a beautiful time with Stella Franklin. How she has improved, matured and softened and yet lost none of her brilliance."[3]

Immediately after the convention there was much work to be done, proceedings to be written up, correspondence to be answered. A comprehensive report on the convention later appeared in the July issue of *Life & Labor*. And Stella Franklin had made a decision. At the executive board meeting on 15 June she presented her resignation as editor of *Life & Labor*. It was a shock and a problem for the league. After much discussion she was prevailed upon to hold her resignation in abeyance until after a three-month vacation with full pay, to begin on 12 September. The board members requested that she not mention the matter and the discussion of it in her minutes. As well as a reluctance to lose her services there must surely have been some guilt about her treatment to produce this generous settlement and odd request. But that night she wailed: "Oh how I expected to be free . . . and they tied strings on me. So exhausted that I was ill."

Next day with Robins she called on the great Gompers, then worked for two weeks on proofs and letters. After visiting Carrie Catt on the twenty-ninth and seeing *Birth of a Nation* the next day, she left New York on 1 July. In Chicago she helped arrange a peace demonstration to welcome Jane Addams home, and worked on the convention article. She took comfort in the affection of the Pischels, seeing Pavlova with them, and going driving with Fred. But she thought matters were past mending with the magazine.

When unsuspecting Margaret Robins returned from New York on 7 July she found that though her sister Mary had sent $500 in January to pay the printers' bill, there was still $500 owing on other accounts. Financially things were in as bad a state as ever. Naturally she was displeased. Stella Franklin took over as editor on the twelfth and handed over the secretaryship to Emma Steghagen on 15 July. By the end of the month both Franklin and Mary Galvin were determined to make Robins consult about the winding up of *Life*

& Labor, for they felt the magazine was not operable without more attention to financial planning.

At conferences on 29 July and 7 August, where Mary Anderson and Elizabeth Christman were also present, it was voted unanimously that the magazine be reduced to eight pages and that Miss Franklin, besides writing and editing, attend to the correspondence. On 6 August Stella had decided that she must get away from such a situation. Finally, from various notes and the Sybyl stories, which she had been tinkering with since January 1913, she began to compose *On Dearborn Street*, and also worked on "Chicago trade union women in conference" which appeared in *Life & Labor* in September, in the midst of the squabbling. She felt that Mary Galvin's dismissal on 7 August was brutal, and on the ninth sent in a letter providing for her own "elimination". Margaret Robins was vexed but Franklin insisted. This time she did not change her mind.

One can sympathise with all parties to the hostilities. Robins had thought the financial road ahead was again clear only to find it as blocked with debt as ever. And this after her sister's generosity. Franklin and Galvin felt that Robins would not confer about the problem, would not admit the impossibility of the situation and would keep putting off a final decision. There were other reasons for the president's annoyance, for attitudes to Germany and England still festered, and, in addition, she was disturbed about a strain in relations between the league and the American Federation of Labor in which Stella Franklin had figured.

From its earliest days the federation had supported the unionisation of women in theory, and even in practice to a small extent, appointing Mary Kenny as a women's organiser for a few months in 1892, and Annie Fitzgerald to a similar position for a period in 1907. The activities of the league in the garment workers' strikes, and in the strikes of the button makers and the carpet makers, as well as in the aftermath of the Triangle fire disaster raised Samuel Gompers' opinion of league members, though he had disliked the league's interest in a labour party as he thought industrial action should be entirely separated from political action. After the national league supported the American Federation of Labor against the radical International Workers of the World group in the controversial Lawrence textile strike of 1912 the federation made a grant of $150 a month to the league to be used in organising women workers. The Lawrence strike was a dividing line, as other women activists such as Mother Jones and Elizabeth Gurley Flynn and even Mary O'Sullivan, founding league member, were pushed further into the IWW and radicalism as a result.

In his early years of power Samuel Gompers had the reputation of believing that a woman's place was always in the home, but by 1914 he was urging the organisation of women in the *American Federationist*, the journal of the AF of L. The question remained: Who was to do the organising? Gompers distrusted intellectual feminists and opposed the protective government legislation for women and political action which Margaret Robins and Stella Franklin favoured. In their struggle with the mighty federation Margaret Robins had proposed embarrassing it by promoting closer ties with Canadian Labor, and her secretary had backed her. Gompers feared that the league might split the workforce, that influenced by the "allies" it might be more a women's movement concerning itself with suffrage and the education of women than with trade union matters. As a trade unionist "first, last and always", as he described himself in his autobiography, he was convinced that the fight for industrial freedom should not be confused with other matters. Many of the league members, for their part, suspected that while to Gompers trade unionists could be of either sex, a trade union leader should be male. Some were inclined to believe that, with his conservative rank and file fearful of the effect women might have on conditions in their trades, Gompers paid merely lip service to the idea of organising women. Though Margaret Robins disagreed with him by demanding a minimum wage for women, she had recognised always the enormous strength of the AF of L and had sought association with it from early days, setting league conventions and conferences to coincide as often as possible with those of the federation. By September 1915 she was writing in the *American Federationist* that problems of working women would only be solved when they became part of the American labour movement. Yet while she was warring with the editors over *Life & Labor* a storm blew up involving the AF of L and the league, and Stella Franklin in her capacity as secretary-treasurer.

It started with a donation from a male union towards the task of trade-unionising women. Frank Duffy of the United Carpenters and Joiners wrote to Gompers on 5 March, 1915, and also to the league secretary-treasurer, offering to donate $500 to the league for work to be done by and through the AF of L. Margaret Robins and other league members felt slighted that they were not entrusted with the money. At a meeting of her national board on 4 June Robins reported on the matter and on attacks made on the league by Samuel Landers, with whom she had clashed during the garment workers' strike. A letter was read and approved at the Fifth Biennial Convention and sent to Frank Duffy by Secretary Stella Franklin. It was decidedly stiff-necked in tone in thanking the Brotherhood, for it said that no money sent to another organisation could be regarded as a contribution to the league. Any contribution must be sent to the secretary-treasurer of the league.

Duffy's reply to Miss Franklin on 18 June was long and indignant. Among a number of complaints, he asked if the league questioned the honesty of President Gompers and Secretary Morrison. He reminded them that his union was one of the few to have helped the league in the past, and commented sarcastically that, if his union had not given them a cent, then it would not be in trouble with them now. He was also angry about the way in which past donations had been spent. "We were under the impression they were to be utilised for organising purposes, at least, we were led to believe that. Imagine, then, our surprise when through the AF of L by your own published statement we learned different."[4] Robins, Melinda Scott and Franklin conferred with Gompers, as reported in his letter of 24 June, 1915, and the matter was smoothed over with an apology to the offended Duffy, acknowledging his generous co-operation, and with an agreement to appoint a woman organiser jointly.

But it had brought Secretary Franklin under Gompers' eye and his irritation must have been added to by one of the discussions at the June convention. There the league's committee on judicial decisions, of which Stella Franklin was a member, had dared to endorse a report in opposition to AF of L policy. The committee had criticised one of the labour sections of the Clayton Arbitration Act, which had AF of L approval. The radical *New Republic*, of 3 July, 1915, seized on the disagreement over the Clayton Act and applauded the courage of girl delegates Louisa Mittelstadt and Agnes O'Brien in opposing the powerful Gompers.

Gompers, in a strongly-worded letter to Margaret Robins on 31 August expressed the view that this difference would furnish ammunition to opponents and should have been discussed in private conferences, not publicly at the convention. He hoped his letter would receive the earnest consideration not only of Margaret Dreier Robins but of those associated with her in responsible positions in the league.

This certainly included the ex-secretary who had taken a large part in arranging the convention and its discussions and who remained a member of the executive board. When league board members Robins, Steghagen and Nestor called on Gompers for a conference on 9 September, 1915, Stella Franklin, though still a board member, was left out.

When Franklin finally cut the painter Gompers agreeably helped her on her way with letters of introduction to leading British trade unionists. But at the moment she was out of favour with the league and with the federation. The new career built with so much effort and distress was blowing away about her as were some of the friendships she had made. The employer-friend who had welcomed her so warmly was now coldly antagonistic. Despondently Franklin wrote to an old friend in Australia, Kate Baker:

> Nothing seems to matter now as it did then—and the dreams and ambitions and glee in life of the old 'Merrily Miles'—could they ever have been . . . Oh if I could only go again to Melbourne town in all its glory of Toorak Road and St Kilda Road. My, my heart grows faint with longing and nostalgia and life is such a wistful little phantom.[5]

Though she had published two novels since leaving home (one recently) and was working on another, she mourned: "I have written nothing since I came over—nothing to speak of—it is impossible to write and live as full a life as I have been doing. I was going to take this year off to scribble but the war again has ruined all.''[6]

Stella Franklin had been with the league for seven punishing years which had ended in dismissal and defeat. It was more than nine years since she had seen her family and her homeland, but it was still impossible to return, to admit that the green promise of young Miles had been blackened and broken. But the publication of *The Net of Circumstance* at least gave her some hope, and in her baggage was a new novel. Away from the hammering demands of ''reform'', and from the tossings and turnings of her emotional relationships in Chicago, in a more tranquil, withdrawn atmosphere she might yet do that something ''great and good'' that had once been expected from her. But it needed time and rest. She had burned the candle at both ends for so long, worn too many confusing hats, and now paid the price in exhaustion and disappointment.

The words she wrote about a character in her novel *All That Swagger* may express her feeling at this nadir of her life: ''He had lost the rewards of both the careful and talented and the daring and the gifted. He must flee from the scene of his immediate defeat; nor could he face return to Australia with empty hands and no definite profession seeing the flourish with which he had departed.''

Franklin had decided to try her luck in Britain. It was a matter now of tying up a few loose ends. Margaret Robins had pursued a policy of ignoring her while she worked out her notice but said goodbye on 17 September, and the next day Franklin rallied her women friends for a farewell tea-party, in the south-east corner of the Narcissus Room at Fields. The copy of the invitation to Lola Lloyd is surprising in its insensitive tone towards that good-natured lady, for it reads:

> Perhaps it was the general war poison which has affected me this last year to the extent of feeling that I had never met one single human being not excepting my mother who would not exploit me to the last inch for what of usefulness and entertainment was in me and then throw me on the scrap heap without qualm.[7]

At almost thirty-six the bitterness of the little girl about her mother remained. Whether she received the invitation or not, not surprisingly Lola did not come, but the party was a great success with Editha Phelps, Margery Curry, Mrs Pischel and Emma, Agnes, Ethel, Mary Galvin and Leonora Pease all gathering to say goodbye, while social leader Mrs Medill McCormick wrote in October about her distress at Stella's leaving.

The last pages of her 1915 American diary are happy ones. W.B. Lloyd took her to a farewell dinner at the Automobile Club, followed by *Watch Your Step* at the Illinois Theatre, Fred came and they ''fooled around in auto'', she had dinner at Hull House with Jane Addams on 18 October and stayed the night, then on the twenty-third Emma Pischel and Editha Phelps saw her off on the train with violets. In New York she dined with Alice Henry, lunched with Helen Marot, and on 30 October Alice Bean and Leonora (O'Reilly) and her mother escorted her on board the *St Paul*, which pulled out at noon. In the calm, mild evening she went to bed early.

Courageous and alone, as she had started her journey to the great republic, she left, jumping into the future again, across another sea, the U-boat-infested Atlantic. She had arrived in the United States at the time of the San Francisco earthquake, full of youthful hope. She left it in the midst of the gigantic catastrophe of the First World War, weary, disillusioned, but not defeated. There was always the future.

21 London postscript

On board ship, Stella Franklin's immediate reaction was joy at the release from pressure. "Off I set. Oh, the relief to be on the high seas where the war was never mentioned."[1] The *St Paul* docked on 7 November, and she went to a friend, Nell Malone, at 23 Woburn Place in London. She met Aileen Goldstein again and found a room in Holland Park. War or no, London rang with music and she saw *La Bohéme* on 17 November and heard Clara Butt on the twentieth.

She had little idea of what she planned to do. That ever-good-natured gentleman, Lord Tennyson, offered to put her in touch with people at the universities, Sir Arthur Quiller-Couch at Cambridge and Sir Hubert Warren, Professor of Poetry at Oxford. A university course would cost about £80 a term and give her a good training in literature and writing, but, however attractive a prospect, it was an impossibility in her narrow financial circumstances.

So, after spending a few days with the McMillan sisters, old friends from the Chicago days, active in the day nursery movement, she settled at Deptford, working at a "baby camp". As a pacifist she wanted no part in the war but Fred Pischel writing to her at 353 Evelyn Street, Deptford, was gently critical of the fact that she should mind babies so that their papas could go out to kill other babies' papas while their mummas made the bullets. As a relief from the children, or for her conscience, she attended anti-conscription meetings in the evenings.

The first euphoria of escape had passed off and she recalled: "God, how unhappy I was when I left America. I was thoroughly Americanised and had to make myself over."[2] A letter from her agent A.P. Watt of 25 November, 1915, brought little cheer, as he reported that Mills and Boon had returned *On Dearborn Street*, though they were prepared to consider a revised form eliminating the Americanisms. Then Franklin caught German measles, convalesced at Newport where she addressed the local Trades and Labor Council on America and the war, decided she had had enough of babies and returned to settle in London at Milton Chambers, 128 Cheyne Walk, Chelsea. She looked up Bernie Wise, the politician she had met in the old days at Rose Scott's, who was now Agent-General in London, and he gave her a reference.

She delighted in the old city, its nooks and crannies, and the beauty of its parks in spring. Brief diary entries show that she studied French, wrote articles for *The Sydney Morning Herald*, worked on a play *The Jackeroo* and on *On Dearborn Street*, went swimming in the Chelsea baths, started learning shorthand and formed a warm friendship with Lady Byles, taking tea with her at the House of Commons. (Lady Byles, friend of Ramsay McDonald and Prince Kropotkin, was the probable model for Lady Courtley of *Prelude to Waking*, "taken without subterfuge from another of my choicest friends".) To earn her keep Stella helped out at the Minerva Cafe, 144 High Holborn, W.C.1, but by May her money was running out (£5-13-0 from *The Sydney Morning Herald* and £6-2-6 royalties from *The Net of Cirumstance* noted in her 1916 diary was scarcely wealth). May was not a good month. A.P. Watt wrote to her cover, G. Marriott (an interesting echo of the name of her former admirer Guido Mariotti), at 37 Beaumont Street, Marylebone, saying that Duckworth had declined *On Dearborn Street* and she received word of the Lloyds' divorce.

She wrote to Agnes Nestor on 26 May, 1916 of her feelings on the *Life & Labor* imbroglio. On 20 December, 1915, she had tendered her official resignation as editor on completion of her three months' leave. Amy Field who had been acting editor was appointed as editor. In February 1916 Margaret Robins wrote to secretary Emma Steghagen, informing her that she was now in a position to cancel the debts of the magazine and the league and had paid the notes of $1,000 for the league and $2,000 for *Life & Labor*. The exasperated ex-editor fumed:

> There is nothing I should have liked so much as to edit *L & L* and try to make it a real working women's publication and because I had put my youth into it and it is hard to start all over again in these times, but Mrs Robins having expressed her desire to exterminate me, among others, and having acted accordingly there was nothing else to be done. She has produced funds now that she has got her own way and I hope all goes well. She is a powerful engine to the cause of the emancipation of working women in its present weak and initial stages and to be valued accordingly.[3]

Life & Labor, though revived, soon fell ill again. Field resigned as editor in November 1916 and Robins took over. In October 1921 it was suspended for some years owing to financial stringency.

Though Franklin was rather homesick for Chicago she had no plans to return. In London she felt happier and calmer, grew fatter and stronger, putting on seven kilograms, but by October 1916 she was once more very dispirited, particularly on the fifteenth when she "opened Marriott letter at last", and on 31 October there is a familiar ring about the diary entry, "feeling utterly down and out".

As winter approached she "found no comfort in the windy holes that the English have instead of homes", and when she went with radical suffragist Cobden Sanderson whom she had met in Chicago, to hear famous socialist Sidney Webb speak on conscience she "found him an awful frost". In view of a decision made some months later perhaps her blood was warmed more by a passionate Serbian meeting she had attended a few weeks previously.

In the cold, black city she tended her guttering literary candle, sending off *Net of Circumstance* to the Paget Agency in the hopes of an American edition, and "Diary" to Watt & Son. In her "little dugout", surrounded by the photographs of her American friends, Agnes, Ethel, Alice Henry, the three Dreier women, and of her family and Keir Hardie, she wrote to Agnes, ill in the Sacred Heart Sanitarium, that she hated to think of Agnes' vacations merely being a sort of massage to get ready to sacrifice herself again and that they had to trust in God a great deal more to do his work in his own way. The reforming fire was burning rather low. She cut her final tie with her future in the NWTUL when she resigned from the executive board on 31 December, though she sent Emma Steghagen $1 for simple membership. The Chicago career had vanished into the past, buried in the files of the league and *Life & Labor*.

The literary progress had come to a halt too. In May 1917 the Paget Agency sent back the two Ogniblat L'Artsau novels to G. Marriott care of Franklin's friend, H.F. Malone, 42 Stevenage Road, S.W. with a stinging report attacking the workmanship, characterisation, plausibility and vocabulary, as well as the academic, didactic, "highbrow" manner and the preoccupation with sex. A play, *Virtue*, was returned in May 1917 also. By this time Franklin had made another decision, for after eighteen months of striving there was no sign of encouragement in her literary career. On 12 March, 1917 she applied to serve with the Scottish Women's Hospitals for Foreign Service. On 6 April her beloved America, under one of her heroes, President Wilson, declared war on Germany, and in June 1917 the first United States division arrived in France.

On 8 June, 1917, Stella Franklin, ex-labour leader, still pacifist trade unionist and writer, was accepted for service in Macedonia with the Serbs as a cook with the America unit of the Scottish Women's Hospitals. "I suppose that just means American money, and no such luck as it being run really by Americans," she reflected.[4] But, at least it was a women's organisation, formed by the National Union of Women's Suffrage Societies, and Serbia was highly regarded by the women's movement as a "suffragette nation", particularly so by jingoistic Christabel Pankhurst.

In high spirits, with a postcard from Agnes from Kansas City and Olive Sullivan's folding cup in her knapsack, proud of her boots and jolly, short skirt, she sent her address for the next six months ("if I survive," was her light-hearted rider) to be passed on to league friends. Her arm was in a sling

Stella as a war-time orderly.

due to inoculations but she was happy to be setting out on a new adventure. "Merrily Miles" had recovered her élan, and, faced with the dangers of the Serbian front and the hard work of hospital service (all for £25 a year, which she never received), she was cheerfully undaunted.

Still searching for excitement and achievement, the brave little girl of the Monaro ranges was now a woman of thirty-eight, weakened by the strenuous efforts of the Chicago years. She began service on 28 June, and travelled through Paris and Rome to Taranto in southern Italy. From there she crossed to Salonika, then moved up country to Ostrovo, near Monastir, to serve with the Serbian army in the field. In July 1917 she wrote to her mother: "I am quite well and happy for me, trying to pick up a little Serbian as one is perfectly helpless without it. I am enjoying the old Australian heat and we go swimming nearly every day in Lake Ostrovo."[5]

In some ways, though, it seems to have been a brutal experience. In later years Franklin told of seeing, as the snows melted, the bodies of soldiers still in battle lines. Something of this grim atmosphere is caught in her Mayfair novel, *Prelude to Waking*, where the heroine Merlin, "a bright young thing", is said to have:

> . . . achieved the Balkan fronts during some of the first great battles and retreats . . . Persuaded to collect funds in North America for the Women's War Hospitals she explained that it took more courage than to cross the Plain of Kossovo in a blizzard, to gather up human fragments under shell-fire around Bitolj, or to go on retreat from Ushtsche to Podgoritza over a trail where the howls of the wolves sometimes blotted out the sound of the pursuing guns, where the lorries decorated the sides of the icy precipices, and where the weak dropped out continuously.

Franklin wrote elsewhere: "I have seen so much of life, so many men dead, heard their shrieks when suffering wounds."[6]

Yet, in general, the period in Serbia, as recorded in the unpublished manuscript *Ne Mari Nishta, It Matters Nothing*, was a happy one, reasonably peaceful and interesting "after the fret and worry of reform drudgery, a royal holiday". Yet Stella left the posting within a year,[7] though she had been moved from the role of cook to that of orderly, for she contracted malaria, and "they ran an exploding needle of quinine into the region of the sciatic nerve . . . and murder I never suffered like it. . . . and had to be drugged at last".[8]

It was three months before she could walk without dragging a leg. She applied for release from service, and on 4 February, 1918 sailed with wounded troops on the hospital ship *Lafayette*, for Marseilles. She passed through Paris "once more" on 13 February, leaving through the Gare de Lyon for Le Havre and London. By April she had handed in her badges, but possibly continued in some kind of war work, for in March 1919, in cold foggy London she wrote to her mother: "must have a little malaria or flu . . .

I find it such a torture to keep on my feet ... shall certainly be glad when I work out my sentence.''[9]

After a visit to Ireland in August 1919, she settled into employment in post-war London as a secretary to the Finance Committee of the National Housing and Town Planning Association in Russell Square, an organisation of a welfare and reformist tone. Franklin's role here was much more low key than it had been in the National Women's Trade Union League, and, taking lodgings at 23 Harley Road, South Hampstead, she began writing obsessively in her free hours. She sent some ten articles to Rose Schneiderman in New York in 1919, hoping that Francis Hackett, a former Hull House resident, might be persuaded to print them in the *New Republic*, which he edited. He was not, but suggested she try the *New York Journal* or *World*. Her Mills and Boon royalty statement for 1917-18, recording no sales for that period for her novel, may have turned her attention more emphatically to the theatre, but she bombarded agents with manuscripts of all kinds. *Virtue*, a play by Mr and Mrs Ogniblat L'Artsau, was returned in March 1919 as too American. She used the same nom-de-plume for an unpublished short story, "A Business Emergency". In June 1920 she sent *Love Letters of a Superfluous Woman* to Huebsch in New York and to an English publisher. Her mood in the (presumably) accompanying letter, signed only "The Writer" was caustic: "Must we forever simper and smirk and hide under vapid conventional phrases what rages in our hearts?"[10] Not accepted. Similarly with some Irish-based sketches and a series, "Hold Tight: Life on a London Bus". Yet the demon drove her on: *Sammies in London, Dentist in Macedonia, John Stuart Mill, Arnold Bennett and Time* (by Mrs O. L'Artsau). None appealed.

Theatre in London was booming in the twenties, with reputations and fortunes to be made. Stella Franklin approached most of the famous actors and managers of the day with scripts—unsuccessfully. A play about a bush girl who became a *prima donna* was returned by Neilson Terry in September 1922, and also by Viola Tree. This may have become *The English Jackeroo*, about a squatter's daughter with musical ambitions, which A.E. Matthews and the Royal Magazine sent back to "J. Verney". In February 1922 Watt had informed "G. Marriott" that he had offered *Sam Price from Chicago*, a turgid novel about an Anglo-American war-time romance with pacifist overtones, to eleven publishers and all had declined it. Perhaps this was the final indignity which turned Stella to the theatre so furiously. But in 1923-24, *Phoebe Lambent and Love* found no favour with Beatrice Campbell, Violet Vanbrugh and Nigel Playfair.

On 15 October, 1923 Stella Franklin left England for a brief visit to first the United States and then to Australia.[11] The Pischels farewelled her from America on 21 November, by telegram to the S.S. *Tahiti*: "Bon voyage".[12] After seventeen years abroad she sailed back to her homeland. Her parents

top: Stella's parents' house, "Wambrook", Carlton, Sydney.
bottom: Stella Franklin at the end of World War I.

had been living since 1915 in Sydney, in the modest suburb of Carlton, in a cottage, Wambrook, called after Susannah Franklin's birthplace. They welcomed her lovingly and she wrote: "I had a wonderful reunion with my dear old father and mother and two brothers. My parents are strong and active and comfortable in a small way so that I feel content about that and shall be freed for adventures and experiments that entice me."[13] Like Dick Mazere in *Back to Bool Bool* she must have wondered on the voyage out: "Could old scenes survive the test of time. Had imagination enshrined a beauty which reality must shatter leaving adolescent memories bankrupt."[14] She visited Goulburn, the Brindabellas and her old haunts, "rushed all over the country seeing old friends"[15], went riding and swimming with her brothers, then in March 1924, boarded the *Moreton Bay* to return to London.[16]

There she kept up her dogged efforts, submitting *Three Women*, by J. Verney, to the Q Theatre in June 1924, with the customary lack of success. A play, *Old Blastus of Bin Bin*, was unwanted in January 1925, and a Mayfair novel, *Not the Tale Begun* (probably a first version of *Prelude to Waking*—another version was entitled *Merlin of the Empiah*), was returned by Blackwood in January 1926. *Prelude to Waking*, with a preface dated December 1925, but not published until 1950, is an attempt at a smart social comedy of twenties London, which ends with the married narrator, Nigel Barraclough, bidding farewell to love, for the heroine Merlin Giltinane "was not one to accept romance from any old father of another woman's children". He reflects: "There was no refuge for me now but Fortitude and Time."

Mostly set in West End apartments and English country houses, with British, Australian and American characters exchanging their pompous and prosy ideas on post-war relationships between their homelands, and their cranky notions on the problems of eugenics and social reform, the book is stiff and artificial in style, the tone being set by the names allotted the characters, such as Lady Pamela Clutterbuck-Leeper, Mex Tarbuck, Lord Montraven of Tintwhistle, and Esme la ffollette. But it contains a significant phrase from writer Nigel, who states after a visit to Australia: "I'll begin my great Australian series." Though all through 1926 Stella Franklin continued to approach actors like Sybil Thorndike, Oscar Asche and Gertrude Forbes Robertson with works bearing the name of J. Verney or Sarah Miles, another project had been forming and had begun to absorb her.

The visit home had stirred the well of her being. Going back to the countryside of her childhood, seeing again her plains and ranges, experiencing again the simplicity and hardship and isolation of life there, soaking again in the beauty of the bushland released a torrent of nostalgia for the country and its pioneers, for her forebears and their way of life.

In 1928 a novel, *Up the Country*, by a pseudonymous author, Brent of Bin

Bin, was published by Blackwood of Edinburgh. (By this time Stella Franklin was home again, for on 11 March, 1927, Kate Baker had welcomed back ''Merrily Miles'' to ''God's own country''.[17] Stella's brother Tal had died suddenly in 1925, and her parents needed her.)

The book was very well received, especially in Australia, where *The Bulletin* of 2 January, 1929, thought it in the running as an Australian classic, but the identity of the author was kept a close secret. The novel dealt with the history of pioneer squatters in the Murrumbidgee-Monaro district in the 1850s and 60s. In simple language and believable dialogue, it recreated the world of the first settlers in that area. A famous old bushman and squatter, P.S. Watson, a friend of Franklin's in Chicago and London (through his feminist wife Nancy Lister Watson), has been credited by P.R. Stephensen with providing some of the anecdotes and atmosphere of this work. But the vitality of the background and the characters, particularly chivalrous young Bert Poole and stout-hearted matriarch Mrs Mazere, spring from the depths of the author's spirit, from her love of the country and probably from her feeling for her father and grandmother.

In 1930 *Ten Creeks Run*, by the same mysterious author, appeared, and carried the saga of these families, Mazeres and Stantons and Pooles and Healeys, further, to the middle of the 1890s. It too won applause. Its simple love story, in which mature Bert Poole, now ''Uncle Bert'', and somewhat dulled by being over-idealised, plays hero to lively young Milly Saunders, is set against a realistically sketched panorama of bush life with its severe sexual codes.

Back to Bool Bool, published in 1931, jumped some thirty years from the late nineties to the late 1920s, and, though it was not as highy praised as its predecessors, *Punch*'s reviewer on 18 November recommended it in some doggerel verse:

> Deep drama and laughter
> Our author can mix
> An hour with him better
> Than three at the Flicks
> We commend to the full
> Back to Bool Bool
> A book to go after
> It's seven and six.

The book was prompted probably by the Tumut centennial celebrations of 1924, the year of Stella Miles Franklin's visit home. A number of offshoots of the original intertwining squatting families of the two previous books return from overseas, where they have made careers, to join in the celebrations of the centenary of Bool Bool, and to make their judgments again on the land of their birth. They include poet Dick Mazere, journalist Freda Healey, prima donna Mollye Brennan, and London man-about-town Major-General Sir Oswald Mazere-Poole. As a critique of Australia in the changing twenties,

when the old bush life was being supplanted by suburban values, it has a good deal of interest, if one overlooks some embarrassingly bad dialogue and a certain amount of preaching by the author. Still, as well as being entertaining reading, it completes the saga, and so has its place. But the first two of the series drew hearty acclaim.

Little Miles Franklin, distressed and discouraged at her seeming failure after her early brilliant success, had fled the Australian scene to face the challenge of the mighty United States, as Stella Franklin, labour leader and feminist. Stella Franklin, in turn, had disappeared from America to surface after years of striving at Seat S9, in the reading room of the British Museum, as that secretive old gentleman, Brent of Bin Bin.

A new novelist had been born, lacking in that silvery trumpet note of youth that had sounded in *My Brilliant Career*, without that breath of childish genius that had stirred the early work, but more generous in attitude and wider in range. Miles Franklin's most probing critic, Ray Mathew, said of her that from a literary point of view nothing ever happened in her life after the publication of *My Brilliant Career*, in 1901. In a sense this is true, for it is the period before that date which lives in her work, whether as Miles Franklin or as Brent. The experiences of her childhood and youth, including the stories of the immediate past handed down to her, left the deepest marks of pain and happiness. All the drama of America and Europe did not move her to its genuine expression in writing. It was as though all life was a charade after the idyll of childhood and the anguish of adolescence, that truth was buried back in time in the ranges of her homeland.

Three other works were to be added to the Brent of Bin Bin series: *Cockatoos* (in previous forms *On the Outside Track* and *Exodists*, an unsuccessful entry in a *Sydney Morning Herald* novel competition in 1947), which dealt with the period of the Boer War and of Franklin's youth and still retained some of the passion of that age; *Prelude to Waking,* that impossibly mannered and artificial Mayfair novel; and *Gentlemen at Gyang Gyang*, set in the Monaro district, written in the late 1920s. The latter is positively, puzzlingly bad, though it may give a clue to the author's hopes, for the heroine, an artist of "unusual promise, which suddenly dried up", leaves "London and Paris and old wounds and sordid mistakes" and in her homeland not only regains her creative abilities, but also finds her great love in Peter Poole. These two last mentioned books have the most exiguous connection with the main series, which in order of time runs *Up the Country, Ten Creeks Run, Cockatoos* and *Back to Bool Bool*. There is no coverage of the years from the turn of the century to the late twenties, for those were the years of Chicago and England.

The exact solution to the riddle of the masquerade of Brent of Bin Bin remains unknown. Yet, as with Mr and Mrs L'Artsau, the clues were there, and they were more obvious. Bin Bin appeared in *My Brilliant Career*, Brent

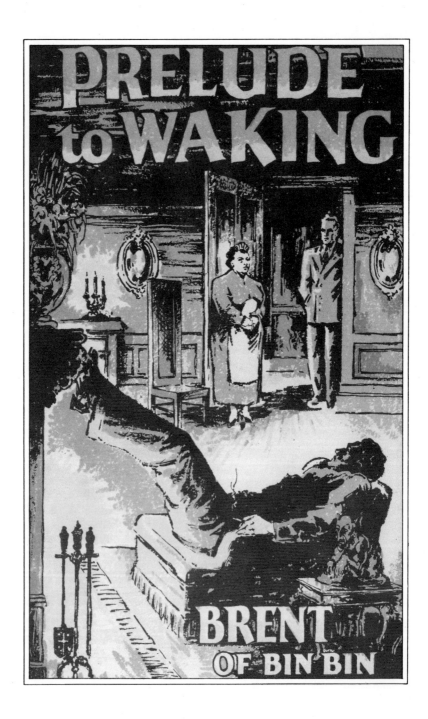

means steep or high and Bin Bin was her home station. Still Stella clung to her mask. In London there were friends in the secret, including Lady Byles. Writer and friend Mary Fullerton acted as agent with Blackwood in the first negotiations, and was joined later in the thirties by Jean Hamilton. But in Australia she was determined, despite the enthusiasm of the critics, to deny the true identity of Brent of Bin Bin. There were the memories of the family unhappiness about *My Brilliant Career*, and the pain of the years of disillusion and failure. It was almost twenty years since her last, almost unnoticed publication as Miles Franklin, and over twenty-five years since her dazzling debut. To seek shelter under an alias against failure, or worse, pity and regret, was natural to someone of her intense sensitivity and pride.

There were also financial reasons for the secrecy:

> If the public suspected that I had a hand in it even as editor or agent I am so situated that it would finish me and frustrate all my plans … No one in Australia has been confided in. The publishers advertise that they know the author and have told someone in confidence that as far as they know it is an elderly man of the pioneering sort. That idea must be confirmed—a sort of Australian Trader Horn appeals to me.[18]

She seems to have been the captive of one of her own jokes. Still the game amused her to the end of her life, and among her belongings she kept a man's outsized stiff collar, size nineteen, marked Brent of Bin Bin.

Whatever the reasons for the imposture, in the early Brent of Bin Bin books the phoenix had risen, even if disguised. Confident enough to return to her own society and drawn too by the problem of ageing parents, Stella Franklin became again Miles Franklin, writer and something of an Australian institution in her devotion to the cause of Australian literature. She published under her own name again, beginning with *Old Blastus of Bandicoot* in 1931, a rural romp in the vein of *On Our Selection*. In 1936 with her prize-winning novel *All That Swagger*, based largely on her Irish grandfather's life, she paid her debt to the Franklin side of her family. The brave, clever little girl who never gave up her particular fight though she turned her back on the world of action, persevered in her task whatever the cost in loneliness and weariness. "The prelude to life with its flowering morning and perfumed zephyrs had passed; she had learned that life was an isolating monster; that those worthy of maturity—the givers—must ever meet it separate and alone."[19]

22 Epilogue

It would be mistaken to think that with her renunciation of the wider world, her retreat from active involvement as a labour leader in the United States in order to concentrate her talents as a writer, Stella Franklin cut all lines of communication with her American past. The opposite is the case. The friends she had made in the league remained dear to her and memories were treasured. She is said never to have talked about her American experiences, yet she corresponded over the years with many of those with whom she had worked and lived during those fervid days, and longed at times to be with them again in America.

In the early years after her withdrawal she contacted a number of league visitors to London. Mary Anderson and Rose Schneiderman, delegates to the Peace Conference, representing women, had a happy day with her at Hampton Court and Kew Gardens on Easter Sunday, 1919. Franklin, looking charming in a brand new rose-coloured suit and hat, was accompanied by a young man from the US, undoubtedly Fred Pischel. The only blot on the day was that Hampton Court was not open, and rain and snow swamped the party before Kew Gardens opened in the afternoon. Stella also saw Doctor Alice Hamilton from the Hull House set, who was impressed by her shrewd assessment of the conservative isolationism to be expected from the dough-boys when they returned home.

Fred Pischel had continued to write during the war years and saw her in London in 1919. He had not given up hope, though returning home on board the RMS *Caronia* on 16 August, 1919 he complained he was desolated without a word from her. Once established in the Office of the Director of Consular Services at a better salary than in London he begged his twin-being to pack her little trunk and join him in America, assuring her he had not given away the secret of her writings. He beseeched her not to neglect him for too long or he would wither up and die. Stella kept her friendship with his sister Emma alive but any romance with Fred shrivelled away.

Her final letter to another old admirer, Demarest Lloyd, was one of her

W.B. Lloyd in court, 1923—"the millionaire red".

masked pranks. Demy had turned from a flighty young man-about-town into a settled and solid citizen. He had married Katherine Nordell in December 1916, had joined the Central Officers Training School at Camp Zachary in Louisville, Kentucky in October 1918, was a member of the Military Training Clubs Association and was prominent in the American Liberty League and the Taxpayers' Union. In May 1920 he became president of the Loyal Coalition and in that capacity sent a telegram to Lloyd George on the Irish question. Among letters he received on this matter at his home in Mt Vermont Street, Boston, was one dated 27 August, 1920 from an unknown O. L'Artsau reading:

> It is good to see the name [Henry] Demarest Lloyd as president of a league that points towards democratic internationalism. A more recent cablegram announces a sentence upon another of the Lloyd family which would seem to indicate that he too is due for congratulations for his courage in holding up the banner of freedom.[1]

That "another" was yet one more former escort, W.B. Lloyd, whose socialist leanings had tilted him finally all the way into the Communist Party. In 1920 he was charged, in company with nineteen other alleged members of the Communist Party, with violating the Illinois Espionage Act. Demarest seemed none too happy about his brother's notoriety as "reddest of the reds," for in his reply to Mr D. L'Artsoll on 11 January, 1921 he observed that while the writer's remarks on the Irish question agreed with those of his organisation (that Sinn Fein propaganda must be defeated by Americans in America), whether his brother was due for congratulations or not was open to question.

Demarest Lloyd continued his serious interest in Christian Science and became diplomatic correspondent for the *Christian Science Monitor* from 1922-24 and was the European cable editor in 1924-25. From 1926-31 he was a director of the Chicago *Tribune* and from 1931 edited and published *Affairs*. He died in 1937.

W.B. Lloyd, whom the press had pleasure in labelling "the Millionaire Red", was convicted after his trial in 1922, in which he was defended by Clarence Darrow, and was sentenced to one to five years in the state penitentiary at Joliot. An appeal to the Illinois Supreme Court failed but after serving one month of his sentence he was pardoned by Governor Small. Volatile William had yet another turn in his political stance later in life, for Emma Pischel reported in 1940 that William Bross had turned conservative. He married again after splitting with Lola and died in 1946.

The men disappeared but the women were friends for life. Through irregular letters and a few brief visits, Stella Franklin kept in touch with Agnes Nestor, Mary Anderson, Elizabeth Christman, Editha Phelps, Louise Dresden, Pauline Newman, Emma Pischel, Alice Henry, Rose Schneiderman and, after the dust from *Life & Labor* had settled, with Margaret Robins in particular.

From afar she watched their careers. Schneiderman grew to almost a cult figure in the women's movement of the US. Eleanor Roosevelt became her friend, Franklin D. Roosevelt read *A Christmas Carol* at the New York league's children's Christmas party in 1925, and in 1929 the league's twenty-fifth birthday was celebrated by President Schneiderman and members at Governor Roosevelt's mansion at Hyde Park. When F.D.R. became President he appointed Schneiderman to the Labor Advisory Board, the only woman. A guest at Hyde Park, at Campobello and at the White House, the blazing, golden-tongued little redhead from the orphanage had made, in worldly terms, the most brilliant career of them all.

Others made their mark too. Steadfast Mary Anderson, a close friend of Franklin's ("Tell Mary Anderson not to forget I'm going to live with her ... when I return," she had written to Nestor), became head of the Women's Bureau in 1920 and served there for twenty-five years, through five presidencies. Radical socialist Helen Marot (who had left the league in 1913, because she felt it should be run by unionist women), through her work on *Masses* and *The Dial*, "at the peak of her career helped provide a bridge between writers, artists and intelligentsia on the one hand and the left-wing labour movement on the other".[2] Agnes Nestor who was appointed by President Wilson to a commission on vocational education in 1914, was elected president of the International Glove Workers' Union in 1915, and was prominent in and remained faithful to the AF of L, whereas Elizabeth Christman joined the rival Congress of Industrial Organizations. Alice Henry followed up her *Trade Union Woman* of 1915 with *Women and the Labor Movement* in 1923. She studied briefly at the Chicago School of Journalism in 1927, then took up residence in Santa Barbara, California where she earned her living by hazardous free-lancing, then returned to live permanently in Australia where Miles Franklin was a helpful and devoted friend.

The longest and most serious correspondence, in spite of the angry parting in 1915, was with Margaret Robins. The tides of the passionate heart wash back and forth, and though this talented pair had found it finally impossible to work peaceably together, once apart each recognised again the special quality of the other. Mrs Robins saw that even though Stella with her casual attitudes had gone, *Life & Labor* still had financial and other difficulties. Stella, after her experiences in London and Serbia, her encounters with British complacency and with the horrors of war, became less attached to her British empire and more appreciative of the crusader quality of Margaret Robins in her battle for the less fortunate and for peace—describing her as "a centre of warm and nourishing association—a fire at which many will revive."[3]

By April 1920 they were writing to each other on good terms about the help Franklin could give to Robins' aunt in Germany. In 1922 Robins resigned from the presidency of the league and in 1923 visited England. Franklin, in the midst of dental troubles, was unsure whether she would see the Robins ("It is all up to the dentist whether I ever smile again"). But American know-how ("I wouldn't have an English dentist inside my head") must have solved the problem, for Franklin, bearing a beautiful bunch of sweet peas and accompanied by Elizabeth Robins, met them at the station.[4]

In 1927 Margaret regretted Stella was going to Australia to live as it seemed so far away. She wished that she would visit Florida for she was so full of wit and the joy of living. "Do come back to us Stella for we need you."[5] They continued to exchange long letters which were of great comfort to Stella in her difficulties with her elderly parents in the stringent early Depression years. The confidence between the two was such that Margaret Robins was one of the handful of people who knew the identity of Brent of Bin Bin—"Even Miss Henry has no inkling of me there. You know more than all of them about me. Perhaps because we were together during some of our formative younger years."[6] When Margaret sent a cable on 24 January, 1930, "Congratulations your great new book *Up the Country*. Three cheers ordering for bookshop lovingly Robins," Stella flew to the Sydney General Post Office under cover of seeing the doctor to reply, by AWA beam wireless, "Loving thanks. Please keep absolutely secret or all ruined financially."[7] Margaret Robins recalled the wonderful times they had working together and said that Stella Franklin had certainly been the most stimulating of her fellow workers, while Franklin remembered "the warmth and effulgence of my beloved Americans",[8] and averred, "If anything happened to you the light would have gone out of my America."[9]

Her attitude to her American experience was decidedly ambivalent. To Alice Henry she wrote: "For a literary artist to be drawn away by causes is a form of infidelity and has its punishment."[10] Of herself she said: "You might say she started to write as a girl in her teens and gave promise, many including Lord Tennyson and Prof. David called it genius. Then was diverted to sociology and was swallowed by the social movement in USA and London."[11] To Nettie Palmer she wrote: ". . . you were the wise or lucky one not to have gone working with dear Vida or anyone else in reform."[12] Yet she had loved the reformers, had revelled in their companionship and the excitement of the struggle. She missed them badly. To Elizabeth Christman she wrote: "You are still in your circle but you see all those warm full years of adventure and struggle and comradeship are cut right out of my life and kept over there."[13] In her later years she reflected, "I think I love the Americans best of all the people that I know,"[14] and: "The memory of what USA meant to me then and my friends is too poignant to be dwelt upon."[15]

In January 1931 Stella Franklin, despite financial problems, prepared to visit the United States and England again.[16] She saw Alice Henry in California in March 1931,[17] stayed some days with Doctor Young in Chicago and by May was in London, where she shared a flat in High Street, Kensington with Mabel Singleton, Mary Fullerton and a monkey. In September 1932 Franklin was filled with joy to be on her way back to America again, to be about to see Margaret and Raymond Robins once more and to be their guest in their dream world of sunshine and magnolias at Chinsegut. But on arrival in New York on 15 September, 1932 she was met with the startling news of Mr Robins' strange disappearance.[18]

Raymond Robins, a shadowy figure in her diaries of the Chicago years, was a man of great force and magnetism. He had headed the American Red Cross Mission to Russia in 1917-18 meeting Kerensky, Lenin and Trotsky, and had advocated recognition of the Soviet Union. He had been prominent in Theodore Roosevelt's Progressive Party, and then a member of the Republican National Committee in the campaigns of 1920 and 1924. He was also a leader in the National Christian Evangelistic social campaign and at the time of his disappearance was involved in a fight against bootleggers.

He checked out of his New York club on West 44th Street on 3 September, saying he was going to keep an appointment with President Hoover, and disappeared completely. When Franklin reached New York Margaret Robins was distraught, fearing he had been murdered because of his anti-liquor campaigning. The two women met in these unhappy circumstances at Mary Dreier's home at East 61st Street but the visit to Chinsegut was cancelled. Franklin returned to Australia. Some two months later Raymond Robins was found in the mountains of the Carolinas, living in a boarding house under the name of Rogers, bearded, dressed in overalls, posing as a mining engineer and prospector. When confronted with his wife he said ''I don't know the lady!'' He regained his memory in time at home in Florida but it was an extraordinary episode. One cynical newspaper woman remarked to Franklin ''he always was daft''.

After his wife's death in 1945 Raymond Robins carried on the cor- respondence with Franklin. She sent him a copy of *My Career Goes Bung* when it was published in 1946, with the comment, ''I think that you will perhaps understand it better than most people.''[19] There seemed to be a search for friendship between the two. He said of his meeting with Lenin that it was one of the two great moments of his life, asked if Stella Franklin would tell of her great moments in her journey in time, and invited her to be a guest at Chinsegut as long as was convenient for her. But Franklin never found her way to the Robins' beloved refuge and her own former haven, Talbingo Station, disappeared beneath the waters of Jounama Dam in 1967.

Stella Miles Franklin died in Sydney on 19 September,1954, a few weeks before her seventy-fifth birthday, leaving as her memorial her works, and also a fund to provide an annual award for an Australian novel. No monument marks her grave, for, as she had requested, her ashes were scattered on the

Stella Miles Franklin in 1948.

banks of Jounama Creek, near the site of the old homestead where she had been born.

If Stella Franklin had not been drawn, partly by force of circumstance, partly by bent of character, into the cause of women's trade unionism in her American years would her energies have been more satisfyingly used? In Australia she never spoke of her years in Chicago and regretted the waste of her resources in reform. The first youthful, romantic dreams of Sybylla-Stella of great fame and a great love died there under the pressures of reality. The loneliness of the girl in Stillwater became the loneliness of the woman in Chicago. The driving egotism which had brought her there could not be satisfied by imperfect suitors and a modest success. Caught in a mesh of poor health, loneliness, overwork and frustration she dashed and fluttered as best she could until she fled Chicago, under the impetus of war-time emotion.

When she turned outwards from the insoluble problems of self and backwards to her unsophisticated childhood and girlhood her gift returned, a gift now not for the heroic gestures of the great world but for the loving understanding and re-creation of the simple country people of the Monaro, seen through a golden glass of memory. The blazing anger of *My Brilliant Career* died down to a gentle warmth of affection in *Up the Country*.

> They hurried up from the rivers and ridges, the plains and gullies and peaks keen to escape oblivion. The old hands who had outlived their mates, the lonely ones from graves that were never fenced with none to know or mourn their passing, the little ones that had snuffed out before they were christened. All were there, reproachful if overlooked. 'Not one of you' I assert 'ever blew out another's brains, none of you was murdered or committed murder or rapine or political intrigue or took any part or felt any interest in the big wars (American and European) that raged in your day.
>
> They persist earnestly, emphatically, reassuringly that they have only to be kept true to life to make a book. They are equally insistent that they must be transcribed day by day as they lived. Tenderness these characters are entitled to, as are all that have gone their way to silence after gallant discharge of life, but it is not meet that they should be subjected to caricature.[20]

In spite of the significant contribution which she had made to the women's labour movement in the United States, Stella Miles Franklin found her second subject as a novelist not in the causes for which she had battled so hard there, not in the sorrows and pleasures of her years there, not in the glamour, the sophistication and the drama of the great materialistic city of her second homeland, but in the unremarkable simplicity and stoicism of the life of the pioneers, her own people, of the isolated ranges and plains of the distant continent of her birth.

Notes

NOTE: Except for letters to her relatives (vols. 108, 113x) the letters of Miles Franklin quoted from the Franklin Papers are hand-written drafts to 1906, and typescript copies after. Other letters are originals.

Chapter 1
The main source for the early years is Miles Franklin's *Childhood at Brindabella*. Other sources are the Franklin Papers, v.113x, Jack Bridle's *My Mountain Country*, *Talbingo*, and talks with Miss Leslie Bridle concerning the manuscript on the Franklin and Bridle families by her sister, Ruby Bridle.
1. *Back to Bool Bool*, p.251
2. *Childhood at Brindabella*, p.10
3. Franklin Papers, v.7, 163
4. *Childhood at Brindabella*, p.73

Chapter 2
Sources as for Chapter 1. Also letters of Charles Blyth, Franklin Papers, v.6, 1-168.
1. Franklin Papers, v.49, 53
2. *Laughter Not For a Cage*, p.99
3. Franklin Papers, v.49, 51
4. *Childhood at Brindabella*, p.85
5. Franklin Papers, v.6, 89
6. Ibid, v.6, 90
7. Ibid, v.6, 113
8. Ibid, v.6, 70
9. Ibid, v.6, 81
10. *Childhood at Brindabella*, p.41
11. Franklin Papers, v.113x, 163-5
12. Ibid, v.113x, 167-9
13. *Childhood at Brindabella*, p.158
14. Franklin Papers, v.6, 81-2

Chapter 3
Sources as for Chapters 1 and 2. Also letters of T.J. Hebblewhite, Franklin Papers, v.6, 307-334.
1. *Childhood at Brindabella*, p.158
2. Ibid, p.158
3. Ibid, p.141

4. Miles Franklin's scrapbooks, Australian National Library, 477/1
5. *My Brilliant Career*, p.4
6. Franklin Papers, v.6, 397-8 (overwritten by a draft of a letter to Lawson)
7. Ibid, v.6, 114
8. *Cockatoos*, p.23
9. Franklin Papers, v.49, 47 and 57

Chapter 4
Letters of Henry Lawson, Franklin Papers, v.6, 357-406; letters of Bertha Lawson, Franklin Papers, v.6, 416a-424; letters of E. O'Sullivan, Franklin Papers, v.6, 343-356.
1. Franklin Papers, v.80, 81
2. Ibid, v.6, 357-8
3. Ibid, v.7, 163
4. Ibid, v.6, 377
5. Ibid, v.80, 27
6. *My Career Goes Bung*, p.55
7. Franklin Papers, v.49, 65-76
8. Ibid, v.49, 102
9. Bread & Cheese Club: *Miles Franklin: A Tribute by Some of Her Friends*, p.37
10. Franklin Papers, v.49, 119-122
11. *New Idea*, 6 December, 1905, p.547
12. *Cockatoos*, p.42
13. Franklin Papers, v.7, 1-4
14. *My Brilliant Career*, p.137

Chapter 5
Letters of A.G. Stephens, Franklin Papers, v.7, 5-60.
1. Franklin Papers, v.8, 1-4
2. Ibid, v.8, 413-21
3. *My Brilliant Career*, p. 222
4. Earle Hooper in *Southerly*, 1955, no. 2, p.85
5. Franklin Papers, v.7, 135, 173, 199-202
6. Norman Lindsay; *Bohemians of the Bulletin*, p.144
7. Leon Gellert, *Sydney Telegraph*, 2 October, 1966
8. Franklin Papers, v.7, 66
9. *Laughter Not For a Cage*, p.218

Chapter 6
Letters of A.B. Paterson, Franklin Papers, v.7, 249-310; letters of Jessie Paterson, Franklin Papers, v.8, 221-274; letters of Fred Maudsley, Franklin Papers, v.7, 73-88.
1. Mitchell Library Mss Af 64/8
2. Franklin Papers, v.49, 93-96
3. Ibid, v.49, 114
4. Ibid, v.49, 115c
5. Ibid, v.7, 295
6. Miles Franklin wrote to Elsie Belle Champion on 31 January, 1936: "Do you know that I have found the companion volume to M.B.C. . . . No one ever saw it but George Robertson and he is dead." Franklin Papers, v.8, 355.
7. Franklin Papers, v.84, 175-177
8. *My Career Goes Bung*, p.211
9. Ibid, p.161
10. Lindsay: op. cit., pp.78-79

11. *My Career Goes Bung*, pp.206-7
12. Franklin Papers, v.84, 179-185b
13. Ibid, v.80, 41
14. Ibid, v.80, 105

Chapter 7
The letters of Rose Scott, Franklin Papers, v.8, 1-179; *When I Was Mary-Anne, a Slavey*, Mitchell Library Mss 445/23-241 n; letters of Elsie Belle Champion, Franklin Papers v.8, 351-370, and of Vida, Aileen and Isabella Goldstein, Franklin Papers, v.10, 1-145.
1. *My Brilliant Career*, pp.31-2
2. Ibid, p.33
3. Ibid, p.72
4. Miles Franklin and Kate Baker: *Joseph Furphy*, pp.116-7
5. Franklin Papers, v.49, 371
6. Ibid, v.59, 21
7. Ibid, v.51
8. Ibid, v.49, 123c
9. Ibid, v.48, 161a
10. Ibid, v.48, 161c-163

Chapter 8
Letters of Joseph Furphy, Franklin Papers, v.9b, 1-191.
1. Franklin Papers, v.51, 125
2. Mitchell Library Mss Af 64/4
3. Kate Baker Papers, Australian National Library Mss 2022, 1/103-4
4. *My Career Goes Bung*, p.206-7
5. Franklin and Baker: op. cit., p.118
6. Franklin Papers, v.80, 45-49
7. Ibid, v.49, 129c-140
8. Ibid, v.9b, 26-7
9. Kate Baker Papers, Australian National Library Mss 2022 1/472
10. Franklin Papers, v.8, 121
11. Ibid, v.55, draft on verso 289-293
12. Letters of Edwin Bridle, Franklin Papers, v.47, 37-88
13. *Cockatoos*, p.237
14. *Some Everyday Folk and Dawn*, p.320
15. *Cockatoos*, p.63, 198
16. *My Career Goes Bung*, p.93
17. Franklin and Baker: op. cit., p.99
18. *My Career Goes Bung*, p.233
19. *Back to Bool Bool*, p.401-2

Chapter 9
Correspondence with Mrs H. McKenzie, Franklin Papers, v.10, 367-394; letters of Edwin Bridle, Franklin Papers, v.47, 37-88.
1. Margaret Robins Papers, Florida Universities, 8 November, 1930
2. Franklin Papers, v.10, 249
3. Ibid, v.51, 133-135
4. Ibid, v.12, 26
5. *Colliers*, 6 February, 1909, p.16
6. Henry B. Fuller: *With the Procession*, p.363
7. Ibid, p.108

8. Franklin Papers, v.51, 135

Chapter 10
1. *Net of Circumstance*, p.238
2. *Ne Mari Nishta*, Mitchell Library Mss 445/4, p.188
3. *Net of Circumstance*, p.1
4. James Weber Lion: *Jane Addams; A Biography*, p.239
5. *Chicago Tribune*, 29 December, 1907
6. Mitchell Library Doc. 812
7. Winifred E. Wise: *Jane Addams of Hull-House*, p.168
8. Mitchell Library Doc. 812
9. Franklin Papers, v.108, 85
10. Ibid, v.51, 133
11. Ibid, v.11, 131
12. *Life & Labor*, February, 1913
13. *Cockatoos*, p.154
14. *Net of Circumstance*, p.19
15. Ibid, p.189
16. Franklin Papers, v.9b, 57
17. *On Dearborn Street*, Mitchell Library Mss 445/6
18. Franklin Papers, v.48, 167
19. *Back to Bool Bool*, p.40
20. Franklin Papers, v.111, 14 November, 1907
21. Kate Baker Papers, Australian National Library Mss 2022, 1/103-4
22. Franklin Papers, v.10, 255-7
23. *Red Cross Nurse*, Mitchell Library Mss 445/3

Chapter 11
Papers of the National Women's Trade Union League, Reel 1; letters of Margaret Robins, Franklin Papers, v.10, 255-311.
1. Franklin Papers, v.10, 255-7
2. Allen F. Davis: ''The Women's Trade Union League: origins and organization'', *Labor History*, v.5, no. 1, 1964
3. *Life & Labor*, February, 1913
4. *Woman at Work. The Autobiography of Mary Anderson As Told To Mary N. Winslow*, p.37
5. Alice Henry: *The Trade Union Woman*, p.76
6. *Dictionary of American Biography*
7. Caro Lloyd: *Henry Demarest Lloyd: A Biography*, p.174
8. Helen Marot: *American Labor Unions*, p.76

Chapter 12
Pocket diaries of Stella Miles Franklin, 1909, 1910, Mitchell Library Mss, Franklin Papers, 364/2.
1. Franklin Papers, v.24, 489
2. Eleanor Flexner: *Century of Struggle*, p.245
3. Margaret Robins Papers, 30 January, 1930
4. Franklin Papers, v.24, 141
5. Ibid, v.12, 26dd
6. Ibid, v.24, 141
7. Ibid, v.24, 159

8. Mary Dreier: *Margaret Dreier Robins, Her Life, Letters and Work*, p.61
9. National Women's Trade Union League papers, 19 May, 1910
10. *The Net of Circumstance*, p.19
11. Ibid, p.189
12. Ibid, p.50
13. Franklin Papers, v.80, 57, 59, 105

Chapter 13
Pocket diaries 1910, 1911.
1. John R. Commons: *History of Labor in the United States*, v.4, p.305
2. Mary Dreier: op. cit., p.72
3. John R. Commons: op. cit., p.307
4. Franklin Papers, v.111. p.c. 28 January, 1911

Chapter 14
Pocket diaries 1911, 1912.
1. Franklin Papers, v.90, 11
2. Ibid, v.111
3. National Women's Trade Union League papers, Reel 1, 4 November, 1911
4. Ibid
5. Rose Schneiderman: *All For One*, p.4
6. National Women's Trade Union League papers, 24 January, 1912
7. Franklin Papers, v.59, 35-47

Chapter 15
Pocket diary 1913.
1. Letter from W.B. Lloyd, Jnr, 17 December, 1979 to author
2. Margaret Robins Papers, 7 May, 1920
3. Franklin Papers, v.24, 137
4. Mary Dreier: op. cit., p.169
5. Cecyle S. Neidle: *America's Immigrant Women*, p.125
6. Flexner: op.cit., p.245
7. Marot: op. cit., p.75
8. *American Federationist*, August, 1913, pp.625-7
9. Baxandall, Rosalyn ed.: *America's Working Women*, p.159
10. Franklin Papers, v.10, 365
11. Ibid, v.24, 445
12. Margaret Robins Papers, 30 December, 1911
13. Franklin Papers, v.24, 487
14. Ibid, v.24, 149
15. National Women's Trade Union League papers, 8 May, 1908
16. Franklin Papers, v.24, 489
17. Ibid, v.10, 259
18. Ibid, v.63, 53-65
19. Ibid, v.10, 269b
20. Margaret Robins Papers, 17 June, 1913
21. Ibid, 25 July, 1913
22. Schneiderman: op. cit., p.167

Chapter 16
Pocket diary 1913.
1. Margaret Robins Papers, 17 June, 1913
2. Franklin Papers, v.11, 525
3. Ibid, v.11, 251

Chapter 17
Pocket diary 1914; letters of Demarest Lloyd, Franklin Papers, v.12, 27-261.
1. Franklin Papers, v.11p.c. 22 January, 1914
2. Ben Hecht: *A Child of the Century*, p.216
3. Franklin Papers, v.51, 133
4. Ibid, v.13, 117
5. Marot: op. cit., p.76

Chapter 18
Pocket diaries 1914, 1915.
1. Franklin Papers, v.13, 117-119
2. Mitchell Library Mss 445/6
3. Franklin Papers, v.10, 57
4. Mitchell Library Mss 445/3
5. Philip Whelan Papers, Australian National Library Mss 24991/400

Chapter 19
Pocket diaries 1914, 1915.
1. National Women's Trade Union League papers, Reel 1
2. Ibid
3. Ibid
4. Ibid
5. Ibid
6. Franklin Papers, v.12, p.26
7. Mitchell Library Doc. 812
8. *Prelude to Waking*, p.7
9. Kate Baker Papers, Australian National Library Mss 2022, 1/103
10. Franklin Papers, v.13, 117-119

Chapter 20
Pocket diary 1915; National Women's Trade Union League papers.
1. Proceedings, National Women's Trade Union League Convention, June, 1915, p.68
2. Ibid
3. Margaret Robins Papers, 17 December, 1932
4. National Women's Trade Union League papers
5. Kate Baker Papers, Australian National Library Mss 2022, 1/103
6. Ibid, 1/102
7. Franklin Papers, v.13, 5

Chapter 21
Pocket diaries 1915, 1916; Scottish Women's Hospital Papers, Franklin Papers, v.104; letters of Fred Pischel, Franklin Papers, v.13, 27-88; publishing papers, Franklin Papers, 80, 84, 88.

1. Franklin Papers, v.13, 117-9
2. Ibid
3. Agnes Nestor Papers, Chicago Historical Society, 26 May, 1916
4. Ibid
5. Franklin Papers, v.108, 21
6. Australian National Library Mss 2449, 1/400
7. Franklin Papers, v.104, 9c
8. Margaret Robins Papers, 7 May, 1920
9. Franklin Papers, v.108 p.c. 13 February, 1918, p.c. 18 March, 1919
10. Ibid, v.84, 193
11. Ibid, v.88, 53
12. Ibid, v.15, 109
13. Margaret Robins Papers, 1924
14. *Back to Bool Bool*, p.10-11
15. Margaret Robins Papers, 1924
16. Franklin Papers, v.48, 179c
17. Ibid, v.9, 225
18. Margaret Robins Papers, 30 January, 1930
19. *All That Swagger*, p.343

Epilogue
The letters of Margaret Robins, Franklin Papers, v.10, 253-365; the letters of Raymond Robins, Franklin Papers, v.39, 51-71.
1. Franklin Papers, v.12, 261c
2. E.T. & J.W. James and P.S. Boyer: *Notable American Women*, p.500
3. Margaret Robins Papers, 2 February, 1942
4. Ibid, 11 July, 1923
5. Franklin Papers, v.10, 279
6. Margaret Robins Papers, 4 March, 1932
7. Ibid, 28 January, 1930
8. Ibid, 30 October, 1930
9. Ibid, 8 November, 1930
10. Franklin Papers, v.11, 11 (verso)
11. Ibid, v.11, 131
12. Ibid, v.24, 511
13. Ibid, v.24, 144
14. Ibid, v.13, 119
15. Ibid, v.13, 141
16. Ibid, v.108, 71
17. Ibid, v.51, 157
18. Ibid, v.108, 117
19. Ibid, v.39, 59
20. *Up the Country*, p.vii-viii

Bibliography

Works by Miles Franklin

Miles Franklin's manuscripts and typescripts, Catalogue no. 47. Sydney, Messrs Berkelouw [1962]

Note: except for letters to her relatives (vols. 108, 113x) the letters of Miles Franklin quoted from the Franklin papers are handwritten drafts to 1906, and typescript copies after. Other letters are originals.

All That Swagger, Sydney, Angus & Robertson, 1947 (first published 1936)
Bring the Monkey, Sydney, Endeavour Press, 1933
Childhood at Brindabella, Sydney, Angus & Robertson, 1974 (first published 1963)
Laughter Not For a Cage, Sydney, Angus & Robertson, 1956
My Brilliant Career, Sydney, Angus & Robertson, 1974 (first published 1901)
My Career Goes Bung, Melbourne, Georgian House, 1946
Old Blastus of Bandicoot, London, Palmer, 1931
Some Everyday Folk and Dawn, Edinburgh, Blackwood, 1909
Sydney Royal, Sydney, Shakespeare Head, 1947 (?)

With Kate Baker
Joseph Furphy, Sydney, Angus & Robertson, 1944

With Dymphna Cusack
Pioneers On Parade, Sydney, Angus & Robertson, 1939

As Brent of Bin Bin
Back to Bool Bool, Edinburgh, Blackwood, 1931
Cockatoos, Sydney, Angus & Robertson, 1954
Gentlemen at Gyang Gyang, Sydney, Angus & Robertson, 1956
Prelude to Waking, Sydney, Angus & Robertson, 1950
Ten Creeks Run, Sydney, Angus & Robertson, 1952 (first published 1930)
Up the Country, Edinburgh, Blackwood, 1928

As Mr and Mrs Ogniblat L'Artsau
The Net of Circumstance, London, Mills & Boon, 1915

Articles
"Rose Scott" in *The peaceful army, a memorial to the pioneer women of Australia, 1788-1938*, Sydney, 1938
"Henry Lawson", *Meanjin*, no. 12, Christmas, 1942

Works on Miles Franklin

Marjorie Barnard, *Miles Franklin*, New York, Twayne, 1967

Bread & Cheese Club, *Miles Franklin, a tribute by some of her friends*, Melbourne, 1955

Ray Mathew, *Miles Franklin*, Melbourne, Australian writers and their work series, OUP, 1963

State Library of New South Wales, *Catalogue of Miles Franklin centenary exhibition*, Sydney, 1979

State Library of New South Wales, Mitchell Library, *Guide to the papers and books of Miles Franklin*, Sydney, Library Council of New South Wales, 1980

Articles on Miles Franklin

Alan Ashworth, *Southerly*, 1948, no. 2

Australian Woman's Sphere, 5 April, 1904

Marjorie Barnard, *Meanjin*, 1955, no. 4

The Bulletin, 31 March, 1904

Thelma Forshaw, *Nation*, Sydney, 10 August, 1963, letter 2 November, 1963

The Home Queen, 18 December, 1903

W. Moore, *New Idea*, 6 May, 1904

Jill Roe, ''The significant silence: Miles Franklin's middle years,'' *Meanjin*, vol. 39, no. 1, April 1980

Douglas Stewart, *Meanjin*, 1962, no. 4

Bruce Sutherland, ''Stella Miles Franklin's American years,'' *Meanjin*, December 1965

Tributes to Miles Franklin, *Southerly*, 16 February 1955

Books consulted

Edith Abbott, assisted by Sophonisba Breckenridge, *The tenements of Chicago*, New York, Arno, 1970 (first published Chicago, University of Chicago, c.1936)

Jane Addams, *Twenty years at Hull House*, New York, Signet Classics, c.1960

Jane Addams, *The second twenty years at Hull-House*, New York, Macmillan, 1930

John D. Andrews and W.D. Bliss, *History of women in trade unions*, Bureau of Labor report, 1911. Reprint, New York, Arno, 1974

Wayne Andrews, *Battle for Chicago*, New York, Harcourt, Brace c.1940.

Rosalyn Baxandall, Linda Gordon and Susan Reverly (eds.), *America's working women*, New York, Vintage Books, 1967

Gladys Boone, *The women's trade union leagues in Great Britain and the United States*, New York, Columbia U.P., 1942

William Bronson, *The earth shook, the sky burned*, New York, Doubleday, c.1959

John R. Commons, *History of labor in the United States. 1896-1932*, vol. IV, New York, Macmillan, 1935

Clarence Darrow, *The story of my life*, New York, Charles Scribners, c.1956

Allen Davis, *American heroine: life and legend of Jane Addams*, OUP, 1973

Emmett Dedman, *Fabulous Chicago*, New York, Random House, 1953

Mary Dreier, *Margaret Robins*, New York, Island Press Coop., 1950

Theodore Dreiser, *Newspaper days*, New York, Beekman, 1974

Theodore Dreiser, *Sister Carrie*, Doubleday, 1900

Bernard Duffy, *The Chicago Renaissance in American letters*, 1954

Eleanor Flexner, *Century of struggle: the women's rights movement in the U.S.*, Cambridge, Mass., The Belknap Press of the Harvard U.P., 1966

Henry B. Fuller, *With the procession*, New York, Harper, 1895

Harry Golden, *Carl Sandburg*, Cleveland, World Pub. Co.

Samuel Gompers, *Seventy years of life and labor*, New York, Dutton, 1925

Alice Hamilton, *Exploring the dangerous trades*, Boston, Little Brown & Co., 1943

Ben Hecht, *A child of the century*, New York, Simon & Schuster, 1954

Alice Henry, *The trade union woman*, New York, Burt Franklin, 1915

Alice Henry, *Women and the labor movement*, 1923

Hull House maps and papers by residents, Chicago, c.1895

Hull House Year Book, 1906-7, Chicago, 1907

Edward T. James, Janet W. James and Paul S. Boyer, (eds.), *Notable American women*, 3 vols, Cambridge, Mass., Belknap Press in the Harvard U.P., 1974

Rudyard Kipling, *From sea to sea*, Doubleday, Page & Co., 1909

James Weber Linn, *Jane Addams; a biography*, New York, Appleton, 1936

Caro Lloyd, *Henry Demarest Lloyd, 1847-1903*, New York, Putnam, 1912

Helen Marot, *American labor unions*, New York, Arno, 1969

Harriet Monroe, *A poet's life*, New York, Macmillan, 1938

Cecyle C. Neidle, *America's immigrant women*, New York, Hippocrene, 1976

Agnes Nestor, *Woman's labor leader: an autobiography*, Rockford, Ill., Bellevue Books, c.1954

Frank Norris, *The pit*, New York, Doubleday, Page & Co., 1903

Judith Papachristou, *Women together*, New York, Knopf, 1976

Ernest Poole, *Giants gone: men who made Chicago*, New York, c.1943

Patricia Rolfe, *Journalistic javelin*, Sydney, 1980

Rose Schneiderman, with Lucy Goldthwaite, *All for one*, New York, Paul Eriksson, 1967

Upton Sinclair, *The jungle*, New York, Doubleday, Page & Co., 1906

Martha Jane Soltow and Mary Wery, *American women and the labor movement, 1825-1974; an annotated bibliography*, Metuche, N.J., Scarecrow Press Inc., 1976

Helen Sumner, *History of women in industry in the United States*, Bureau of Labor report, 1911. Reprint, New York, Arno, 1974

Lincoln Steffens, *Autobiography*, New York, Harcourt, Brace, c.1931

Barbara Mary Wertheimer, *We were there: the story of working women in America*, New York, Pantheon Books, c.1977

Winifred Wise, *Jane Addams of Hull-House, a biography*, New York, Harcourt, Brace, c.1935

A.M. Wheeler, with M.S. Wortman, *The roads they made in Illinois history*, Chicago, Charles Kerr, 1977

Woman at work: the autobiography of Mary Anderson, as told to Mary N. Winslow, Minneapolis, University of Minnesota Press, 1951

National Women's Trade Union League. Proceedings of Biennial Conventions. 1909, 1911, 1913, 1915

Training school for women. Preliminary report, 1914. Chicago, 1914
WTUL of Chicago. Official report of the strike committee, 1910-1911

Articles consulted

Jane Addams. Interviewed in *Ladies' Home Journal*, March 1906
Allen Davis, "The Woman's Trade Union League: origins and organization," *Labor History*, vol. 5, no. 1, winter, 1964
"Democracy at work," *New Republic*, July 1915
Robert Dvorak, "The fighting garment workers," in *International Socialist Review*, January 1911
Robert Dvorak, "The garment workers strike lost. Who was to blame," in *International Socialist Review*, March 1911
Samuel Gompers, "Women's work, rights and progress," *American Federationist*, August 1913
Samuel Gompers, "Working women organize," *American Federationist*, March 1914
Samuel Gompers, "Coming into her own," *American Federationist*, July 1915
Francis Hackett, "Hull-House — a souvenir," *Survey*, June 1925
Will Irwin, "The First Ward ball," *Colliers*, 6 February 1909
James J. Kenneally, "Women and trade unions, 1870-1920," *Labor History*, winter, 1973, vol. 14, no. 1
Milton Plumb, "Records of the National Women's Trade Union League of America," US Library of Congress, *Quarterly Journal of Current Acquisitions*, August 1951
Mary T. Waggaman, "National Women's Trade Union League, *Monthly Labor Review*, US Dept. of Labor, 8:1183-1190, April 1919

Manuscript sources

Franklin Papers, Mitchell Library, State Library of New South Wales
Margaret Robins Papers, University of Florida Library, Gainesville, Fla.
National Women's Trade Union League papers, Library of Congress, Washington
Kate Baker Papers, National Library, Canberra
Agnes Nestor Papers, Chicago Historical Society
Other manuscripts are noted individually

Newspaper sources

Chicago *Tribune*, 1906-1915
*Life & Labor**, January 1911-September 1918
New York *Herald Tribune*, September-November 1924
San Francisco *Examiner*, April-May 1906

* In the State Library of New South Wales

Index